PALGRAVE STUDIES IN THEATRE AND PERFORMANCE HISTORY is a series devoted to the best of theatre/performance scholarship currently available, accessible, and free of jargon. It strives to include a wide range of topics, from the more traditional to those performance forms that in recent years have helped broaden the understanding of what theatre as a category might include (from variety forms as diverse as the circus and burlesque to street buskers, stage magic, and musical theatre, among many others). Although historical, critical, or analytical studies are of special interest, more theoretical projects, if not the dominant thrust of a study, but utilized as important underpinning or as a historiographical or analytical method of exploration, are also of interest. Textual studies of drama or other types of less traditional performance texts are also germane to the series if placed in their cultural, historical, social, or political and economic context. There is no geographical focus for this series and works of excellence of a diverse and international nature, including comparative studies, are sought.

The editor of the series is Don B. Wilmeth (EMERITUS, Brown University), Ph.D., University of Illinois, who brings to the series over a dozen years as editor of a book series on American theatre and drama, in addition to his own extensive experience as an editor of books and journals. He is the author of several award-winning books and has received numerous career achievement awards, including one for sustained excellence in editing from the Association for Theatre in Higher Education.

Also in the series:

Undressed for Success by Brenda Foley
Theatre, Performance, and the Historical Avant-garde by Günter Berghaus
Theatre, Politics, and Markets in Fin-de-Siècle Paris by Sally Charnow
Ghosts of Theatre and Cinema in the Brain by Mark Pizzato
Moscow Theatres for Young People by Manon van de Water
Absence and Memory in Colonial American Theatre by Odai Johnson
Vaudeville Wars: How the Keith-Albee and Orpheum Circuits Controlled the Big-Time and Its Performers by Arthur Frank Wertheim
Performance and Femininity in Eighteenth-Century German Women's Writing by Wendy Arons
Operatic China: Staging Chinese Identity across the Pacific by Daphne P. Lei
Transatlantic Stage Stars in Vaudeville and Variety: Celebrity Turns by Leigh Woods
Interrogating America through Theatre and Performance edited by William W. Demastes and Iris Smith Fischer
Plays in American Periodicals, 1890–1918 by Susan Harris Smith
Representation and Identity from Versailles to the Present: The Performing Subject by Alan Sikes

Directors and the New Musical Drama: British and American Musical Theatre in the 1980s and 90s by Miranda Lundskaer-Nielsen

Beyond the Golden Door: Jewish-American Drama and Jewish-American Experience by Julius Novick

American Puppet Modernism: Essays on the Material World in Performance by John Bell

On the Uses of the Fantastic in Modern Theatre: Cocteau, Oedipus, and the Monster by Irene Eynat-Confino

Staging Stigma: A Critical Examination of the American Freak Show by Michael M. Chemers, foreword by Jim Ferris

Performing Magic on the Western Stage: From the Eighteenth-Century to the Present edited by Francesca Coppa, Larry Hass, and James Peck, foreword by Eugene Burger

Memory in Play: From Aeschylus to Sam Shepard by Attilio Favorini

Danjūrō's Girls: Women on the Kabuki Stage by Loren Edelson

Mendel's Theatre: Heredity, Eugenics, and Early Twentieth-Century American Drama by Tamsen Wolff

Theatre and Religion on Krishna's Stage: Performing in Vrindavan by David V. Mason

Rogue Performances: Staging the Underclasses in Early American Theatre Culture by Peter P. Reed

Broadway and Corporate Capitalism: The Rise of the Professional-Managerial Class, 1900–1920 by Michael Schwartz

Broadway and Corporate Capitalism

The Rise of the Professional-Managerial Class, 1900–1920

Michael Schwartz

BROADWAY AND CORPORATE CAPITALISM
Copyright © Michael Schwartz, 2009.
Softcover reprint of the hardcover 1st edition 2009 978-0-230-61657-8

All rights reserved.

First published in 2009 by
PALGRAVE MACMILLAN®
in the United States—a division of St. Martin's Press LLC,
175 Fifth Avenue, New York, NY 10010.

Where this book is distributed in the UK, Europe and the rest of the
world, this is by Palgrave Macmillan, a division of Macmillan Publishers
Limited, registered in England, company number 785998, of Houndmills,
Basingstoke, Hampshire RG21 6XS.

Palgrave Macmillan is the global academic imprint of the above companies
and has companies and representatives throughout the world.

Palgrave® and Macmillan® are registered trademarks in the United States,
the United Kingdom, Europe and other countries.

ISBN 978-1-349-38004-6   ISBN 978-0-230-62332-3 (eBook)
DOI 10.1057/9780230623323

Library of Congress Cataloging-in-Publication Data

Schwartz, Michael, 1963 Oct. 18–
    Broadway and corporate capitalism : the rise of the
professional-managerial class, 1900–1920 / Michael Schwartz.
        p. cm.—(Palgrave studies in theatre and performance history)
    Includes bibliographical references.

    1. Theater and society—New York (State)—New York—History—
20th century. 2. Theater management—New York (State)—New York—
History—20th century. 3. Class consciousness—New York (State)—
New York—History—20th century. 4. American drama—20th century—
History and criticism. 5. Class consciousness in literature. I. Title.

PN2277.N5S37 2009
792.09747—dc22   2008051654

A catalogue record of the book is available from the British Library.

Design by Newgen Imaging Systems (P) Ltd., Chennai, India.

First edition: August 2009

Contents

Acknowledgments	vii
1. Introduction: A Matter for Experts	1
2. The Growth of Broadway, the Emergence of the PMC	23
Brave New York: Nowhere to Go But Up	23
The Show Business	24
Who Were the PMC?	29
Meet the Experts	39
Where the Actors Stood: The Actors' Strike	47
3. The Problem of Nerves	51
Dim Shadows: Pre-PMC Consciousness	51
Modern Men and Modern Nerves	57
Gillette as Sherlock Holmes, Super Expert	61
Fitch and the Psychological Moment	63
Neurasthenics Caught on Kodak	71
4. Muckraking the Playing Field: Emerging PMC Class Consciousness	77
The Freshest Kids in Town	77
Fair Play: *The College Widow*, *Strongheart*, and *Brown of Harvard*	80
Sweepings from the Muckrakes: *The Lion and the Mouse*	94
Strikers, Gentlemen, and Toughs: *The Boss*	97
5. A Size Thirteen Collar: Musicals and PMC Class Consciousness	101
The Musical: Pre-Postmortem	101
The Providences of God: *The Sultan of Sulu*	105
Musicals Grow Up for a Moment: The Princess Shows	109
Showing a Class How to Move: The Castles	118

6. **System and Farce: Emerging PMC Habitus**   **125**
   Cohan as Super Model—Positive and Negative   125
   F.W. Taylor: A Scientific Call for PMC   136
   Losing and Making a Fortune: *Brewster's Millions*   139
   Grant Mitchell—PMC Poster Boy   142
      Humbugging Prelude: *Get-Rich-Quick Wallingford*   142
      Mitchell on the Rise: *It Pays to Advertise*   143
      PMC Apotheosis: *A Tailor-Made Man*   147

7. **Conclusion: Business as Usual**   **153**
   Clarence: Leading the U.S. Safely into the 1920s   153
   Freud and the PMC   154
   O'Neill and Psychological Capital   155
   Other Cures for Nerves: A Look at the 1920s   159
   Postscript: The Return of the Tailor-Made Man   168

Notes   169

Bibliography   195

Index   209

Acknowledgments

This book required a great deal of help in many different forms and attitudes—firm, gentle, friendly, stern, exasperated, patient, and impatient. Irrespective of how I might have felt about the different kinds of help at the time, it is safe to say that I required every bit of it, and it is truthful to say that I am grateful for all of it. Bruce McConachie provided invaluable chapter-by-chapter guidance and organizational suggestions. Attilio Favorini, William Scott, and Lynne Conner gave me terrific information regarding the drama, dance, and literature of the period. The graduate students of the University of Pittsburgh Theatre Department were a tremendous source of assistance and insight. At Palgrave, Don Wilmeth most generously gave me pages of great notes and practical advice, and Brigitte Shull and Lee Norton never failed to get back to me no matter what dumb question I asked, often in a matter of minutes. I am also greatly indebted to all the participants of the ATHE-ASTR Publication Workshop—especially Patricia Ybarra, for organizing it, as well as E. Patrick Anderson, Harvey Young, Andrew Sofer, LeaAnn Fields, Dr. Wilmeth (again), and Ramon-Rivera Servera for their input and advice.

Not all the help had to do with academia and publishing. Greg and Sue Watts let me use their computer (a lot). Dana Popovic, Daniel Damiano, and Judy Alvarez gave me a place to crash in the New York City area. My wife, Kathleen Kerns, made sure and continues to make sure that I stay on track. And finally, major thanks to Howard (may he rest in peace) and Shirley Schwartz, my parents—they always knew I could do something like this.

All of the above gifted and brilliant people, and more whom I've inadvertently left out, did their best to help me avoid errors. For such errors, I take sole credit.

1. Introduction: A Matter for Experts

The early twentieth century is a problematic era in American theatre. A key critical commonplace is that the work of this era avoided or simply ignored the seismic shifts of the world beyond the Great White Way. A few scholars, however, have shown some appreciation of the pre-1920 years of Broadway. Brenda Murphy, for example, acknowledges the period as one of transition—crucial years for establishing realistic principles in American drama (Murphy 86). John Gassner makes a case for the "sweepings" of Progressive muckraking that "fell" on the early twentieth-century American stage (Gassner viii), and the controversial feminist heroines of Rachel Crothers have garnered more than cursory interest in the past 25 years. Nevertheless, it is fair to say that Ronald Wainscott's summation of the period is representative of—an era given "short shrift" because "what is clearly missing in most of the work is a direct assessment of or confrontation with the obvious vicissitudes and tensions of the larger world surrounding the microcosm of the American theatre" (Wainscott, "Plays" 263).

In terms of the plays themselves, or the tangible theatrical product that audiences were watching, the argument denying the lasting significance of the first years of twentieth-century Broadway is a strong one. A cursory reading of surviving scripts reveals a great deal in the way of giddy, airy entertainment and considerably less in the way of serious thought. The plays that did venture a "confrontation with the obvious vicissitudes and tensions of the larger world" were frequently saddled with melodramatic conventions and tacked-on happy endings. Moreover, dramas and comedies alike were structured and paced in ways that would tax the patience of a twenty-first-century audience used to the speed and economy of television, music videos, and Internet-streamed entertainment.

There are, nevertheless, alternative ways of understanding and appreciating the years of American theatre around the turn of the twentieth century. The fact that the pre-Eugene O'Neill years still serve as a common mode of periodization for American theatre studies is the result of a myriad of emerging social forces that Broadway responded to and acted upon during the years 1900–1920. My proposition is to examine (and further problematize) this era in terms of class formation—specifically, the formation of the Professional Managerial Class (PMC) of New York City.

As Alfred Chandler Jr. writes in *The Visible Hand: The Managerial Revolution in American Business,* modern business enterprise as we know it can be defined as an entity containing many distinct operating units, which are managed by a hierarchy of salaried executives. By World War I, the firm following the modern corporation model became, in many sectors of the U.S. economy, the dominant business institution (Chandler 1–3). Business history shows us where and how the need arose for a new class of professional managers and planners—experts who knew, because they helped to create, the new American bureaucratic machinery. The emergence of this class of experts provides the foundation of my general thesis. *Broadway and American Corporate Capitalism: The Rise of the Professional-Managerial Class 1900–1920* will demonstrate (1) that the formation and rise of the PMC shaped the Broadway theatre of this era and (2) that Broadway in turn, played a large role in creating and affirming PMC class identity. A fruitful and rewarding way of teasing out this mutual influence is through a close examination of bodies, and how the body literally "embodies" the acquisition of cultural competence.

What do historians mean by "Professional Managerial Class"? My definition of the PMC begins with the one set forth by John and Barbara Ehrenreich: "salaried mental workers who do not own the means of production and whose major function in the social division of labor may be described broadly as the reproduction of capitalist culture and capitalist class relations" (Ehrenreichs 18). The Ehrenreichs are to be commended for their precision and relative brevity, but the definition, understandably, is a loaded one.[1]

Problems arise when the historian attempts to keep job classifications consistent using the Ehrenreichs' definition. As Pat Walker points out, using the example of the engineer, much depends upon which theory of technology one uses, and how one defines "productive" and "reproductive" labor. If the engineer is seen as someone who is exclusively a productive laborer (that is, one who produces surplus value for the capitalist), then the engineer is just like other workers, with the exception of being more highly skilled (and, generally, more highly educated). In contrast, other theories stipulate that the engineer's function is primarily to control and suppress labor, and is therefore reproductive (or reproducing capitalist culture, as per the Ehrenreichs). Still other theories find separable functions for the engineer—he or she is a worker, and the reproductive function could conceivably be eliminated. Finally, there are those who would argue that the "productive" and "reproductive" functions of the engineer's position are inseparable. Each approach places the engineer in a different class position (Walker xvi–xvii).

Indeed, in terms of the PMC itself, there is by no means a clear consensus that we are even talking about a "class." Is the PMC, in Robert Wiebe's words, "a class only by courtesy of the historian's afterthought" (Wiebe 111)?[2] Jean Cohen and Dick Howard question the importance, and even the common sense, of trying to study these "mental workers" in terms of class in the first place (Cohen and Howard 77). David Noble charges the Ehrenreichs with hiding behind the notion of class as a mere "analytic abstraction" (Noble 129). And the Ehrenreichs themselves are the first to admit that because the PMC "includes people with a wide range of occupations, skills, income levels, power and prestige," class boundaries are necessarily "fuzzy" (Ehrenreichs 13). Is there a meaningful way to discuss the PMC?

We can, and probably should, go back even further: what makes a class? Erik Olin Wright, in his entry in *The Encyclopedia of Social Theory*, posits five key questions "within different agendas of class analysis" (Wright 717). Any discussion of class, class formation, and class identity must deal with at least one (and in most cases, all) of these questions.

And, in one way or another, they all play a role in working up a definition of "Professional Managerial Class":

1. Class as subjective location, or, "How do people, individually and collectively, *locate themselves and others* within a social structure of inequality?"
2. Class as objective position within distributions, or, "How are people *objectively located* in distributions of material inequality?"
3. Class as the relational explanation of economic life chance, or "What *explains* inequalities in economically-defined life chances and material standards of living of individuals and families?"
4. Class as a dimension of historical variation in systems of inequality, or, "How should we characterize and explain the variations across history in the social organization of inequalities?"
5. Class as the foundation of economic oppression and exploitation, or, "What sorts of transformations are needed to eliminate economic oppression and exploitation within capitalist societies?" (Wright 717–719, author's emphasis)

In this study, my main concerns will involve people locating themselves as a class (#1) and the notion of life chances and their effect on class embodiment (#3). Nevertheless, objective positioning, a sense of historical variation, and the factors of economic oppression and exploitation will no doubt prove pertinent as well.

Marx, of course, asks the question "What makes a class?" at the end of the third volume of *Capital*. He began his answer, logically enough, by discussing "revenues and revenue sources." Marx immediately acknowledged the problems inherent in defining class through revenue: "From this point of view...doctors and government officials would also form two classes, as they belong to two distinct social groups, the revenue of each group's members flowing from its own source." As Marx extends the example to consider "vineyard-owners, field-owners, mine-owners...[and] fishery-owners," Engels's editorial note follows immediately after: "At this point the manuscript breaks off" (Marx 1026). Theoretical disputes regarding the concept of class, to understate the obvious, have since proliferated greatly.

If we keep in mind Marx's stated purpose in writing *Capital*, we can not only get a handle on a meaningful discussion of class but also begin to gain an understanding of why a basically Marxist (or, at least,

Marx-inspired) approach to the PMC has value. In Volume I, Marx notes, he "investigated the phenomena exhibited by the *process of capitalist production*, taken by itself." In Volume II, he took up the "process of circulation" in further investigating the "life cycle of capital." In the third volume, Marx writes, the idea is

> to discover and present the concrete forms which grow out of the *process of capital's movement considered as a whole*…The configurations of capital…thus approach step by step the form in which they appear on the surface of society, in the actions of different capitals on one another, i.e., in competition, and in the everyday consciousness of the agents of production themselves. (Marx 117, author's emphasis)

Marx also allows for flexibility in class articulation as follows:

> Class articulation does not emerge in pure form…middle and transitional levels always conceal the boundaries…We have seen how it is the constant tendency and law of development of the capitalist mode of production to divorce the means of production ever more from labour and to concentrate the fragmented means of production more and more into large groups, i.e. [,] to transform labour into wage-labour and the means of production into capital. (1025)

These quotes, taken together, provide a great deal of the foundation of the "class" aspects of my thesis. Throughout this study, I will be discussing class, including the PMC, as a "form" that grows from a process—in particular, a capitalist process that removes the means of production from "labor." To explain the existence of the PMC (and subsequently to analyze both its influences and its influence), there needs to be an acknowledgement of "middle and transitional levels" that classical Marxist analysis might not always allow. Harry Braverman, in *Labor and Monopoly Capital: The Degradation of Work in the Twentieth Century*, provides additional helpful context when writing about the term "working class:" "It never precisely delineated a specified body of people, but was rather an expression for an ongoing social process" (Braverman 17). It is similarly helpful to think of the PMC as a description of "an ongoing social process"—a process that occurred in the midst of rapid and explosive social change.

I also should provide a few words of clarification regarding the players in my book. On those occasions when I have been obliged to provide some description of my study, the question I am most often asked is "Do you mean theatre managers?"—an understandable assumption, given that I am dealing extensively with "theatre" as well as with "managers." However, the focus of this book concerns neither the "theatre manager" in the modern sense, that is, those workers who are responsible for day-to-day theatre operations, nor the celebrated "actor-managers" of the nineteenth and twentieth centuries around whom (and for whom) a production was created. I am chiefly concerned with this "fuzzy" and "transitional" group of manager-experts, the PMC as a whole, including their theatre-going practices and moments of self-recognition—seeing themselves, or broad cartoons of themselves, represented onstage.

More specifically, when I write about PMC class formation, I am describing (again with reference to the Ehrenreichs) an ongoing social process that encompasses two key conditions. The first is economic necessity in the history of capitalism. In this case, the PMC were needed to manage the machinery, science, and technology of burgeoning corporate capitalism, as well as to mediate and circumvent potential conflicts between the capitalist and working classes. This mediation found much of its application in the sweeping reform programs of the Progressive Era. "Social defense," as Progressive professor Edward A. Ross wrote in his 1907 book *Sin and Society*, "is coming to be a matter for the expert." For Ross, as well as for many PMC progressives, social defense referred to preserving capitalist culture from the potential uprising of the poor—particularly unhappy immigrants and workers (Ehrenreich 19).[3] The second condition is a performative one, that is, the articulation of self-identification. The PMC gradually recognized themselves as a separate class and began elaborating and justifying their class identity through a variety of social practices, including theatregoing.

It is the second condition in particular that raises the most interesting challenges for the historian. There is a need to identify evidence of such self-identity, as well as a need to determine if there are recognizable stages in the course of this class identification. A great part of this identity lies in emerging notions of profession and training:

> The defining characteristics of professions should be seen as representing simultaneously both the aspirations of the PMC and the claims which are necessary to justify those aspirations to the other classes of society. These characteristics are, in brief: a) the existence of a specialized body of knowledge, accessible only by lengthy training; b) the existence of ethical standards which include a commitment to public service; and c) a measure of autonomy from outside interference in the practice of the profession (e.g., only members of the profession can judge the value of a fellow professional's work). (Ehrenreichs 26)

There had, of course, been "professions" and "training" long before 1900 and the PMC. What distinguishes "PMC" professions (and training) is the context of American corporate capitalism as a culmination of the urban-industrial system that had been growing since the mid-nineteenth century. By 1900, the population of these "salaried mental workers" had either expanded enormously (in the cases, for example, of college faculty and engineers), or proliferated in areas where just 20 years before, their numbers were too small to measure in any meaningful way (in the cases of auditors and accountants, as well as government officials, administrators, and inspectors). In ten more years, the latter would be true as well of manufacturing managers and social workers (Ehrenreichs 18). Again, while the occupational net is wide, these "experts" can all be said to owe the existence of their positions—the demand for their expertise—to the boom in technology and science, the increasing centralization of business and industry, and the need to address the issues of the poor and the immigrants that marked the early twentieth century.

In terms of training, the universities had been gearing up for the emergence of the PMC as early as a generation ahead of schedule. As Robert Wiebe writes,

> The universities played a crucial role in almost all of these movements. Since the emergence of the modern graduate school in the seventies, the best universities had been serving as outposts of professional self-consciousness, frankly preparing young men for professions that as yet did not exist. By 1900 they held

8   *Broadway and Corporate Capitalism*

an unquestioned power to legitimize, for no new profession felt complete—or scientific—without its distinct academic curriculum. (Wiebe 121)

A university degree, membership in a professional organization, and independent legal standards for entry and proficiency were a few of the key signifiers of the PMC. The experts reaped the benefits of the new administrative, technological, and political machinery:

> The more intricate such fields as the law and the sciences became, the greater the need for men with highly developed skills. The more complex the competition for power, the more organizational leaders relied on experts to decipher and to prescribe. Above all, the more elaborate men's aspirations grew, the greater their dependence upon specialists who could transcribe principles into policy. (Wiebe 174)

And, through a peculiar kind of cultural evolution, the male PMC body began to "embody" its newly found cultural competence. In terms of self-identification and location, the PMC had to position themselves in distinct ways from the elite class above and the working class below, allowing for ever-permeable and shifting class boundaries. Such delineations are especially challenging to track inasmuch as the growing ranks of professionals often sought to emulate the elite class in terms of dress and the kinds of entertainment they could afford.[4]

The roles of the PMC speak directly to the relationship between class and habitus, or for the purposes of this study, a PMC and a *PMH*—a Professional-Managerial Habitus. By applying several of the concepts of Pierre Bourdieu's sociology, the historian can negotiate between the larger social world of class formation and the presence and significance of popular theatre within that social world. Bourdieu's concepts of "habitus," "cultural field," and "cultural capital," among others, are germane to a class-oriented theatrical study. Here, as with Marx and the Ehrenreichs, it will be helpful to remember that we are using Bourdieu's terminology to describe ongoing, and swiftly moving, social processes. Once again, a degree of flexibility is called for—not enough, certainly, to render useful and specific terminology meaningless, but enough to push Bourdieu's ideas beyond his sometimes rigid orthodoxy. For example, Bourdieu writes this about taste, class culture, and habitus:

> Taste, a class culture turned into nature, that is, *embodied*, helps to shape the class body.... It follows that the body is the most indisputable materialization of class taste, which it manifests in several ways. It does this first in the seemingly most natural features of the body, the dimensions... and shapes... of its visible forms, which express in countless ways a whole relation to the body, i.e., a way of treating it, caring for it, feeding it, maintaining it, which reveals the deepest dispositions of the habitus. (Bourdieu 1984, 190, author's emphasis)

For Bourdieu, generally speaking, bodily habitus begins with childhood, and this concept can prove troubling when attempting to apply it to a burgeoning class formation:

> Habitus is an internalized, embodied disposition toward the world. It comes into being through inculcation in early childhood, which is not a process of deliberate, formal teaching and learning but, rather, one associated with immersion in a particular socio-cultural milieu—the family and household. Through observation and listening, the child internalizes "proper" ways of looking at the world, ways of moving (bodily habits), and ways of acting. (Reed-Danahay 46)

As Deborah Reed-Danahay acknowledges, "newer forms of hybrid identities, shifting forms of subjectivity related to either geographical mobility or rapid social change, cannot easily be accommodated with this view of habitus as something inculcated in early childhood and then providing a set of dispositions that guide a person's life trajectory." Nevertheless, Bourdieu allows for a degree of flexibility as to when and how the habitus is formed—including immersion in a higher education or university milieu, or even times of "rapid social change" (Reed-Danahay 156). Then, too, the period under study allows for a new generation of children raised by PMC families to embody "taste" at an early age. In other words, Bourdieu should indeed be helpful in showing that the Broadway stage of 1900–1920 gave its audiences live demonstrations of "ways of moving... and ways of acting." One might then think of Broadway in terms of a "cultural field," that is, a site of cultural practice, or "a series of institutions, rules, rituals, conventions, categories, designations and appointments which constitutes an objective hierarchy, and which produce and authorize certain discourses and activities" (Webb, Schirato, and Danaher x–xi). As Bourdieu elaborates with regard to history and social conditions as follows:

> Habitus is very similar to what was traditionally called character, but with a very important difference: the habitus... is something *non natural*, a set of *acquired* characteristics which are the product of social conditions and which, for that reason, may be totally or partially common to people who have been the product of similar social conditions (such as individuals occupying petty bourgeois positions in different societies or at different epochs). There is another difference which follows from the fact that the habitus is not something natural... being a product of history, that is of social experience and education, it may be *changed by history*, that is by new experiences, education or training. (Bourdieu, "Habitus" 29)

PMC habitus, as well as PMC class consciousness, were indeed greatly shaped and changed by history.

In considering how the emerging PMC found ways to play upon the Broadway field, the historian discovers several resources—elements of capital—that the PMC attained as it grew and matured. These resources were, in turn, appropriated by most of the players on the field of Broadway. Such resources included the role of "expert," the jargon of the scientist and the (scientific) manager, and the industry of advertising.

For example, by appropriating the role of "expert," the PMC was able to create a pervasive and persuasive rhetoric of "thinking" as opposed to "unthinking," and "scientific" as opposed to "instinctive" or "unskilled." In the management literature of Frederick Winslow Taylor, for example, the manager's job was to guide the "unthinking" worker.[5] Similarly, in theatre criticism, critics assumed the responsibility and vocation of "thinking" in order to guide "unthinking" audiences. Brander Matthews wrote in his book *On Acting*, of "subtleties of the histrionic art which are never suspected by the ordinary playgoer, who comes to the theatre in search of unthinking recreation" (Matthews 7). Matthews later noted that an actor typically needs guidance "by a wiser head," which could conceivably refer to producers, playwrights, and directors (38). While the vocabulary of "thinking" and "brain work" was not exclusive to the PMC, "brain working" became the foundation of a PMC "life-style." Or to put it another way, various theatrical professionals could and did appropriate elements of a PMH, whether or not they fit comfortably within the PMC.

Nevertheless, actors were not about to be lumped together with the "unthinking" workers or audiences. The actors also began to appropriate the rhetoric of the "mental worker"—Mrs. Fiske, in a 1917 interview with Alexander Woollcott, speaks of the actor in terms that would have been at home in Taylor's works on Scientific Management: "As soon as I suspect a fine effect is being achieved by accident I lose interest. I am not interested in unskilled labor…The scientific worker is an even worker. Any one may achieve on some rare occasion an outburst of genuine feeling, a gesture of imperishable beauty…but your scientific actor knows how he did it" (Fiske 585).[6]

The stories of Broadway and the PMC are the stories of numerous "actors" and "players," engaging and confronting one another on various "fields." To develop an informal typology of what constitutes habitus for the purposes of this study, I will be referring frequently to a number of elements while examining plays, playwrights, actors, and audiences of the period. These elements include, among others, models of posture and musculature; costuming; faces ("color," facial hair, etc.); and social manners. Good manners, for example, were a vital component in the 1890s conception of onstage manliness, as demonstrated in such plays as Fitch's *Beau Brummell*. The position of facial hair and the presence (or lack) of sideburns were key indicators of social position in plays including *The College Widow* and *A Pair of Sixes*. Long before the concept of "theatre semiotics," theatre practitioners and critics wrote specifically regarding "the actor's symbols," including "voice and look and gesture" (Matthews 43). With an understanding of the varying and various players on the cultural fields, the historian can then further appreciate the role the theatre plays by presenting, and representing, these elements. In some cases, the representation is faithful and admiring; at other times, plays and productions proved subversive, either through the plays themselves or by the presence of the actors. As Laurence Senelick writes, "however much the theatre has been pressed into service to endorse and advertise society's values, it is staffed by a suspect and marginal personnel" (Senelick 9). One might add that those observing the theatre and criticizing it frequently find themselves "suspect and marginal" as well.

It is important to make the necessary distinctions between emerging class consciousness and emerging habitus when discussing the PMC and Broadway. Perhaps because of the salient element of consciousness in the PMC's development—the choosing of a necessary role in the worlds of American corporate capitalism and of Broadway—there is the danger of confusing and conflating the conscious (class consciousness) and unconscious (habitus) components of this emerging class. In discussing the plays, the performances, and the performers (as well as the responses to them) during this period, I will be frequently pointing out potential moments of class consciousness on the part of the PMC segment of the audience. Often these moments of recognition were painful, as when onstage characters dismissed the necessity of a college education, or openly mocked those who took their studies seriously (the "grinds" of the college dramas, for example). There were also moments of pleasurable, satisfying recognition as well, when PMC heroes led the befuddled capitalists down the path of success. Of course, the history is not so neat as to present a clear-cut, gradual process of PMC characters gaining respect—plays that represent progress for the PMC types often immediately preceded plays where the PMC characters received the fuzzy end of the lollypop. Nevertheless, the historian can trace patterns that lead to the PMC attitudes that defined, and placed its stamp of approval on, a modern American drama.

With regard to habitus, the historian is dealing with the outward, visible, but unconscious manifestations of class on the body. I will be referring to particular types of PMC characters and audience members, which I hope will illustrate different aspects of this class habitus in a meaningful and accessible way. During the era under study, I will be referring to three distinct PMC "types" that appear on, behind, and in front of the Broadway stage: Mr. Nervous, Mr. Grind, and Mr. Can-Do.

Mr. Nervous, as his name indicates, is defined by his nervousness. This manifests itself in neurasthenia roughly from the end of the Victorian era up until the American embrace of psychoanalysis and Freudian theory (that is, from the 1880s until the 1920s, allowing for some inroads of Freudian influence dating from the 1910–1920 period). This time frame, in fact, is significant because Mr. Nervous bridges the Victorian and the modern eras—he is partially a Victorian gentleman type, and partly a PMC type. By the 1920s, the neurasthenic had evolved, with considerable help from the PMC who were the first to Americanize Freud, into the neurotic. Mr. Nervous is closely related to the "tired businessman" so often written about in reviews of the frivolous Broadway fare of the period. He is usually stooped, embodying the cliché of carrying the weight of the world on his shoulders. He speaks quickly, and often haltingly or jerkily, with bodily movements to match—a result of his nerves and his overly taxed intellect. A mere laborer was not smart enough to have nerves, but a mental worker was particularly susceptible to nervousness. He wears a typical suit as befits his profession, and manages to appear respectable until a crisis causes the final break, frequently leading to a crime, drug addiction, or suicide. Mr. Nervous appears onstage most frequently in serious plays involving business and finance, and often in the plays of Clyde Fitch.

Mr. Grind is a figure of the Broadway college campus. He is the student who is never in step with the gentlemanly athletic heroes of the college plays. The grind's intelligence, wealth of information, and advanced vocabulary are all fodder for jokes perpetrated by the athletes. He shares the physical posture of the neurasthenic, that is, he also walks with a distinct stoop. The difference is in how and when the stoop evolved—the grind has been leaning too intensely over his schoolbooks, whereas Mr. Nervous has been crippled by his nerves as well as, perhaps, leaning for too long over important books and papers. Furthermore, while the neurasthenic can usually still function fairly smoothly in social situations, the grind is hopelessly awkward with everyone except fellow grinds. In other words, the neurasthenic has learned social skills, most likely from an early age, whereas the grind has never learned anything outside of the textbook and the classroom.

Handsomeness, or lack thereof, is also a key factor in distinguishing Messrs. Nervous and Grind. Mr. Nervous, while weakened by pressure and nerves (often noted in stage directions describing "weak" chins or mouths, for example), is generally a "good-looking" or a "handsome" man, which helps him at least temporarily to maintain his respectability. The Grind, on the other hand, is typically gawky (comically tall) and would be essayed by a character comedian for whom physical beauty was not an issue. Mr. Grind is never in danger of attaining or losing respectability, and is nearly always a figure of fun, although in *Brown of Harvard*, there is an interesting attempt to make him a three-dimensional, partially sympathetic character (though not, of course, as sympathetic as the hero).

Mr. Can-Do, the expert, comes closest, despite the obvious differences, to resembling the Victorian gentleman who exuded confidence in his carriage and his bearing. For the Victorian gentleman hero would never stoop, and he would always move with grace and with purpose. Mr. Can-Do, for his part, might possibly lean forward while striding quickly, diving into any situation head-first. Nevertheless, he also has the capability of standing erect, particularly when he is espousing or defending an American corporate capitalist principle. The key differences between the gentlemanly confidence and the PMC Can-Do confidence have to do with the different kinds of grace that the characters embody. While the gentleman can frequently take his time and employ the grace of a man who has the time to wait for what he wants, Mr. Can-Do is generally in a hurry—especially the Mr. Can-Do who drives a farce. His speed and no-nonsense speech carries its own grace of a sort, but this grace is that of the modern businessman who has "what it takes." The speech is peppered with up-to-the-minute references and slang, with no time for the elevated Sunday school locutions of Victorian heroes. Through sheer force, he carries the supporting characters along with him, and audiences too were often swept happily along in Mr. Can-Do's wake.

Here again, physical beauty, or "leading man" quality, is an important factor. The Victorian gentleman-hero could vary in size and shape, but was invariably a handsome, "leading man" type. These heroes included

John Drew, Maurice Barrymore, E.H. Sothern, and numerous "matinee idols" of the 1990s who prospered in the early twentieth century as well. Mr. Can-Do, the PMC hero, could be very ordinary-looking—indeed, that aspect accounted for a great deal of his appeal. When one of the most active interpreters of Mr. Can-Do, Grant Mitchell, seized center stage between 1910 and 1920, he was portly, middle-aged, and balding—as were, no doubt, a good deal of the audience. From then on, a Broadway "leading man" could conceivably look like the bank manager, the accountant, or the chief financial officer. That is what made Mr. Can-Do's appearance distinctly PMC.

Broadway in the first years of the twentieth century would see a number of types for the first time, thanks to such personalities as George M. Cohan, Ziegfeld (or more accurately, Ziegfeld's Girls), Vernon and Irene Castle, and a host of others. How were these bodies different from what Broadway had seen before? If, like Brenda Murphy, we view the years 1900–1920 in terms of transition in establishing principles of realism, we can view the era in terms of bodily transition as well. Earlier melodramatic and comic bodies alike found themselves increasingly shaped by the demands of the metropolitan corporate world. Giddy, reckless youth often found themselves in college. The beginnings of the modern business suit and the athletic letterman's sweater costumed bodies that reflected the changing world.

Henry Woodruff, for example, embodied the ideal of higher education with his earnest gaze and manly collegiate sweater with the big "H" in *Brown of Harvard*, a role he played to great acclaim in 1906, despite being a somewhat overage collegian at 36 (Blum 46).[7] According to James Metcalfe's review in *Life*, Brown is "the hero who steps into the 'varsity boat, and, of course, at the vital moment, snatches victory from defeat" (Metcalfe 35–36). Rida Johnson Young's play was sturdy enough to warrant two silent film treatments. Metcalfe's closing paragraph provides a telling view of the state of Broadway in March 1906:

> *Brown of Harvard* is the best in the recent American invasion of the American stage. If it meets with the pecuniary success which seems to await it, the play will probably inspire the Theatrical Trust to follow its usual tactics of imitation

and give us a succession of copies with such titles as *Smith of Yale, Jones of Princeton, Wiggins of Johns Hopkins, McFadden of the University of Chicago, Maymie of Vassar*, etc. (Metcalfe 36)

Metcalfe's review touches on several key currents running through the stream of early twentieth-century Broadway: the rise of the American playwright (in this case, a female), the bottom-line mentality of the Syndicate[8] seen as villainously crippling the American theatre, as well as the introduction of American university athletic life on stage. Metcalfe, in fact, makes the comparison with a play that appeared two years earlier, George Ade's *The College Widow*, a football-themed play that Metcalfe lauded for its faithful and accurate depiction of "pipe-smoking and 'rah-ing' college boys" (Metcalfe 58). Audiences would be re-introduced to the college widow in musical form in 1917's *Leave It to Jane*, one of the successful "Princess" shows of the period.

These "sporting bodies," and the plays that contained them, gave Broadway audiences a full, if jaundiced, view of the athletic "field" on which class identity is often formed and fought over. As Bourdieu notes, "sport, like any other practice, is an object of struggles between the fractions of the dominant class and also between the social classes" (Bourdieu, "Sport" 360–361). The playing field features struggles "over the definition of the *legitimate body* and the *legitimate use of the body*" (361–362, author's emphasis). In one sense, the triumph of the athlete is a triumph of anti-intellectualism—"character" and "will power" trumps instruction and erudition. These aspects of athleticism would seem to leave the "intellectual" PMC on the sidelines, as it were, and in the plays under study, this is indeed the case. PMC characters in the sporting plays tend to appear as misfits—"grinds" (or Mr. Grind) who spend too much time studying to be regular fellows, or stuffy professors and school administrators who have the nerve to insist that the sports heroes attend classes and lectures.

Sport, as performed on stage and on the real-life fields of play, is also a technique of sociability, an important tool in the American corporate capitalist world. Moreover, the sporting bodies, shaped by the particular sport, become valuable as signs—signs of ease, mastery, and the most accomplished realization of the use of the body. In this sense, the "sporting body" served as an aristocratic, gentlemanly ideal (Bourdieu, "Sport" 367–372). The "sporting body" speaks to one of the most significant tears in the PMC fabric—intellectual vs. anti-intellectual, in this case. It was to be one of many inter-PMC disputes that flared during the era, and in the Broadway arena, practitioners, producers, critics, and audiences would all have their chance to complicate matters.

Nor were Broadway's expert heroes solely mythic or athletic. The PMC audience also witnessed more concrete examples of their own ranks in the theatre. A look at the comedy *It Pays to Advertise,* part of a long string of hits produced by George M. Cohan and Sam Harris, will illustrate. In this case, the plot turns on the expertise possessed by advertising executives and copywriters—from the PMC-type professions that had just come into existence in the United States at the turn of the century. In turn, these, among others, were the kinds of businessmen that the Syndicate, and later the Shuberts, would cater to in their production strategies. As Lee Shubert explained,

> We have learned a few things, at least.... We know that people like youth and beauty. We know that they will go down in their pockets and pay gladly, if you give them something that will make them laugh. They like to see a play that holds their attention, keeps it from straying off to their worries and troubles.... People want a play to have plenty of action. A few persons will go to a "talky" play and be interested, if the talk is clever and brilliant. But those persons form a very small group. (McNamara xxv–xxvi)

The narrative of PMC class formation, and the role theatre played in this narrative, is as lively and colorful as it is complex. To witness the evolution of this new class is to witness, in effect, the turbulent evolution of an entire nation as it came to terms with, and ultimately embraced, great advances in technology and science, as well as the perceived need for sweeping social and municipal reforms. The drama of PMC class formation began to play on American stages just before and during the turning of the twentieth century. As American corporate capitalism itself became a subject for American drama, playwrights such as Bronson Howard and Clyde Fitch examined man's relationship with capitalism, profit, and power just as both men and women across the country were forging and renegotiating that relationship (Postlewait 158–159).

In years past, the New York stage featured numerous embodiments of various class formations. Jacksonian heroes led the masses against oppression. Aristocratic benefactors restored fallen middle-class heroes, ravaged by alcohol, back to home, hearth, and society. Sensation melodramas reflected and dramatized current financial panics.[9] The Civil War provided rich material for fairly subtle intrigue as well as the "insane melodramas" that infuriated critic George Jean Nathan and his peers. Following 1920, Broadway saw Babbitized businessmen and their social-climbing wives, increasingly sophisticated musical productions, aristocratic "high comedy," greater strides toward (and as an equal and opposite reaction, away from) realism, and the stirrings of social protest. The years 1900–1920, in essence, constitutes the era when the PMC and the American theatre seemed to hit their respective strides.

At the end of this era, in 1920, Broadway audiences saw, among other events, the successful continuation of Ziegfeld's *Follies,* Marilyn Miller's biggest musical success in *Sally,* John Barrymore's first Shakespearean role (*Richard III*), and two O'Neill plays (*Beyond the Horizon* and *The Emperor Jones*). Perhaps Broadway had at last attained an artistic maturity, but this new beginning was the culmination of emerging class, emerging class consciousness, emerging class habitus, and changing social fields. If not exactly an "invasion of the body-snatchers," certainly newly tailored (and Taylored) bodies were here to stay.

Chapter 2 of this book will set foundations and boundaries concerning New York City and the business of Broadway. This chapter will contain a broad outline of major institutional changes on Broadway, extending somewhat before 1900 to a few years beyond 1920, including theatre building, increase of seats of productions, and such pivotal events as the 1919 Actors' Equity strike. There will also be a more concrete description of the PMC in terms of their probable day-to-day lives, and how often they went to the theatre. I will examine some of the major theatre critics during this era, and the shift in critical tone and emphasis that mirrored (and influenced) the overall shift in the Broadway field from the Victorian gentlemen to the PMC.

Chapter 3 focuses on the class consciousness of the Victorian gentleman, the habitus of the Victorian gentleman, and the emergence of the issue of nervousness and the need for experts to deal with this issue. This chapter will especially delve into the criticism of William Winter and John Ranken Towse, the two exemplars of genteel Victorian theatre criticism. Also, I will explore Bronson Howard's early (1887) take on American corporate capitalism, *The Henrietta*, as the beginnings of the exploration of both American business and of nervousness on the Broadway stage. The chapter will also analyze several plays by Clyde Fitch, who throughout his career placed many neurasthenic males onstage. The neurasthenic (or Mr. Nervous) proves to be an interesting transitional figure between the Victorian and the modern eras, looking back toward Victorian notions of character and integrity, and looking forward to the modern psychological themes O'Neill would pursue. Through his convincing and knowing portrayals of weak, nervous men (in counterpoint to his strong women), Fitch began to delineate the tastes (or habitus) of the emerging PMC.

Chapter 4 explores the emerging PMC class consciousness. Included here will be the collegiate plays. The use of the "fields" of college sports to train future business leaders, and the increasingly popular quest for what Jackson Lears refers to as intense and enjoyable experiences, are two concepts that found representation on the Broadway stage in such plays as *The College Widow* (as well as the later musical adaptation, *Leave It to Jane*), *Brown of Harvard*, and *Strongheart*. Such plays examined the practicality of a college education in ways that suggested that some kinds of expertise were more welcome, and could be taken more seriously, than others. College as a field where class differences play themselves out becomes increasingly important as PMC characters begin to make their presence felt onstage, although the PMC characters do not, for the most part, come out on top. The young gentlemen heroes (and their friends) in these plays still played by the gentlemanly rules their fathers and grandfathers had set, and there was a strong sense of "inside" vs. "outside," and "us" vs. "them." At this point, PMC characters still constituted the "outside" and "them" contingent; excellence in school studies was not a guarantee that one could belong (in fact, frequently the opposite was the case). The proliferation of college enrollment and the growth of professional and "land-grant" schools are noted here as well.

The fifth chapter looks at several of the era's musicals, and how they also shaped PMC class consciousness. Early musical jabs at American imperialism, such as *The Sultan of Sulu,* as well as Ziegfeld's Follies, and the "Princess" musicals, all gave PMC audience members opportunities to recognize themselves as a class—sometimes in an unpleasant way, but at other times, particularly in the case of the Princess musicals, in more pleasant and positive ways. Class consciousness can be painful as well as satisfying, and this chapter will explore the sources of both the pleasure and the pain.

Chapter 6 deals with emerging PMC habitus, with a detailed examination of master showman George M. Cohan as well as dance masters Vernon and Irene Castle—how Cohan challenged the existing Victorian habitus, and how the Castles contributed to the PMC habitus through their expertise in ballroom dancing. Chapter 6 will also provide background on Frederick Winslow Taylor, whose concept of Scientific Management was a distinctly PMC phenomenon, in terms of the stated necessity for educated mental workers to supervise (nonmental) laborers. I also examine several of the successful business farces of the era, when PMC characters became leaders and heroes in their own right. Scientific Management found its way onstage in a number of plays, most often in a joking and ironic atmosphere. In *A Pair of Sixes,* for example, the managers who insist on implementing a "system" cannot even agree which manager has the authority to do so; in *Get-Rich-Quick Wallingford,* the hero-crook rises to captain of industry simply because his con accidentally proved genuinely successful.

The final chapter explores how the class consciousness and habitus of the PMC continues into the 1920s. By this time, the theories of Sigmund Freud had entered mainstream thought and parlance, forming the basis of a "pop" psychology that further identified and defined the PMC. This psychology would complete the transformation of the embodiment of nerves from neurasthenics to neurotics. Moreover, the application of this pop psychology would prepare the PMC theatrical experts and their audiences for the introduction of what would become nationally, and then internationally, accepted as "modern" and "mature" American drama. Chapter 7 includes an examination of the emergence of the chief exemplar of PMC-endorsed "mature" American drama, Eugene O'Neill. In many ways, O'Neill's rise as "the" American playwright was as much a PMC construct as the idea of the Ziegfeld Girl. O'Neill's biggest hit of the 1920s, *Strange Interlude,* gave the playwright and his supporters success and approval on an international level, making the PMC (and PMC-approved) playwright a part of the national pop culture. Nevertheless, while O'Neill reigned as the "leader" of modern American drama, there were still plenty of business and sex farces to temporarily alleviate the ongoing problem of nerves.

2. The Growth of Broadway, the Emergence of the PMC ~

BRAVE NEW YORK: NOWHERE TO GO BUT UP

To elaborate on this project's thesis, we first need to gain some understanding of what New York City was circa 1900. It was a city straining mightily, and often successfully, to compete with and surpass the world's great cities. Three years before the century turned, the five boroughs of New York had been consolidated, giving the city an area of 327 square miles, and a population of three and a half million (Burns & Sanders 206). The litany of opposing superlatives is familiar by now: the wealthiest and the poorest, the classiest and the most vulgar, the highest and the lowest, all commingling within a few miles or even within a few blocks—even in 1900, it was practically a cliché.

By the following year, over a third of the nation's 200 largest companies were located in New York, including Standard Oil, General Electric, American Tobacco, and U.S. Steel (231). The "skyscraper," once a nautical term describing the highest sails of the ships sailing the Atlantic, now referred to structures that followed the only direction corporate buildings could go—as Lincoln Steffens wrote, "Confined on all sides, the only way *out* was *up*" (232, author's emphasis). And in terms of getting around, carriages and ferries would no longer suffice; the most efficient way in and out would soon be *under*. By 1900, citizens could see teams of surveyors laying out the routes of what would become the Interborough Rapid Transit. To paraphrase one *New York Herald* article, Father Knickerbocker would venture underground to travel within four years (255–257).

Immigration would reach its highest levels during this time, and with the mounting numbers came mounting hostility, and often outright hysteria.

As one New York City newspaper editor wrote: "The floodgates are open. The dam is washed away. The sewer is unchoked. Europe is vomiting!" (qtd. in Burns & Sanders 242) One of the most systematic responses to the threat of vomiting continents was implemented in the New York City public school system. The plan was to "Americanize" immigrant children as quickly as possible, with intensive lessons in English grammar, American history, hygiene, and manners. "We were 'Americanized,'" one immigrant explained, "about as gently as horses are broken in" (252).

It is difficult to exaggerate the explosive growth and development of New York City in these early years of the twentieth century. A great deal of what we generally consider "modern American life" begins during this period, and for the most part, it was in New York City where this development either originated or was first exploited and implemented on a mass scale. It seemed that everyone, from Victorian elites, to new immigrants, to old merchants, and those somewhere in-between, was swept into a modern era somehow not of their making. Wary and uncertain voices came from all sides. In the words of Henry Adams: "The city had an air and movement of hysteria, and the citizens were crying, in every accent of anger.... Prosperity never before imagined, power never yet wielded by man, speed never reached by anything but a meteor, had made the world irritable[,] nervous, querulous, unreasonable and afraid" (Adams 499).

Nor was this irritability and nervousness strictly a patrician response, as witnessed by John Dos Passos's question in the Thorstein Veblen vignette in *The Big Money*: "Was there no group of men bold enough to take charge of the magnificent machine before the pigeyed speculators and the yes-men at office desks irrevocably ruined it?" (Dos Passos 854). One can appreciate the aptness and accuracy of the title of Robert Weibe's account of the Progressive Era: "The Search for Order." Not a few of the paths and byways of this search led through Broadway and the Professional Managerial Class. An understanding of the business of Broadway will shed some light on the territory the searchers for order had to explore.

THE SHOW BUSINESS

In 1900, the "business" of theatre meant two things in particular. One was that a producer did not count on the New York City run to make money—the profits were to come from "the road." The other was that "the Theatrical Syndicate" had firmly established itself as the dominant producing force. As the *Chicago Tribune* noted in November 1900: "It may safely be said that not one play in twenty of those produced in New York, whatever its kind, leaves that city with one cent on the profit side of the ledger of its business manager. The managers do not, as a rule, hope to make money there" (qtd. in Bernheim 49).

By 1920, the business state of affairs would change: the "road" would no longer generate the majority of the profits. Motion pictures were a significant factor in "killing" the road, but the movies never interfered with Broadway profits, either in their initial silent form or in the panic-inducing introduction of "talkies." Indeed, Broadway saw a boom of theater building between 1900 and 1920 (which would continue throughout the 1920s), allowing more bodies to see more shows.

The use of the term "business manager" is of interest here, because it speaks to the kind of "industrial revolution" the theater business experienced in the last generation of the nineteenth century. As Jack Poggi points out,

> What happened to the American theater after 1870 was not very different from what happened to many other industries. First, a centralized production system replaced many local, isolated units. Second, there was a division of labor, as theater managing became separate from producing. Third, there was a standardization of product, as each play was represented by only one company or by a number of duplicate companies. Fourth, there was a growth of control by big business. (Poggi 26–27)

The same sort of necessity in the history of corporate capitalism that helped give rise to the PMC existed in the business of theatre as well.

The decline of the stock system and the rise of the combination system in the theatre industry in the second half of the nineteenth century have been well-documented.[1] In terms of the evolution of the theatre business and where things stood by 1900, what is of chief interest to us is the creation of a new middleman in the theatre: the booking office. Bernheim, in his 1932 study of theatre business, dates the first booking agencies around 1859. These agencies established contacts between the theatres and the attractions by taking charge of the scheduling of attractions in the theatres. The men who would come to form the Theatrical Syndicate learned the lessons of other American industries, recognized the financial advantages of concentration and consolidation, and pooled the resources of their existing partnerships to come to the first official Syndicate agreement in August 1896 (Bernheim 34–41).

The Syndicate's methods of operation in many ways parallel the development of other industries during this era. The Syndicate would pave the way for future producing organizations, complete with executive levels of management: departmental managers, auditors, and bookkeepers overseeing clerical staffs (Bernheim 110). Although there are and were legitimate legal and moral objections to the Syndicate itself,[2] the Syndicate's existence as a de facto trust in the field of theatrical booking was a logical outgrowth of already existing changes in the theatrical industry. It was, in Bernheim's words, "the clearest manifestation of an evolutionary process working within an institution that we can expect to find" (Bernheim 60–61).

The business of theatre was growing more "corporate" across the board, as an examination of "executive staffs" for producers reveals. In many cases, identifying members of these "executive staffs" with the burgeoning managerial class would be a mistake; just as the theatre used the terms "manager" and "management" for both owners and workers, many of the new theatre "executives" would soon identify themselves with workers through unionization. Nevertheless, the nomenclature is not insignificant in terms of theatre's ongoing and evolving relationship with business management. George M. Cohan and his partner Sam Harris, for example, listed an "executive staff" for *Little Johnny Jones* that included the stage manager, master machinist, master of properties, chief electrician, and wardrobe mistress. Such people did "manage," of course, in the sense that they were responsible for crews, but their clear-cut identification with a "managerial class" as such did not occur.[3]

Other "executive" positions, on the other hand, jibed fairly well with the "salaried mental worker" element of the burgeoning PMC. In 1906, for example, the theatergoer enjoying *Brown of Harvard* could take the time to notice in the program the "executive staff" for the Princess Theatre: Lee Shubert and Chas. E. Evans, lessees; Thomas L. Nelson, business manager and treasurer; and Chas. E. Evans Jr., assistant treasurer.

Both Nelson and Evans Jr., it could safely be said, fulfilled the "mental" operations of money and business management for the Shuberts.[4]

Arguably the key figure in the evolving theatre business was the press agent—so much so that as late as 1929, Alfred L. Bernheim could remark with all due seriousness that "the producer may try to get along without a director, a business manager, an art director—but under no circumstances will he do without the services of a press agent" (Bernheim 112). The press agent came into his own as the century turned as the rise of advertising whetted the public's appetite for eye- and ear-catching publicity. Colorful (and often tasteless) stunts and promotions, and exaggerated (or downright false) claims were among the tools of the press agents' trade. The public would resent lies about the quality or content of upcoming shows, and this was one of the key factors that irreparably damaged the "road" business. But generally speaking, a press agent could seldom go wrong with well-executed outrageousness.[5] Such outrageousness, in the sense of gaiety and frivolity, was never far from Broadway.

And what exactly was "Broadway" in 1900? Geographically, what was known as "Broadway" or the "theater district" in 1900 followed Broadway (the thoroughfare) from 13th to 45th Streets. New electric street lights gave rise to the now-familiar Broadway nickname "Great White Way" in 1901. Broadway was still a few years away from the completion of the Times Building that would convert Longacre Square into Times Square (Atkinson 3–7; Trager 284). The chief mode of transportation to get to a Broadway show was still the carriage, although surveyors and city planners were already working on ways to transport the growing workforce underground. Nevertheless, producers, architects, playwrights, performers, and audiences were all forging and expanding "Broadway," not only as a geographic location but also as a theatrical image.

As the new century turned, two dollars bought the theatergoer the best orchestra and first balcony seats. There were still vestiges of earlier times when the wealthiest set bought the most conspicuous seats in the theatre in order to be seen as much as the performers. Fifteen dollars would secure you that luxury at the Princess Theatre in 1906, if you were inclined to purchase a box seat.[6] Audiences were treated not only to eye-catching and ostentatious theatre design but also to the most up-to-date methods of climate control. When James A. Herne's *Sag Harbor* opened in September 1900 at the Republic Theatre, the audience felt the effects of cold air circulating through floor ducts to ventilate the house—or rather some time after the play opened, when this system malfunctioned on opening night. Backstage, the engineering and mechanical experts made their presence felt in the operation of curtains and scenery—one man at an onstage switchboard could do the work of a curtain and scenery crew by operating an electric motor (Trager 267).

The era under study was also the busiest time for new theatre building. From 1900 to 1925, the number of Broadway theatres jumped from 20 to a high of 80 (Lewis 9). Concurrently, the number of Broadway productions increased, allowing for some fluctuation. Eighty-seven productions reached the Broadway boards during the 1899–1900 season; in 1927–1928, there were 254 (Atkinson 11). The rise in the number of available theatres and theatre seats was considerable. During the years 1903–1918, for example, new theatre openings included the New Amsterdam, the Lyceum, the Belasco, the Globe, the Winter Garden, the Little Theatre, the Cort, the Longacre, the Shubert, the Booth, the Broadhurst, the Plymouth, and the Selwyn (Botto 27, 35, 43, 51, 57, 73, 79, 89, 99, 109, 119). The openings were so frequent that the *Times* laconically commented in October 1917, "It is a dull week when no new theatre opens" (Botto 109). Seating ranged from 299 at the Little Theatre to a high of 1,750 at the New Amsterdam (Botto 7, 51). By way of contemporaneous comparison, the New Theater, built in 1909 in an early attempt by New York aristocrats to create an American modern repertory theatre, seated 3,000 (Wilson 196).[7] The seating sizes and arrangements, if not all the theatres, remain with Broadway even today, including an emphasis on clearer sightlines and an attempt to bring the public closer to the actors.

Of principal import is the fact that thousands of new seats were available for an increasing theatregoing public during this period. Among the increasing theatregoing public were the PMC. Here, the historian is obliged to move from a somewhat abstract concept of PMC—a way of describing a social and historical movement—to a more concrete picture of, at least, some of these men who were experiencing class consciousness in ways that defined their identity and their habitus. To fill in such a picture, one must answer several questions concerning the quotidian life, regarding salary, shopping habits, shelter, and other clues to identity.

WHO WERE THE PMC?

In 1900, the U.S. Census determined that the average American (excluding farm workers) was making $490 per year, or roughly $9.42 per week. The PMC mostly earned well over the average, with the notable exception of schoolteachers, who generally pulled in $328 annually. If our PMC representative was an average player in the world of finance, insurance, or real estate, he could expect a $1,040 annual salary ($20 per week). Federal employees and clerical workers made slightly less, with $1,037 and $1,011 yearly incomes respectively. In the following ten years, these salaries would rise somewhat, but by 1920, the clerical workers made $2,160 annually, overtaking both the federal employees ($1,648) and those in the finance/insurance/real estate fields ($1,758) (*Historical Statistics* 2–271–273).

The PMC man during this period worked harder, or at least longer hours, than his present-day counterpart, although, in general, his hours were still more regular than those of the labor class. Working hours tended to average between 55 and 60 hours per week around 1900, but the eight-hour day had at last prevailed by around 1919—48–50 hours per week, over a six-day working period—possibly comparable to a twenty-first century "workaholic" (Whaples "Hours of Work"). On the PMC man's day of rest, there was a good chance he could be found in one of New York's many churches—there were some 983,000 Presbyterians in the United States in 1900—third in terms of total U.S. church membership, behind Southern Baptists and Catholics (*Historical Statistics* 2–906).

The question of religion brings up the issues of exclusivity and discrimination. The members of the elite classes were what we would now call WASPs (White Anglo-Saxon Protestants), as the term in its common parlance did not exist until the early 1960s. Nevertheless, discrimination regarding social membership based on race, religion, and ethnicity, or, in E. Digby Baltzell's words, a "caste" system had been in place long before, and certainly during the era under study.[8] The PMC, on the other hand, was a class of expertise, education, and achievement, fulfilling a specific function in American corporate capitalism. In theory at least, there seemed to be no reason why the PMC could not be inclusive of all races, religions, and ethnic origins.

Nevertheless, there were rules and norms that the PMC had to follow, even as many of them insisted on greater autonomy as a necessary condition of their work. Although the ideals of objectivity and rationality frequently placed the PMC on opposite sides of capitalist class interests, they still had to work and operate by the rules established by the dominant class. In other words, as the Ehrenreichs write: "To the extent that the PMC established itself as a major class in twentieth-century American society, it did so on terms set by the capitalist class" (Ehrenreichs 25). Therefore, although the PMC could afford to be slightly more accommodating in terms of ethnicity and religion than the elite classes, the outsider was still obliged to fit himself to "team" standards. The outsiders, meanwhile, were obliged to climb or descend, in Mary Brewer's words, a "ladder of Whiteness." Brewer explains:

> Compared to both "Indian" and "Negro" identities, constructions of Whiteness in the nineteenth century proved conveniently flexible, prone in their historical terms to rapid fluctuations in signification, due to the necessity of assimilating a host of immigrant communities that were deemed racially/culturally different. As a result, for most of the period and continuing into the twentieth century there existed a ladder of Whiteness in U.S. racial discourse. That White Anglo-Saxon Protestants should occupy the top rung passed for the cultural common sense. (26)

"Whiteness," therefore, becomes a category that is not merely racial but social as well.[9] As David Roediger points out, "The racial landscape discovered gradually by new immigrants to the United States was a mess.... Expert opinion divided the world into either a handful of races or several dozen.... Race was at once biological and cultural, inherited and acquired. Race identified, depending on context, both a category and a consciousness" (Roediger 35). Thus, each "outsider" group, occupying what Roediger calls an "in-between" position between races, had to consciously embrace the concept of "Whiteness" in order to be considered white (20–21). In many cases, this embrace entailed approving of and participating in discrimination against blacks. As Noel Ignatiev writes in *How the Irish Became White*, "They [the Irish] came to a society in which color was important in determining social position. It was not a pattern they were familiar with and they bore no responsibility for it; nevertheless, they adapted to it in short order" (Ignatiev 2). An embrace of "Whiteness," however, by no means guaranteed acceptance. In 1912, for example, "congressional hearings on immigration restriction debated whether Italians were 'full-blooded Caucasians'" (Roediger 67).

Nevertheless, inasmuch as college educations and professional-management training was available to the "in-between" immigrants and their progeny, there were some PMC openings for the new immigrants. Immigrant Jews and Catholics, for example, could conceivably rise in the PMC if they practiced assimilation strategies such as changing their names or even rejecting their religion outright. As Ignatiev notes, Catholics were "suspect as Mary-worshippers and idolaters.... The Catholic Church was for many Protestants the Whore of Babylon" (148). "White" immigrants, especially their sons, who rose to obtain college educations and the jobs that required them, could also belong to the PMC, with some likely modifications of speech (losing or toning down an accent, for example) and dress (looking the part of an American man of business). The necessity of the PMC provided the new immigrants another rung on the "ladder of Whiteness," although the rung was not always near the top, and the position was not always steady. Nonwhites, meanwhile, were met and blocked by the ceiling of race, despite the growing numbers of blacks in positions of law, education, and engineering during the period under study.[10] For all practical purposes, the PMC consisted of white men.

With regard to living and transportation, the burgeoning PMC could take full advantage of the equally burgeoning transportation booms in the City, even before the first subways were completed in 1904. As Elizabeth Collins Cromley writes,

> Access to New York's districts was enhanced by an elevated railroad system that had been completed by 1878. City dwellers were also served by 135 miles of horse-car lines charging five or six cents a ride, and by the 1,500 cabs and hacks licensed in 1890. Newly constructed streets complemented the elevated

rail lines, opening whole new territories to the west and north of Central Park for residential development. (Cromley 128)

With some 300,000 white-collar workers (many of whom could be included in the PMC) in Manhattan by 1910, the need for apartments and apartment houses grew (Cromley 172). For those PMC workers on the lower end of the wage scale, but presumably on their way up, the rooming or boarding house was available—and most PMC men could, at least, avoid the tenements.[11] The PMC worker found reliable and swift transportation from his home to his office; sometimes this was a matter of taking the train downtown, and sometimes, especially from the 1910s and beyond, home would be in one of the boroughs—Queens, Brooklyn, the Bronx, or Staten Island. Those PMC workers on the upper end of the income scale were also becoming the proud owners of automobiles—those on the lower end mastered the fine art of straphanging.

With orchestra seats at $2.00 each, where the price would remain until the mid-1910s, a night out on Broadway for an unaccompanied PMC patron came to 10 percent of his weekly salary—20 percent of that salary, if a date or a wife accompanied him. To make a broad contemporary comparison, the ratio would be roughly the equivalent of someone making $52,000 annually paying $200 for a pair of tickets to a Broadway show—or, allowing for taxes (which, of course, PMC men did not have to worry about until the passage of the 16th Amendment in 1913), someone making in the $65,000–$70,000 range buying the tickets for a night out. The orchestra seats remained steady at $2.00 per head from 1895 through the 1914–1915 season (Hischak 3).

Whether or not the PMC men took their place in the orchestra was largely a matter of priorities. If they were regular theatre fans and did not mind going up to the balcony (seats ranging from 50 cents to a dollar during this period), it is certainly conceivable that they could indulge at least once a week. On the other hand, if the PMC audience wished to keep up with (and sit next to) their bosses in the capitalist class, the indulgence would be somewhat more of a financial strain. By the 1915–1916 season, prices began a fairly steady increase, with top prices reaching $3.50 and remaining there through the 1920–1921 season. Prices would continue to increase, with an interruption (and decrease) during the Depression. Thus, while salary for the clerical workers more than doubled from 1900 to 1920, the ticket prices after 1915 almost proportionately matched the increase. Some PMC men could keep up fairly comfortably, while others could do so only with some strain—with quite a few settling for taking over the role of gallery god, a privilege that by 1920 did indeed cost a dollar.[12] A good deal of this ticket price increase was directly related to the rise of the motion pictures and the "death of the road"—a play now had to make its profits in New York, on Broadway. The play also depended more heavily on newspaper advertising and positive quotes from reviewers to generate business.

Another way to gain an understanding of the day-to-day lives of the PMC is to examine the program ads of the plays they went to see. While examining these ads can give no more than an impressionistic portrait of the theatergoer/consumer, the historian can begin to get a sense of what audiences were interested in and how local merchants catered to them.[13] Today's programs frequently feature the kinds of ads one might also see nationally, through magazines or television. In 1890 New York, the bulk of the ads were still composed fairly modestly by the entrepreneurs themselves (Lears, "American Advertising" 50). The bulk of the ads in 1890–1891 programs catered strongly to the elite gentlemen and their wives, the ones who could afford pianos (and had places to live big enough to fit them) and double-breasted sack suits for twenty dollars and up—somewhat more than a week's salary for many early PMCs. Celebrity endorsements enhanced the elite appeal of indulgent items—Sarah Bernhardt, for example, assured audiences that indulgences such as Lowney's Chocolate Bonbons were well worth the investment (Goodrum and Dalrymple 28). Nevertheless, even some twenty years before Frederick Winslow Taylor wrote his book on Scientific Management, there was some advertising copy that espoused the efficacy of departmentalization. Sohmer Pianos ads, for example, assured its audience that "each member of the firm [is] in charge of a special department to which he devotes his entire energies."[14]

As early as the 1890s, program advertisers acknowledged the existence, concerns, and growing purchasing power of PMC men. Many ads were for products that addressed the kinds of illnesses that beset busy mental workers—for example, Garfield Tea for "sick headaches" and constipation (signs of stress and working too hard). PMC men also had the opportunity to dress like the Victorian gentlemen, but for less money. One of the most striking ads in the early 1990s programs is one for Velutina, a material that was "about one-quarter the cost of Silk Velvet." The example is interesting for its message—a man and his wife could *look* like the upper class while paying only 25 percent as much for the material. In the words of the Billy Joel song "It's Still Rock and Roll to Me" (evoking one of 1890's big hits, written by a young Clyde Fitch), "you could really be a Beau Brummell, baby, if you just give it half a chance"—or even a quarter of a chance.[15]

The distinction between ads for "reasonably priced" clothes and accessories after the turn of the century and this 1890 Velutina ad is subtle but full of import in terms of self-identification. The 1890 ad encouraged imitating one's "betters" while staying within a more modest budget, in this case, by purchasing less expensive material. Although the notion of looking "elite" (or simply looking "better") for less money would still be a viable selling point in the early twentieth century, the growing ranks of advertising professionals would soon shift the emphasis to how the clothes affect the shape of the individual body. In a real sense, the road to positive class identification for the PMC was paved with clothes and textiles, and part of the roadmap can be found in theatre programs.

Neither was business and travel ignored by the theatre program advertisers. Couples could "see Niagara Falls in 12 hours" for $17.00 roundtrip.[16] This trip was a "budget" version of a quick getaway excursion—still a fairly luxurious expense for many PMCs, but not inconceivable for a special occasion. Nor were young, growing families ignored in the programs of the early 1990s. A number of stores advertised children's clothes. The New York Building Loan Banking Company could help a couple attain what might now be called a "starter" home, as evidenced by their ad promising to show "how to purchase a $1,000 home for $9."[17] Providing for the family in case of emergency was a concern addressed by the Travelers Insurance Company of Hartford, "the largest and strongest company in the world."[18]

By the twentieth century, personal health, hygiene, and appearance took on an even greater importance in theatre ads.[19] As in 1890, programs provided a rich assortment of advertisements for products of varying degrees of luxury, convenience, and practicality. One item that bears particular examination in the theatre ads is that of soap.[20]

"Cleanliness" as such was not a new concern at the turn of the century (or in the previous decade), nor was it exclusively a "PMC" concern. It is fair to say, however, that the concern for cleanliness was a key component in the changing culture on several levels, including the "Americanization" (and cleaning) of the increasing numbers of immigrants, as well as the elimination of personal odors related to being unclean. Cleanliness was another way to impose order in an increasingly disorganized world. A 1900 Ivory Soap ad, for example, credited soap for cleaning up (both literally and spiritually) the Plains Indians: "And now we're civil, kind and good/And keep the laws as people should" (Lears, "American Advertising" 56). By 1905, soap copy addressed the rising man of business: "Personal appearance is a prime factor in business or social success. Nothing retards a good impression like a bad complexion."[21] Men wishing to become professional-managers and professional-managers wishing to attain even greater positions needed to start with soap and water.

Making a "good impression" figured prominently in clothing ads as well. By 1905, programs regularly carried features for both men and women—"What the Woman Will Wear" and "What the Man Will Wear." Men received such tips as the following: "A turnover collar should be worn only with a jacket, and not with a tail coat. Such collars are sometimes seen with frocks and cutaways, a fashion not accepted by the man who knows."[22] The way a man's appearance—his physicality—was "sold" in theatre ads was undergoing a subtle change.

One of the most graphic examples of such a change is the Ovalesque Dress Shirt ad. The term "ovalesque" was used to describe how the shirt fit the man's body—"it just ovalesques into place," without bands, buckles, or other fastenings. A particular ad illustrating the shirt cut right to the heart of the matter: "It exalts an ordinary dress suit, justifies a brave front, and fixes a man's social position as no other article of dress can." The picture illustrating the copy shows the ovalesque shirt worn on a well-formed male torso, no head, and hands casually placed in the pants' pockets (we see just enough of the pants to show the hands in the pockets). The man's face, included with comic features in earlier ads, was by now completely superfluous. Only the very tops of the legs were needed to convey the man's confidence and "brave front."[23]

This was an ad that sent a clear message of class embodiment that placed physical signs of confidence ahead of actual monetary wealth—cultural capital could be attained and maintained with the right shirt. The question remains, however, as to exactly which class embodiment—the "old" carriage trade crowd, or the "new" PMC (or both)? In 1890, the question as to the intended audience for program ads is relatively simple. The new professionals at that time could fairly easily be grouped, as potential customers, with the old carriage trade— the idea was to look as "elite" as possible and enjoy as many of the entertainments as the elite class could. Exceptions included specific ads for cheaper clothing materials, such as Velutina, which played specifically to the desire to look "elite" on a less-than-elite budget.[24]

To a large degree, the same could be said of program ads as the century turned. With the "ovalesque" ad, however, the old idea of looking "elite" for less money underwent an important change. The emphasis was now on the body rather than the material. The selling point of the ovalesque shirt was that it could fit the body the way a tailor-made shirt could and automatically straighten the wearer's posture. The ads and those who were creating them were beginning to display an awareness that it was not enough to be able to purchase or make nice-looking clothes out of cheaper material. The suit or shirt had to fit properly on the individual body in order to present the "correct" or "brave" front.[25] Characters who could present a "brave front" would figure prominently in the comic business plays of the 1910s. Perhaps not surprisingly, the man largely responsible for these plays, as writer and/or producer (and occasionally performer), was George M. Cohan.

As for other program ads, as befits the period, the automobile made its timely appearance, with ads for cars and tires joining regular features such as "For the Automobilist." The car might have been out of reach for many PMC workers, but, again, the range of salary for the PMC was and remains quite wide. The varying salary positions of PMC workers had a strong influence with regard to when and how often PMC experts found themselves opposing the capitalist class, as well as whether or not the PMC worker could afford to emulate the typical capitalist. Book recommendations, short stories, travel recommendations, and jokes (usually at the expense of Irish or colored servants) rounded out the reading material.

By the 1910s and including 1920, the ad copy was taking a decided turn from the language of the elite gentleman to the rhetoric of management. These changes simultaneously reflected, and were effected by, the PMC. "Probably not *all* the best things are advertised in this program," reads the typical program copy a playgoer might read in 1920, "but all the things advertised are the best."[26] Pianos were still an advertising presence, but not as dominant as before—one or two moderate ads now surfaced in the programs, as opposed to the several large ones (including full-page back cover ads) that typically appeared in the 1990s and early twentieth century. Roughly speaking, in terms of size and quantity of ads, it is fair to say that ads for cars, tires, and automotive supplies were taking the place of the piano ads. The "Standard Eight" was a "powerful" car, and the Essex Sedan and the Hudson Super-Six offered the new car buyer additional options. Tires, from Goodrich, United States Tires, and Kelly Springfield, along with antiskid chains, found a place in the programs to further support the motorist.

In terms of making a connection between fewer piano and greater car ads, there is a contemporaneous clue in an essay from The New York Theatre Program Corporation entitled "Why Is New York City the Theatrical Center of the World?" The article appeared in programs following the 1919–1920 season. "Not because it has so many visitors," the essay explains in answer to its titular question, "for visitors constitute but 25 percent and New Yorkers 75 percent of theatre patronage." The reason, according to the essay, had more to do with the geographical area of Manhattan and its effect on living space: "New York, because of its small area, limited by natural boundaries, is a city of apartments. Apartment life is different from home life as the term is understood in other communities. We...spend most of leisure outside the home."[27] For the growing middle class that included the PMC, leisure and smaller living space meant less and less playing and singing around the piano at home and more and more travel.[28]

The car ads are significant for another reason. An examination of the copy, particularly when read along with men's clothing ads in the same programs, reveals a rhetoric that defined manly and managerial authority. In the case of the Standard Eight, for example, the ad informs the reader that although some drivers might enjoy the quick "flourish of speed," most drivers would prefer the "easy authority" that would guide the driver and its passengers over rough roads and steep hills.[29] Difficult roads, in other words, could be managed with the proper "authority," a helpful message for current and future managers.

Similarly, clothing ads promoted manly grace, an "up-and-coming" attitude, and the ability to be a regular fellow. Union suits, for example, "are on the hustling, bustling chaps—the live-wires in the game for fame. Up-and-doing men find free play and sway of muscle and mind when they've 'Got 'em on.'"[30] As for what the up-and-doing man wore over the union suit, there were business jackets featuring "a style of shoulder treatment which gives the breadth and grave now considered important." Meanwhile, the ever-helpful "What the Man Will Wear" articles emphasized strength and freedom in men's quotidian life: "A certain easy freedom best comports with that brawn and biceps which underlies manhood, whether in a backwoods camp or on the ball room floor."[31] PMC men could go camping and dancing with equal ease, if they followed the right advice from the right experts.

Nor did the program fashion experts neglect one of the chief fields of the up-and-coming and established men of business, the golf course: "plainness and practicalness [sic] are the cardinal considerations in sporting dress. The dandiacal [sic] *poseur* may be inoffensive on the Avenue, but he is insufferable on the links. Unless he plays miraculous golf, you itch to send him sprawling." The message was clear—men were authoritative, practical, graceful (in a manly way), on the ball, and ready to punch a dandy in the face if he got in the way. The dandy, in this case, might not necessarily have been gay, although he certainly could have been so. The chief crime, in this case, is wearing too self-consciously and flamboyantly "sporty" golf clothes. Dandies, and by extension, homosexuals, were figures of fun in the programs and were starting to be so onstage as well.[32]

Two rival forms of entertainment found their way into the theatre programs by 1920. One was Columbia Records, whose artists, including Al Jolson and Bert Williams, appeared prominently in full-page program ads.[33] For 85 cents, fans could bring their favorite entertainers and bands home and listen to their favorite acts as often as they liked, including "jovial, rollicking, unexpected, spontaneous, ingratiating, friendly Al." The other entertainment interloper was the movies—specifically, Selznick Pictures, whose pictures were "now showing at theatres where quality rules." Budding and rising movie stars received the publicity department push for the benefit of the theatergoer who was also the moviegoer. Ads in 1920 programs plugged, among other cinematic highlights, the last films of Olive Thomas, "loved—now mourned—by a nation."[34] The movies, one of the chief culprits in the death of the "road," had come to an arrangement with the theatrical world, at least in the programs. Increased attendance, increased productions, and, soon, increased prices would ensure that Broadway could avoid "fabulous invalid" status without the road, at least for a while.

The PMC men who attended the Broadway shows were increasingly influenced by the experts—PMC in their own right—who wrote about the opening nights.

MEET THE EXPERTS

The stirrings of the Professional Managerial Class in and around Broadway are tightly linked to the evolution of American theatre criticism. By the 1890s, newspaper readers were consulting critical "experts" who were beginning to have some influence on where the prospective theatergoers might best spend their evenings as well as their admission money. This positioning of critic as expert bears elaboration. The play reviewer's status remained low well into the nineteenth century, as editors sent untrained reporters to cover theatrical openings, and as critics often favorably reviewed (if they reviewed at all) only those productions that advertised in their paper. While moral censorship and paid puffery dominated the newly expanding amusement departments of newspapers, a small but influential group of critics emerged in New York City shortly before the onset of the Civil War. This witty, irreverent group, often referred to as "Pfaffians" (so named for their favorite Lower Broadway hangout), championed theatre on the basis of artistry and entertainment, rather than moral value. The group was effectively destroyed by the Civil War.

There emerged a new "school" of critics who shared and espoused the moral and conservative values of the cultured elite. Such "genteel" critics as William Winter and John Ranken Towse retained their posts for generations, lasting in tenure (if not necessarily in influence) into the early twentieth century.[35] Winter stayed at his post at the New York *Tribune* until 1909 (writing his reviews standing up—the *Tribune* never gave him his own office); Towse wrote for the *New York Evening Post* until 1927. Both papers, and their respective critics, "shared the values of the cultured elite and endured until these values changed" (Miller, "Criticism" 132). These "values," and their subsequent change, are in large part the story of the Victorian gentleman class and habitus, and the emerging PMC habitus. Towse and Winter chronicled this change, one might say, from the losing side.

It is fair to say that both Towse and Winter shared the belief that "the theatre should illustrate and enforce the soundest principles of art, morality, and social law under the seductive guise of entertainment" (Miller, *Bohemians* 86). Such "genteel" positions in particular are helpful in understanding the shifts between eras that exist in the years 1900–1920. In discussing the rise of the Professional Managerial Class in the context of Broadway, there are three key shifts that one can trace in theatre criticism. One is the shift from "Victorian" to "modern"— Winter's as well as Towse's tastes and opinions represent the vestiges of the fading Victorian era. The second is the shift from character to the aesthetic. Winter knew and associated with many of the actors of the day, and their character, for Winter, was inseparable from their artistic achievement. As Tice Miller writes, "His most demanding principle for determining the worth of an actor was personal integrity. He did not separate an actor's personal and professional lives. He believed that an actor's stage characters were but a reflection of his personality" (Miller, *Bohemians* 89). The third change relates to the shift of importance from the actor (and his character) to the playwright.

Theatre history has made and accepted some broad generalizations regarding Broadway theatre criticism in the first part of the era under study. Brooks Atkinson sums up the critical atmosphere: "In 1900, there were fifteen newspaper drama critics in New York, and Broadway took the normal theatrical attitude towards them—it disliked them.... Until World War I shook America out of its complacence, Broadway was a stuffy and bigoted midway. In every period, newspaper critics are traditionalists who resent and resist new ideas and new styles" (Atkinson 87–88). This view is corroborated by George Jean Nathan's biographer Thomas F. Connolly: "up until 1915 there were two sorts of drama critics: anonymous puffsters and scholarly, genteel types exemplified by William Winter and J. Ranken Towse" (Connolly 47). What appeared in hindsight as bigotry and stuffiness (and "gentility," used as a pejorative) was an important element of the Victorian habitus that would soon either fade from the scene or suffer a violent overthrow, depending upon one's perspective.

The newer critics—those who started toward the end of Winter and Towse's tenures and continued after their retirement—were returning to the earlier, "Pfaffian" spirit. This was partly due to the growing demands of the popular press for "bright and clever reviews, not moralistic essays" (Miller, "Criticism" 252). This demand stemmed largely from the fact that newspapers were conforming to the "big-business" model initiated by William Randolph Hearst's *Journal* and Joseph Pulitzer's *World* (Conner 14).[36] The critics, university-educated for the most part, assumed the role of "expert" to simultaneously instruct and distance themselves from the "affluent and fashionable" (and unthinking) audience. As Richard Butsch writes,

> The "legitimate" audience was divided between the affluent and fashionable on the one hand and the cultured and educated on the other, or what sociologist

> Pierre Bourdieu distinguished as those with high economic capital and those with high cultural capital. The cultivated took to their pens to criticize the shallowness of the fashionable audience and by contrast to praise the sincerity of the lower-income gallery desirous of cultivation. (122)

This display of expertise among the theatre critics jibes in large part with the growing consciousness of the PMC as a whole. As the Ehrenreichs point out, "The generation entering managerial and professional roles between 1890 and 1920 consciously grasped the roles which they had to play. They understood that their own self-interest was bound up in reforming capitalism" (Ehrenreichs 19). In turn, the critics understood that their self-interest was equally "bound up" in improving the theatre. A great deal of the critics' "improvement" efforts were decidedly misogynistic in tone—not only the matinee girls, but also the fashionable wives whose tastes were (allegedly) guided by passion rather than intellect and who went to the theatre as a form of social climbing rather than to experience art, came in for considerable criticism from the "cultured" (male) critics (Butsch 122–123). The other major culprit was usually the Syndicate—producers such as Charles Frohman who catered to the debilitating, feminine taste.[37]

The emergence of the theatre critic coincided with a boom in newspaper circulation. Dramatic (and controversial) rendering of the news—"yellow journalism" to many—and the advent of regular comic strips made the newspapers accessible and entertaining for the immigrants—a new class of daily English-language newspaper readers in New York. "The yellow journal," Robert Jones writes, "with its pictures, sensation, and easy editorials, brought the immigrant more and more into the newspaper audience" (Jones 598).[38] Joseph Pulitzer and William Randolph Hearst were most responsible for this new sensationalism, and in terms of selling papers, they were immensely successful, whatever one thought of their ethics. In a general sense, however, these were not the newspapers that interested the PMC—not those, at least, who were or considered themselves among the intellectual elite.

Newspapers on the big-city daily level were growing in sheer numbers by the turn of the century. Circulation for English-language daily publications had grown from 489 in 1870 to 1,967 thirty years later (Emery and Emery 155). As the numbers increased, newspapers could target increasingly specialized audiences. Joseph Pulitzer's *New York World* (circulation 189,000 by 1890) appealed primarily to "working class and small businessmen," whereas the *Tribune* (circulation 70,000) held more interest for the "intellectual elite." William Randolph Hearst's *Journal* became Pulitzer's chief competition by the end of the nineteenth century (Miller, *Bohemians* 132). Editor Charles A. Dana of the *Sun* sought the audience of "average New Yorkers: workers and small merchants" during a tenure that began in 1868 and ended with his death in 1897 (Emery and Emery 148). Meanwhile, editor Adolph Ochs defined the *Times'* identity as "a class publication, appealing to the educated, the informed and the well-to-do" (Jones 478). In fact, as a direct response to the growing popularity of sensational journalism (that is, of Hearst's *Journal* and Pulitzer's *World*), Ochs wrote in his initial *Times* editorial (in 1896) that the paper would henceforth be "a high-standard newspaper, clean, dignified and trustworthy, publishing all the news in concise, attractive form, in language that is parliamentary in good society." It was this attitude that led the *Times* to its still current motto: "All the news that's fit to print" (Jones 478).

While the *Times,* the *Tribune,* and the *Post* in particular identified themselves with an audience that could roughly be defined as "educated," it was the *Times* that eventually emerged, shortly before the Great War, as the paper whose dramatic criticism was geared toward the playgoer/businessman. As Elliot Norton explains: "play reviewing was generally unsatisfactory: It was either academic, the work of men far more erudite than the conventional playgoer, or else mere puffery." Managing editor Carr Van Anda, together with Adolph Ochs, determined that plays had to be written about from a more journalistic standpoint—making the point and answering key questions early. The *Times* hired Alexander Woollcott to embody their new idea of the dramatic critic in 1914 (Norton 324).

Woollcott, besides earning "a following almost at once among people who probably had neither the time, the education nor the inclination for the essays of the pundits," found himself at a key turning point in the highly charged relationship between critics and producers (Norton 325). The Shuberts sought to ban Woollcott from all future Shubert productions after the critic panned the play *Taking Chances* in March 1915. The pugnacious producers sent tickets to the *Times* with the condition that some other reviewer would have to cover the play. Adolph Ochs responded with an unprecedented move, sending the tickets back to the Shuberts and ordering Woollcott to purchase his own tickets. The Shuberts fought back by continuing to refuse Woollcott entrance. The impasse grew in size and notoriety, as the *Times* filed an injunction against the Shuberts and subsequently threw out all Shubert advertising. Although the courts upheld the Shuberts' right to ban whoever they chose, the producers found the victory a costly one; there would be neither *Times* reviews nor *Times* advertising, two important components in selling their plays to the public. Consequently, the Shuberts gave up in 1916, agreeing to allow Woollcott or any other *Times* critic into their theatres. Critics had come into their own as an independent, powerful group whose approval was vital for a play to survive in New York, and Woollcott, for his part, earned his own byline (Norton 325–328).

The flamboyant and colorful Woollcott, who might well have been punched on the golf course if he were playing with strangers who had taken the theatre program advice too literally, and later (in the mid-1920s) Brooks Atkinson—considerably less colorful, but steadier, more consistent, and, gradually, more trusted—wrote for "the hurried, harried reader of the *Times*, clinging to a subway strap or standing in a commuter train, or rolling through traffic in a chauffeured limousine," who needed "the gist of it and the spirit, too, in one swift paragraph" (Norton 329–330). The broad description of *Times* readers is indicative of two important considerations regarding the PMC and the gentleman class. The first is that very often the PMC and the gentlemen read the same papers—an understandable and even predictable outcome of harried, nervous businessmen, in striving to get to the top of their chosen business, choosing to read the papers that their bosses read. The second consideration is the remarkably wide spectrum of financial success and security within the PMC itself, encompassing straphanging clerks and teachers as well as executives who enjoyed the perks of the company limousine.

The "newsman" critics collectively held sway over the newspaper readers on a day-to-day basis. There were, however, other venues for critics—the magazines. While newspapers could appeal to the "educated" and the "intellectual," the papers were, by design, meant to be disposable—information disseminated for those who needed to read quickly. The magazines were for home—longer stories, "deeper" essays meant for extended contemplation. It was this environment that proved fertile for George Jean Nathan, the critic most closely associated with bringing wide attention to O'Neill.

Nathan benefited considerably from the burgeoning opportunities in magazine journalism during the period under study. Between 1905 and 1907, when Nathan was with the *New York Herald*, a daily paper, he wrote extensively for *The Bohemian*, *The Century*, *Munsey's Magazine*, *Outing*, *Harper's Weekly*, *The Burr MacIntosh Monthly*, *McLure's*, *Green Book Magazine*, *The Theatre*, *Vanity Fair*, and *Puck* as well as coedited *The Smart Set* and *The American Mercury* with H.L. Mencken.

Just as the received history gives the lion's share of the credit to O'Neill for the maturation of American drama, it is George Jean Nathan, O'Neill's great friend, supporter, and champion, who is most often credited for engineering American dramatic criticism's great shift.[39] As Thomas F. Connolly explains: "Nathan overturned the genteel tradition of drama criticism, exemplified by William Winter and J. Ranken Towse, which focused on acting, and relocated the center of its attention to the playwright" (Connolly, *George Jean Nathan* 19). Nathan himself made the following observation: "Dramatic criticism advances as its concern with the actor recedes.... The critic who treats of the history of the theatre in terms of its great actors is like the historian who treats of the world's wars in terms of their great generals" (Nathan, *The Theatre* 24–25).[40]

Neither was Nathan reticent about criticizing the state of Broadway reviewing or its reviewers. In *The World in Falseface* (1923), Nathan takes his colleagues to task on their inability to judge drama in general and the work of O'Neill in particular:

> Surely if any playwright in America deserves, or has deserved, to be considered as a dignified artist, it must be agreed that O'Neill is that man. Yet...he is

regularly treated not as an artist-dramatist but exactly as if he were a mere box-office jobber... and his plays not as works of artistic merit or demerit but as so many vaudeville jugglers or trained dogs. He is subjected not to the standards of aesthetics, but to those of popular drama.... They [critics] deplore that, unlike the vastly more agreeable and sunshiny Winchell Smith and Edward Childs Carpenter, he seems to see human life chiefly as an inscrutable and gloomy piece of irony on the part of the gods—like Joseph Conrad and Fédor Dostoievski [*sic*].... They deny (and offer the works of Augustus Thomas in proof) that life as O'Neill pictures it is just that way. And when, as in the case of "Anna Christie," he does not see life "that way," but sees it with a touch of rainbow athwart its skies, they recall his past work and snicker self-satisfiedly [*sic*] that he has arbitrarily stuck a theatrical happy ending on to his play. (79–80)

In denouncing criticism that attempted to "straddle" both sides of the issue regarding O'Neill, or any issue, Nathan made clear his personal critical credo: "Criticism may straddle nothing. Positive or not positive, certain or doubtful, enthusiastic or disgusted, it must lead by the head or pull by the tail" (Nathan, *World in Falseface* 80). If critics of the 1890s and the early turn of the century began to see themselves as responsible for educating the theatergoer, Nathan distinguished himself by virtue of his modernity, by leading theatergoers by the head and pulling fellow critics by the tail, and by never looking back on any form of "good old days" throughout his long career.

The shift in theatrical criticism is significant in terms of the Broadway PMC emergence. To extend Nathan's analogy, if the "genteel" critics concentrated on the actors, or "generals," then Nathan concentrated on those "officers" who conceived the scenarios and gave the generals the information needed to maneuver and lead heroically—in this case, the playwrights. The move away from the Victorian critical (or in Nathan's disparaging terms, "Puritan") mindset is linked to the emphasis on and championing of the "mental-worker" playwrights. The fact that many actors saw themselves also as mental workers had comparatively little influence on Nathan and the "modern" dramatic criticism that he helped to create.[41]

It is important to remember the distinction between Nathan's power and influence and those of the daily critics, because this distinction speaks to the ultimate dominance on Broadway of the PMC dramatic expert—in turn, a distinct part of the PMC itself. The daily critics generally held sway over the men in a hurry, who could range in financial success from those who depended on the buses and subways to those who could afford taxis and limos. Nathan, as Tice Miller points out, never had that kind of instant, mass influence. Where Nathan wielded his power most effectively was among the young intellectuals who, quite possibly while catching subways and running for buses, made time for some thoughtful reading of the magazine essays Nathan, H.L. Mencken, and their peers were writing (Miller, "Criticism," 132). Also, it is important to remember that Nathan's viewpoint, particularly on O'Neill, was the one that emerged dominant in the world of Broadway theatre and its criticism by the 1920s—a viewpoint that by the end of that decade had gained acceptance by the daily critics, the straphangers, and the rest of the country.

WHERE THE ACTORS STOOD: THE ACTORS' STRIKE

If, as Ronald Wainscott opined, all too many Broadway plays of the early twentieth century avoided "confrontation with the obvious vicissitudes and tensions of the larger world surrounding the microcosm of the American theatre" (Wainscott, "Plays" 263), the actors themselves could no longer avoid such vicissitudes, particularly when the vicissitudes involved class, labor, and fair pay. Actors were, willy-nilly, workers paid for their craft. Producers, perhaps also willy-nilly, were management—the ones who did the paying or chose, in some situations, not to do so. The spirit of smiles, handshakes, and let's-put-on-a-show camaraderie could no longer exist apart from, in Howard Zinn's words, "the class anger that came from the realities of ordinary life" (Zinn 321). Broadway, of course, was neither Haymarket Square nor Homestead, PA. The actors had nothing to fear from Pinkerton detectives or overzealous police (unless they appeared in plays that were deemed "immoral"). Nevertheless, the thespians at last had to acknowledge that to guarantee fair treatment, they would have to adopt one of the most powerful and effective tools of the worker—the strike. The vicissitudes of the working actor were something of a surprise to long-established stars such as Ethel Barrymore, who, in fact, did not even realize she was an Actors' Equity member. As she admits in her autobiography,

> I...had no grievances of my own It was something of a shock when Georgie [cousin George Drew Mendum] explained the grievances that had brought about the strike, to find out that the members of the Actors Equity were asking for so very, very little, for things that, it seemed to me, should in common decency have been theirs without the asking. It seemed a shameful thing that people should have to go on strike to gain assurance that they would be brought back to New York when a play closed on tour instead of being left penniless in Texas, that they should be offering to rehearse without pay for four weeks—six weeks for musicals—and after that to go on rehearsing for half pay! (Barrymore 220)

To strike, the actors had to at least partially admit to a brotherhood with other workers—a comedown for many actors who relished embodying the artist-as-aristocrat. The actors found their own way to reconcile the difficult identity adjustment. They put on a show.

In the face of cavalier treatment by theatre management, including rehearsing and playing extra matinees without pay, getting stranded on the road with no return fare, and paying for costumes, the acting community had a choice to make in August 1919. The actors, through Actors' Equity, set out to determine their new class identity. Understandably, they were not all in agreement as to how best to negotiate the necessity of organizing with their status as artists. Benjamin McArthur describes the situation:

> Actors were broadening their notion of the behavior appropriate for professionals. Sociologists have noted that an overriding concern for professional status hinders unionization. Moreover, the exalted sphere of the artist...had always been thought to be above the mundane concerns of the laboring man. But actors were willing to bend their professionalism to harmonize with the economic situation they faced. (McArthur 227)

The strike, fittingly enough for a group of actors, was in itself a grand performance, full of songs, parades, and "good-natured banter" between the actor-picketers and the general citizenry. Such gregarious and entertaining displays won the actors considerable support (McArthur 230).

Actors gained the concessions they had asked for after a month of striking—fairly modest demands, as Barrymore had noted. The actors received full pay for rehearsal extensions and for Christmas and Easter weeks, and managers were to pay for outfitting the chorus girls (McArthur 232). Nevertheless, the disagreement was big enough not only to prompt the strike but also to goad the acting profession to adopt the habitus of the professional. In McArthur's words, "Art had come to terms with labor. Most actors now accepted unionism. But it was unionism in the service of a higher ideal: professionalism" (233). As the actors embraced the ideals of the PMC, the "PMC-ing" of Broadway took a substantial stride forward.

Nevertheless, in the process of unionizing, the actors left behind an old friend. Broadway's ultimate triple-threat performer, composer, and playwright George M. Cohan never stopped believing in square deals and fair play, but he took the actors' unionization, particularly the strike, as a personal affront. As sympathetic biographer John McCabe writes: "Cohan's word...was an unbreakable bond...He had become a manager by working twice as hard as any actor he knew, and he was willing to be double-damned if he were forced into giving up a jot of his hard-earned prerogatives" (McCabe 148). Actors' Equity frequently offered Cohan the olive branch throughout the remainder of his career, but Cohan steadfastly (or stubbornly) remained a "scab." Cohan spent most of the 1920s as an out-of-step relic, not regaining his combination regular-fellow-great-actor status until his unlikely teaming with Broadway (and PMC) hero Eugene O'Neill in *Ah, Wilderness!*

With this broad overview of the years 1900–1920 in mind, it might well be helpful to examine the class consciousness and the habitus of the Victorian gentlemen who were beginning to make their graceful exits from the scene. These were the gentlemen who bequeathed the legacy of nervousness to the new generation, and this legacy would soon require the attention of experts.

3. The Problem of Nerves ⁓

DIM SHADOWS: PRE-PMC CONSCIOUSNESS

The end of the century encouraged a millennial hopefulness in the era's theatrical reporters and critic-experts. In an enthusiastic tribute to the future twentieth-century actor, *The New York Dramatic Mirror*'s "Matinee Lady" wrote in the first issue of 1900, "It would almost seem certain that the twentieth century were going to evolve an entirely new type of actor," whereas the current male stars seemed only "as dim shadows cast before" ("Matinee Lady" 2). What do the "dim shadows" of the 1890s have to say to us about the period? And how do we know?

The dim shadows left a few clues behind. We know some of the items the elite gentlemen at the end of the Victorian era liked to buy, as well as some of the luxuries they enjoyed. In the 1890 theatre programs, for example, the fashionable men in the menswear ads sported derby hats and kept one hand in the pocket while the other held a walking stick. And if the gentleman had a hair loss problem, hair restorers were available to come to his aid. Cigars (or "segars"), cigarettes, Bass and Guinness, wine and claret rounded out the gentleman's day and evening.[1] One of the chief elements of the Victoria gentleman's class consciousness was the choice of expensive apparel and entertainment. The walking stick was conspicuous, as was the hat, worn with easy, casual elegance (hence the hand—often both hands—in the pockets). This graceful bearing, in turn, unconscious and effortless (after years of learning the moves), is a key element to the gentleman-habitus.

The world in which these gentlemen moved was infused with what could be called a popular Broadway morality. Broadway manners would undergo a seismic shift with the coming of the Great War. However, in

1900, the Broadway theatergoers operated under the influence of an earlier shift: the taming of the audience. As Jackson Lears writes in *No Place of Grace*, "Victorian respectability undergirded the values disseminated by the educated bourgeoisie. Those values were not descriptions of actual behavior; they were official standards of conduct" (14). By the 1890s, B.F. Keith's vaudeville audiences were regularly instructed via placards carried by theatre ushers as to what constituted permissible behavior. Ladies were asked to remove their fashionably large hats out of consideration for the other patrons, and the audience assumed the responsibility of squelching other disruptive noises, from talking and whispering to those noises associated with bodily functions. As Lawrence Levine writes:

> The relative taming of the audience at the turn of the century was part of a larger development that witnessed a growing bifurcation between the private and the public spheres of life. Through the cult of etiquette, which was so popular in this period, individuals were taught to keep all private matters strictly to themselves and to remain publicly as inconspicuous as possible. (Levine 198)[2]

The code of gentility and etiquette held for both sides of the footlights. As unpleasant behavior was banned in the audience, so were unpleasant subjects barred from the Broadway stage. Writing wistfully for *Theatre Magazine* in 1919, Daniel Frohman mourned "the passing of what he considered 'the two prime requirements' of good theater: 'cleanliness and a happy ending'" (Tomkins 55). Those two requirements held sway at the beginning of the century, and from the point of view of the producers, this was not only healthy business but also, they claimed, a boon to the general health of the theatergoer. As Charles Frohman maintained in a 1904 *Harper's Weekly* interview,

> The class of entertainment that is being given is not only satisfactory to the audiences, but is beneficial to their health, and in no way conducive to harm. I am sure that there is more genuine satisfaction and pleasure and help in going to see a George Ade play than in sitting through a performance by Mr. Sudermann. The public seeks entertainment and diversion from care. (qtd. in Poggi 255–256)

Nevertheless, that was 1904, the same year that Marc Klaw championed the heroism of the Syndicate in *Cosmopolitan* for bringing "order out of chaos, [and] legitimate profit out of ruinous rivalry" (qtd. in Bernheim 52–53). By then, the Syndicate representatives found themselves frequently on the defensive. To be sure, as the century turned, the Syndicate had its detractors from within and without the theatre profession. Critics and reviewers would use anti-Syndicate essays, as well as derogatory remarks within reviews, as an important tool in establishing themselves as arbiters of culture. It is, however, safe to say that in 1900 the Syndicate, Belasco, and here and there up-and-comers such as the Shuberts were more often than not capable of providing audiences a good time.

And what constituted a good time for the audience(s)? The "lightness" of the period (as compared with the "depth" of the period that followed the Great War) makes it easy to generalize regarding onstage frivolity and displays of wealthy living.[3] It is just this sort of generalization that has left the period under study somewhat neglected. It is nevertheless the case that the practitioners and personalities of the period were largely responsible for such perceptions (which they often shared). As Lewis Erenberg writes,

> This was the age of the drawing-room drama, the naughty French farce, drawing-room comedies, and the musical stage filled with chorus girls such as the Floradora Girls. A number of popular stars such as John Drew, Maude Adams, Mrs. Fiske, and Lillian Russell brought to the public stage stirring portrayals of the life led by the wealthy. In the hands of the great playwright Clyde Fitch, the drama indulged in examinations of wealthy living and the social aspirations and difficulties of women of the social set. Long before the theatre's star system reached the mass level through vaudeville and movies, it appealed to a carriage trade, featuring players who embodied the drawing room and advertised the nonascetic life possible for the rich and successful. (Erenberg 41)

While the onstage men were embodying the drawing room and advertising the "nonascetic life," they were also embodying (and advertising) something deeper.[4] The Victorian actors embodied a code of behavior and ways of moving, behaving, and, in at least a double sense, *acting*.

The *Dramatic Mirror*'s prediction was correct—these embodiments of Victorian gentleman habitus would indeed become "old-fashioned" and largely disregarded by "modern" critics and audiences. Nevertheless, Victorian class consciousness and class habitus helped to shape the bodies that would follow.

A look back at two of the Victorian "genteel" critics will help to fill in these pictures of class consciousness and habitus, because both Winter and Towse described the Victorian gentleman so eloquently. William Winter's reviews and memoirs call forth a Broadway defined by the actor, and actors defined by their character. Thus, Joseph Jefferson was "a poetic genius and a consummate artist...No deeper feeling, no more sensitive imagination, no finer, more delicate nature, has been manifested by any actor seen on our Stage in the last sixty years." David Warfield, in turn, was not only "a man of exceptional talent and respectable artistic achievement" but also a gentleman possessing "a pleasant personality; an affable disposition; a gentle manner; sympathy with sweet, fine feeling" (Winter 175). Winter's elegiac tribute to actor Frank Worthing provides one example of the Victorian-era, ideal combination of gentleman and actor:

> Mr. Worthing was a gentleman by nature as well as by birth. He recognized the dignity of personal reticence and he observed it in his conduct. There was no affectation in him, no assumption of superiority or importance. He was simple, unassuming, gentle, and kind. He had positive convictions on all subjects that interested him, but...he preferred to listen rather than to speak. He was closely observant. He was greatly liked by persons of taste and discernment....He was keenly susceptible to kindness....His feeling toward...[women] was chivalrous, his conduct deferential. He could easily be led by sound counsel, if it were presented to him with kindness and fortified by reasons....He thoroughly understood and deeply respected the art of Acting. He had a good opinion of his own abilities, knowing himself to be a fine actor, but he was modest and he was aware of his limitations....He bore suffering with fortitude and patience. His influence was strong in the direction of right....Society lost a good and amiable man. (205–206)

John Ranken Towse, Winter's contemporary and co-exemplar of Victorian gentility, also provides a number of portraits of gentlemen-actors—largely forgotten to theatre history, but thriving—perhaps even towering—in Towse's memory. Here is Towse on "old John Ryder": "He was a large, heavy, dignified man...His declamation was fastidiously correct and charged with sonorous music" (Towse 82). In describing Walter Montgomery, Towse recalls, "Nature had bestowed upon him a striking and virile personality, high ambition, energy, and keen dramatic intelligence. His one handicap was a somewhat throaty and unmusical enunciation. But his voice was strong, his carriage gallant, and his gesture bold and free. He had fire, sentiment, and pathos" (Towse 84–85).

Edwin Booth, who was not forgotten by theatre history, likewise earns his own unique analysis through the lens of Towse's nostalgia. Though Booth was "not...a very great actor," according to Towse, he was nonetheless

> a most accomplished artist.... His countenance was handsome, pale, intellectual, and refined. His long black hair, large and luminous dark eyes, somewhat Hebraic nose, and strong mouth indicated a character both poetic and resolute. In frame he was not large, but well knit, nicely proportioned, and graceful; his voice was sonorous and melodious. (181)

The picture of the Victorian gentleman, both on and off stage, emerges: expansive of gesture, gallant of carriage, correct in declamation, and resolute and poetic in character: chivalrous to women and amiable among men. The gentleman was *conscious* of his place in society and particularly conscious of the opinions of the gentlemen around him— being seen in the right places and with the right people, wearing the finest (and perfectly fitting) clothes, treating women with the utmost courtesy, paying debts, and keeping one's word were the major components of gentleman-class consciousness. The gentleman's *speech, face, body*, and the way he carried his body—the music of the actor's voice, the precision of his diction, the strength and resoluteness of his face and posture, the freedom and grace of his gestures, were all in turn the major components of the gentleman habitus.

For both Towse and Winter, it was not only the loss of these specific practitioners but also a loss of what they personified that so greatly reduced the state of Broadway in their eyes. "The wells of histrionic talent have been choked," Towse lamented (88). Winter railed even further against the moral lapse of early twentieth-century Broadway—so much so that his fame largely rests on his attacks against the plays of Ibsen, a testament to an aging critic's doddering intolerance.

To an extent, such criticisms of Winter are justified. His most (in)famous quote with regard to Ibsen renders his judgment of modern drama rather suspect: "A reformer who calls you to crawl with him into a sewer, merely to see and breathe its feculence, is a pest" (Winter 593). For Winter, inasmuch as he examined playwrights and playwriting, held such practitioners to the same standards of character as he did the actors. Winter praised playwright Augustus Thomas with some profusion, not only for the qualities the critic perceived in the plays themselves, but also for Thomas's intentions: "His motives are pure. His aspirations are high" (530). For the most part, one could say the same of Winter himself.

What changed in Winter's (as well as Towse's) lifetime was an awareness of the distinction between introducing and debating "unpleasant" and "immoral" subjects onstage and espousing immorality itself.[5] And, in terms of Winter and Towse's beloved gentleman heroes, they no longer always either emerged victorious or died nobly. In modern tragedies, the hero might rail against or question a capricious, unjust, or nonexistent God. The modern hero might wonder "what's it all about?"—a question that simply did not exist for the Victorian gentleman by virtue of taste, behavior, and understanding. The "PMCing" of Broadway could not have happened without what Warren Susman referred to as the disappearance of the "culture of character...and the resulting call for a new modal type best suited to carry out the mission of a new cultural order" (Susman 274). This "culture of character" encompassed Winter, Towse, and the Victorian stage heroes—it encompassed the ideals that helped to make up the Victorian gentleman habitus. As "character" gave way to "personality," and high, noble locutions gave way to the gift of gab, and integrity gave way to projecting a brave, convincing front, Susman's "new modal type" began to emerge—the emerging PMC habitus. The plays that involved the men of nerves (or Mr. Nervous) featured characters that fell between character and personality, and between Victorian and Modern.

MODERN MEN AND MODERN NERVES

Theatre from the 1890s to the early twentieth century was in a transitory phase. The critics and theatre reporters of the time could feel it, or perhaps it was mostly hope—either way, they spent a great deal of ink on the theatre of the future. As 1890 began, critics were eagerly anticipating a new century of American drama. This anticipation included commentary on theatre technology, acting, dramaturgy, and audience. The expression "fin de siècle" found its way into optimistic and forward-looking theatre commentary. By the 1890–1891 season, most of the major playhouses had made the transition from gas to electric, and most of the playgoers were treated to brightly illuminated stages.[6] Writers for *The New York Dramatic Mirror,* among others, welcomed science to the stage:

> Who should be asked to come upon the stage? Every man of science. The civil engineer, the hydraulic engineer, the mechanical, military and naval engineer; the chemist; the physiologist, and most important of all the physicist, or student of physics. We shall be wise if we also ask the botanist, geologist, zoologist, lest our scene-painter give us the date palm growing beside the cedar tree. (Barnard, "Science")

In this case, the writer is referring to science experts not as onstage characters but rather as consultants ensuring as much stage verisimilitude as possible. How newly mastered stage effects should be implemented did indeed become an issue, as electricians occasionally found reason to show off irrespective of the play's content.[7]

The experts were equally hopeful regarding American playwriting, as witnessed by this column in the *Dramatic Mirror* from the same month: "It seems evident that an era of encouragement for American playwrights is dawning on the dramatic horizon" ("At the Theatres, Star Theatre, 'The Senator'"). William Gillette, for his part, opined, "The drama of to-day cannot live...but I am pleased to be able to add that the dramatist can" (Gillette, "Will It Live?"). And Henry Guy Carleton, with somewhat messianic fervor, predicted that "some day not far distant, the ship of art-supremacy will come to our shores and be long at her moorings" (Carleton, "The Dramatic Millennium").

As for the audience, contemporaneous commentators were divided along now-familiar lines. If Broadway's offerings were not all that they could be, went one argument put forth by the New York *World*, it was not the fault of the producers:

> The people attend the theatres for relief from the excessive strenuousness of their lives. They do not want to be uplifted or educated or subjected to any strong emotion. Their nerves and brains are perpetually on strain, and if they go to the theatre at all it is for the sake of a complete unbending of the mind and soul. They wish to laugh, and the more idiotic the thing they laugh at the better for their purpose. They want nothing serious. ("The Stage To-day" 2)

"Strained nerves" would prove extremely important in the evolution of both the PMC and a PMH, and the above article provides an early hint of that importance. The same columnist, in rebuttal to the *World's* "tired (and nervous) businessman" argument, expressed a higher regard for the Broadway audience:

> It is true that the largest number run after theatrical rubbish and "rot," but it is not true that these are the only requirements of the playgoing classes. There is a numerous public in this city, composed of intelligent and discriminating people, that can be safely relied on to appreciate and support every appeal, having the true elements of success, that is made to refined perceptions and artistic taste. ("The Stage To-day" 2)

Although there was a strong implication that the "intelligent and discriminating playgoing classes" were not the ones that were creating or supporting the big hits of the day, the columnist nevertheless applauded the "generous and continuous patronage that is given to such theatres as the Madison Square, Lyceum and Daly's"—in other words, mainstream first-class theatres ("The Stage To-day" 2).

As for strained brains and nerves, "dean of American playwrights" Bronson Howard provided one of Broadway's first glimpses of a man physically and mentally wracked by the pressures of business. *The Henrietta* was an early, seriocomic treatment of American corporate capitalism, and Mr. Nervous made his first major appearance. Although

Clyde Fitch often turned to stock speculators, nervous and otherwise, to drive his plots, he did not come to the idea first. In Howard's *The Henrietta,* which premiered on Broadway in September 1887, the home phone is always within arm's reach, and the stock ticker provides the onstage tempo, even slowing down and stopping to coincide with the death of one of the major characters.[8]

The machinations of stock speculation provide most of the evening's plot. The eldest wheeler-dealer is Nicholas Vanalstyne, or "Old Nick in the Street," as he is perhaps not so affectionately known by colleagues. Vanalstyne Sr. has his scruples: "I never made a big haul yet, except by telling the honest truth. I only lie between times" (9). He cheerfully suggests buying the Nevada legislature to secure the titular mine deal and apparently enjoys great health and a clear conscience. By contrast, Vanalstyne Jr., embodying Mr. Nervous, is all fragile nerves and suffers an even more fragile health as his shady business and personal dealings inevitably overtake him. As voice-of-reason physician Dr. Wainwright intones as he is warning Vanalstyne Jr. to relax,

> Your father was bred in the country. His nerves were as firm and as cold as steel before he ever came to the city.... The furnace-bred young men of New York are... mere bundles of nerve, that burn themselves like the overcharged wires of a battery. Notice the electric lights at your club. Every now and then one of them fizzles convulsively and goes out. (15)

The doctor's diagnosis, in fact, provides a fair description of how Vanalstyne Jr. moves through the play until his stock ticker–monitored death—overcharged, stooped (under the burdens not only of business stress but his own duplicity against his father), and speaking in angry bursts to those who want to help.

The play alternates, perhaps somewhat jarringly for a twenty-first century audience, between scenes of jovial business parody, melodramatic self-sacrifice with justice meted out to the wicked, and romantic comedy geared to the talents of two notable comedians of the era—W. H. Crane and Stuart Robson. The elder Vanalstyne suited Crane's hale and hearty brand of comedy, with a scene involving Vanalstyne trying to propose marriage and monitor an erratic stock ticker at the same time proving to be a comic highlight.[9] Robson, in turn, scored as Bertie, the youngest Vanalstyne who has no taste for business, and whose idea of a wild time is smoking two whole cigarettes in the same evening—the sort of milquetoast characterization that was Robson's forte. Bertie's business innocence is echoed by his young intended, Agnes, who tries to explain the Street to her fiancé: "Business is very easy, Bertie.... You just speak through the telephone to a man in Wall Street. You say 'sixty-five'—or any other number you choose—and a few weeks afterwards the man gives you a lot of money" (20). The climactic joke of the play is that Agnes turns out to be right—Bertie becomes a Wall Street genius by virtue of flipping a coin to make his decisions, thus saving his father's business and winning the girl. "It takes brain to deal at the Stock Exchange," Bertie sums up, with or without a trace of irony—although certainly Howard, along with the audience, viewed him ironically (82).

Throughout the play, playwright Howard makes several fairly curt and cutting observations about society and business. The Rev. Dr. Murray Hilton, while advocating the distribution of wealth to the poor in his sermons, sweatily speculates based on the elder Vanalstyne's advice. The suggestively named Watson Flint, the broker, gets many of the most cynical lines of the play regarding the vagaries of business in general and the stock market in particular: "Whichever side loses, we brokers win," he notes laconically (50). And while Howard describes Flint as "about thirty, quick, firm and decisive in speech, gentlemanly in manner" and wearing "evening dress," Flint is quick to dismiss any emotions or even humanity from the business equation: "I am a mere business machine" (27, 53). It is perhaps Flint who most closely represents a PMC figure while maintaining a "gentlemanly" habitus, based on his position relative to the high-volume trading that occurs throughout the play, but he does not play an active role in the plot. Bertie, for his part, has "returned from college" (29), and this would prove to be a typical condition of the callow, seemingly useless heroes of the business comedies of the next generation. Colleges and universities, which in Howard's time were beginning to prove so vital in identifying and defining a new business class, were primarily turning out dolts, idiots, and layabouts in the world of Broadway. While it could be argued that Bertie becomes an "expert" by the end of the play, the foundation of his expertise is neither his college education nor even any meaningful business experience—in the end, it comes down to a series of coin tosses. The Broadway stage would not provide a PMC expert in action for almost 30 years, but Broadway playwrights had made a beginning in exploring the business of business.

The nerves that plagued and ultimately killed Vanalstyne Jr. in *The Henrietta* would neither be cured nor subdued. At least one of the Matinee Lady's "dim shadows" threw a compelling light on another kind of hero—equal parts gentleman hero, man of nerves, and consummate mental expert. Although William Gillette fit comfortably also within the habitus of the carriage trade, he brought to one of his particular gentleman heroes an interesting new wrinkle.[10] One could not argue a case for Sherlock Holmes as a PMC type—certainly, Holmes was nothing if not an aristocrat—but he emerged as possibly the greatest expert mental-worker hero. Holmes as a character has the interesting distinction of falling between three distinct "habiti"—Victorian gentleman, Mr. Nervous, and Mr. Can-Do.

GILLETTE AS SHERLOCK HOLMES, SUPER EXPERT

It was the end of 1899 when William Gillette not only found in Sherlock Holmes what was to become his longest-running Broadway success but also created the physicality of Holmes that was accepted as "genuine" by New York and London audiences alike, as well as by Holmes creator Arthur Conan Doyle himself. It was Gillette who gave Holmes one of his trademark visual accoutrements—the drop-stem pipe. Apart from any aesthetic considerations or fidelity to the original stories (Holmes *did* smoke, but not drop-stem pipes), Gillette found it impossible to deliver dialog with his mouth clenched around an ordinary pipe (Kinsey 248). In Holmes, the New York audiences witnessed the theatrical pyrotechnics of the "mental worker" par excellence, a man whose superior powers of observation and deduction prevented even the most ingenious and diabolical criminals from disrupting society for more than four acts.

Holmes, and Gillette's embodiment of him, proves to be a useful theatrical/social marker in other ways. Gillette's cagey "underplaying" of the character, combined with his explicit directions to the supporting cast to "do it up brown" (in other words, to play for maximum melodramatic effect), automatically rendered Holmes the sanest and most rational person onstage. Gillette could exploit the melodramatic conventions of character, structure, and performance style that audiences still enjoyed and simultaneously, in the role of consummate expert, subvert such conventions as well (Kerr 64).[11] Gillette, by virtue of his playing style (which extended beyond his specific characterization of Holmes), contributed to a new phase of stage "realism"—more natural underplaying, photographic realism, and eventually "psychological" realism would all play a significant role in the "PMC-ing" of Broadway.

Indeed, the only "sensational" action Gillette allowed himself as Holmes was to "shoot up" onstage. Audiences received a graphic view of Holmes' notorious addiction to his "seven percent solution" as the great detective, despite Dr. Watson's sensible protests, "throws himself languidly into [the] sofa, leaning back in luxurious enjoyment of the drug" (Gillette, *Holmes* 226). Holmes' defense of his use of his "old love" cocaine is telling: "My whole life is spent in a series of frantic endeavors to escape from the dreary commonplaces of existence! For a brief period I escape!" (227). Here, Gillette and Holmes share a commonality with the neurasthenic heroes of the period. Holmes' seven-percent solution, however, could provide a cure for nerves only "for a brief period." Other solutions, it could well be argued, would not be much more effective.

Not that Gillette's primary physicalization was necessarily "languid." But his was the physicality of a man supremely confident in his abilities—meeting suspects in his brocade dressing gown, pausing in the midst of a tense confrontation to light his pipe, and moving with a "serpentine grace" that matched the grace of an agile mind (Kinsey 248). It is a confidence that falters, somewhat sentimentally, only at the possible onset of falling in love, a prospect more dangerous, one assumes, than a dozen Professor Moriartys.

There is more than a coincidental connection between Holmes' desire to escape and the assumed desires of the audience. The notion of theatre as a primary escape from "dreary commonplaces of existence" is an old one and, arguably, rather dreary in itself. But what were the "dreary commonplaces" for the emerging PMC? Broadway marketing strategies were shifting from courting the elite "carriage" crowd to pitching entertainment for "the family and its tired businessman"—an acknowledgment of the new corporate breadwinners, on various rungs of the corporate ladder, who put in long hours applying their Holmesian expertise to maintaining and improving the capitalist machinery. Lawyers, judges, engineers, professors, administrators, and clerks all needed a brief period of escape.

Gillette's greatest accomplishment in embodying Sherlock Holmes was not necessarily as a playwright. "Buncombe and claptrap" was a characteristic critical comment on the play itself (Cullen and Wilmeth 13). But critics also took sharp notice of the singular character that Gillette brought to life. According to the *New York Journal and Advertiser* of November 7, 1899, "no such type has ever flitted across our vision before" (Cullen and Wilmeth 15). Gillette's embodiment of this type carried him successfully well into the 1930s (he died in 1937, at age 83) and not incidentally made him a wealthy man. Gillette's creation was not merely a gentleman of the John Drew type, for example, who "perambulated graciously" throughout the 1890s (Carroll 73). Although both Gillette and his popular contemporary Drew embodied gentlemanliness and could perambulate graciously, Gillette combined aristocratic manners and values with debilitating nerves as well as extraordinary powers of ratiocination.

While Gillette impressed a nation with what was considered the definitive Holmes, playwright Clyde Fitch found his own popularity in exploring the idea and the bodies of the neurasthenic more thoroughly than anyone before or since.

FITCH AND THE PSYCHOLOGICAL MOMENT

"Well, it was Rand's good luck—to come along at the right psychological moment," a character comments on the hero in Clyde Fitch's final play, *The City* (Fitch, *The City* 513–514). Fitch's terminology is not inappropriate to describe the emerging character of early twentieth-century Broadway. Commercially, Fitch rode the wave of the psychological moment for all its worth.[12]

Fitch did, in fact, possess a few PMC attributes. He was college-educated, a graduate of Amherst. And, by the 1898 production of *The Moth and the Flame,* Fitch occupied something akin to a "managerial" position in terms of play production—he directed and supervised all details with the blessing of the producers (most often Syndicate member Charles Frohman).[13] Such a position was not dissimilar to an executive-level position in other corporations. Moreover, toward the end of his career, Fitch gave lectures on theatre at Yale, Harvard, and other universities—there was some acknowledgment of Fitch as "expert." In these lectures, printed in essay form as "The Play and the Public," Fitch gives his own view of the Broadway audience, referencing "the plush minds downstairs and the unupholstered hearts in the gallery" (Fitch, *Plays* v. 4 xxi).

Fitch's use of furniture metaphors to describe the primary Broadway audience bears some examination. Fitch shared the opinion of many of the audience experts (i.e., the critics) that there was an honest, unadorned (hence "unupholstered") directness to be found in the "gallery gods'" enthusiasm, in contrast with the response of the more fashionable (or "plush") members of the audience.[14] However, Fitch was not pitting one section of the audience against the other—his view of the ideal audience was largely even-handed and democratic, "leavened with a little of every class and kind" (Fitch, v. 4, xxvi). He did not accept the idea that some plays were too good for the public; as a playwright, it was simply his job to please as much of the audience as he could. Fitch even held considerable affection for the infamous "matinee girl":

> Personally I love the matinee girl! She believes in youthful love, ideals, self-sacrifices, and I want to. She believes in romance in real life—I want to. And she is no fool. She is quick with her ridicule, ever ready with her discernment of what is true and what is stage pretense. But granting all her charms and her intelligence, I still do not think she should rule the playhouse. As a matter of fact, she is growing to be an obsolete character! Conditions are such that it is more often mother and father who go to the matinee now; she goes in the evening! (Fitch, *Plays* v. 4 xlvi–xlvii)

Although he dressed too flamboyantly and lived too lavishly to fit comfortably within the emerging PMC, Fitch had one more significant trait shared by the elite and the PMC, that of "nervousness." In the editorial notes accompanying his collected letters, friends Montrose Moses and Virginia Gerson write of "a shorthand quickness which suited his impulsive and nervous nature," which is borne out by Fitch's frequent use of italics and hurried abbreviations (Moses and Gerson, *Letters* xiv). Audiences, of course, did not go to see Fitch (except perhaps on opening nights), but it is worth noting that Fitch had intimate knowledge of his subject. Fitch and his friends were all too aware of this neurasthenic quality that they shared, as evidenced by this excerpt from a 1904 letter to Fitch from Maude Adams: "We live so much among people of morbid tendencies, neurasthenics (I can't spell it), and the like—that we begin to think they are real, and they are real of their kind but it isn't a red blood kind" (Fitch, *Letters* 256). Adams not only spelled the word correctly but also put her finger on a key PMC problem.[15] Nervousness and neurasthenia would prove significant in Fitch's work, in future PMC self-identity, and in the future of "modern" American drama.

Fitch's ability to write a "manly" play, as well as his personal manliness, was called into question throughout his life and career. It might well seem that using the closeted gay Fitch as a key figure in the emerging PMC habitus would be problematic, if not completely counterproductive.[16] However, Fitch's place in the "PMC-ing" of Broadway consists of three elements, or perhaps, three overlapping stages: antimodel, posthumous super-model (the triumph of his final play, *The City*), and unconscious and largely unheralded pioneer in staging a distinctly (if early) PMC type—the "neurasthenic."

The first stage, Fitch as antimodel, is the one with which his contemporaries were most familiar. Although Fitch claimed that he neither wrote for specific actresses nor cared to do so (Fitch, *Letters* 311), he created several winning roles for, among others, Effie Shannon, Ethel Barrymore, Maxine Elliott, Elsie deWolfe, and the unfortunate Clara Bloodgood, who would shoot herself in a theatre in Baltimore before a performance of Fitch's *The Truth* (*Letters* 353–54). Fitch occasionally wrote male-driven vehicles, most notably *Beau Brummell*, his first play, for Richard Mansfield, as well as *Nathan Hale*, Nat Goodwin's successful historical piece. Until *The City*, however, critics primarily characterized Fitch and his plays as facile, artificial, superficial, and distinctly feminine.[17]

Part of Fitch's "superficiality" was a function of what was increasingly recognized by critics and audiences as a "photographic" sense of realism. A significant contributor to the program advertisements that surfaced in 1890 was Kodak. The rise of interest in photography led to the demand for easy-to-use cameras, and Kodak promised these in their advertising: "You press the button, we do the rest."[18] The term "photographic" and even the brand name "Kodak" would soon find their way into theatre criticism and analysis as a way of describing and defining realism. Sometimes the term could be derogatory, as in Eugene Walter's self-criticism of *The Easiest Way*:

> Incidentally, I do not think much of it [the play]. To my mind a good play must have a tremendous uplift of thought and purpose. "The Easiest Way" has none of this. There is not a character in the play really worth while, with the exception of the old agent.... As it is more or less purely photographic, I do not think it should be given the credit of an inspiration. (Moses, *Representative Plays* 707)

Here Walter criticizes one of his biggest successes as being *merely* photographic, something of a sordid and sensational snapshot. More often, however, the term was used approvingly as a way of presenting the kinds of situations and bodies that the audience could conceivably meet and witness outside as well as inside the theatre. Tellingly, Fitch's friend Montrose Moses likens the bulk of Fitch's oeuvre to "excellent Kodak films of the city" (Moses & Gerson, "Introduction" xiii).

Fitch's great subject through the bulk of his career was, in Edith Wharton's words, "humorous exhibitions of human vacuity"—more specifically, the vacuity exhibited by a particular section of New York society (Wharton 160–161, qtd. in Loney 22).[19] For the most part, the Fitch hero, or more often, heroine, could rise above the deadly pettiness to attain a happy ending—a pattern not always to Fitch's liking, but he would generally bow to either a producer's demands (usually Charles Frohman's) or his own sense of what an audience wanted. His output was large, regular (in terms of his plays being performed each season), and generally welcome. This was the Fitch—the "Hustling

Histrionicus"—that the New York *Sun* playfully celebrated in verse: "out of the glittering social grot,/Of the very Fitchiest, fetchingest lot,/ Stirred in the scorching society pot,/Hot,/He plucks a wild, weird name and plot" (qtd. in Atkinson, 55–56).

Fitch, for his part, maintained his breakneck schedule of writing, rehearsing, and traveling. By his early 40s, he had shocked Broadway with his frank depiction of a seduction/near-rape in *Sappho* and had started to show audiences more social unpleasantness than "good taste" allowed.[20] He had not, however, convinced critics or general audiences that he could write a "masculine" play. With the story of the rise and moral corruption of a young, hustling politician, Fitch was able to create the play that at last earned him the "capital" of manhood. He did not live to enjoy it.

As a Fitch character, George Rand Jr. of *The City* was a relative anomaly—a young, striving male with "the New York bee in his bonnet" who held the center of the play and drove the plot (454).[21] Whether or not Fitch realized this would be his final play, he nonetheless deliberately presented the audience with many distinctly "masculine" signifiers. As Rand Jr. rises in politics, the local newspapers refer to him as "Teddy, Jr." (512). Audiences of 1909 immediately knew that "Teddy" could refer only to Theodore Roosevelt, a proponent of vigorous physical exercise whose character was readily identifiable as manly. The public saw him, in Howard Zinn's words, as "the great lover of nature and physical fitness, the war hero, the Boy Scout in the White House" (Zinn 351). Strength and masculinity, for Roosevelt, were integral in the fight for Anglo-Saxons to avoid "race suicide"—decadence and effeminacy left the superior races vulnerable to "inferior immigrant stock" (Lears, *No Place* 30). As an article in a 1905 issue of *The Cosmopolitan* advised: "There is something enervating in feminine companionship.... The genuine man feels that he must go off alone or with other men, out in the open air, as it were, roughing it among the rough, as a mental tonic" (*This Fabulous Century* 43). This love of exercise and physical fitness would largely inform the plays that celebrated college and college athletes.

Nor did Fitch stop there. He not only had the villain curse (earlier in the play, we also see the drug-addicted villain shooting up) but also included what apparently was the first time the Lord's name was taken in vain on stage: "You're a God damn liar!" character actor Tully Marshall uttered as the drug-addicted villain.[22] The harsh language was enough to draw astonished gasps from male and female theatergoers alike.[23] Before the audience had a chance to fully recover from this blasphemy, the villain shoots Rand's younger sister just as she is about to discover that she has married her half-brother. It could be said that Fitch would overpower the Broadway audience with brute strength, or die trying. As it happened, he did both.

Amidst the sensational moments, Fitch set out to tell a story that encompassed everything germane to the new century, the city, and the "clean-cut American" man (462) who would take them on. Fitch establishes the "rat-race" element of the City (New York) early on through the shady pillar of Middleburg society Rand, Sr.: "First, you want to catch up with your neighbor, then you want to pass him; and then you die disappointed if you haven't left him out of sight!" (473). The father must confess to his son that he "ruined" Hannock's mother—Hannock is his son, and Rand, Sr. has been giving him money all his life (Hannock does not suspect his parentage, thus setting up the climactic near-incest) (477–78). The progressive Rand Jr. is understanding: "I'm a twentieth century *son*, you know, and *New York at heart!*" (488, author's emphasis). When Rand, Sr. suddenly drops dead near the end of the first act,[24] Rand Jr. knows he is bound for New York City at last: "He straightens up, and lifts his head; and his face flushes with the uncontrolled impulses of youth and ambition. With a voice of suppressed excitement, full of emotion, and with a trembling ring of triumph, he says... 'The City!'" (502–503).

Act II unfolds "several years later" as the Rands take up residence in New York, with a home befitting a rising politician, complete with John Singer Sargent portrait (503). Here Fitch introduces another "manly" thread into the dramatic narrative, that of politics. The drug-addled Hannock is now Rand Jr.'s personal secretary, and he makes no bones about intending to ride Rand Jr.'s coattails. One can notice Fitch's construction as he takes the old device of the villain talking to himself, while justifying it in a realistic context at the same time: "Humph! 'Teddy, Jr.'

is a good nickname for him,—I guess not! The *public* would put George Rand in the Roosevelt class with a vengeance, wouldn't they!...Damn it, when am I going to stop talking in my sleep when I'm wide awake!...Too much of the needle, I guess!" (512–513, author's emphasis). The steps toward greater realism in dialog, along with the cursing and the "photographic" realism, are evident in Fitch's work and would be expanded between 1910 and 1930.

Rand Jr.'s mentor, Vorhees, appears to be trying to guide the hero away from shady, "end-justifies-the-means" practices in politics, while reaffirming the fundamental dignity of man in the technology-driven machine era: "Man is greater than a machine, because God's soul is in him" (520). Rand Jr. despite the less-than-honorable goings-on that involve practically his whole family, insists that he is ready for "the muckrakes" (522). Just as it appears that Rand Jr. will indeed receive the nomination, Cicely announces that she has married Hannock, leading to the most sensational of all of Fitch's—or anyone else's of the period for that matter—climaxes.[25] Following the shooting of Cicely Rand, the hero must at last confront his own dishonest business dealings in his showdown with Hannock: "You can't alter the diplomacy of the business world—calling it by ugly names!" Hannock replies, in a testament to the high esteem in which Roosevelt was held by Fitch and his audience: "No, I can't, but *Roosevelt did!*" (599, author's emphasis).

In the final act, Rand Jr. takes responsibility for his actions and resolves to start again with a clean slate. At the end of the day (and the play), the emphasis is not on a perceived social or political problem endemic to the City, but rather on personal accountability. As Rand Jr. states famously: "Don't blame the City...What the City does is to bring out what's strongest in us" (628). His girlfriend, Eleanor, stands by her sadder-but-wiser man: "It's the man whom it costs something to be good,—that's what makes real character!" she beams happily (635). The two stand together in mutual love and support as the curtain falls. Rand Jr., throughout the play, has shuttled between two worlds—one of character (honesty and integrity), and one of personality (slickness, glad-handing, and covering up). In the context of later business farces, the ability to be glib and to slide quickly over inconsistencies and improbabilities would be highly prized. Perhaps ironically, the final image in Fitch's most modern play hearkens back to the old-fashioned tableaux of melodramas where father is reunited with wife and family, all heads turned to heaven.

I have devoted these several pages to Fitch's final play because of the rush of "manly" (and posthumous) cultural capital the play brought to him:

> For "The City" was to be a challenge to those who had persisted in saying that Fitch was strictly a "feminine" dramatist. It was to be the proof that he could be strong and forceful, fearless and almost Greek in theme. "The audience roared its approval," said one paper; cheers swept the house from orchestra to balcony. There were combined on that evening the power of the playwright, who was not there, and the power of the actors who at every moment seemed to feel his presence. Another paper declared, "It seems tame to say merely that the play was strong, for in its strongest scene it is tremendous. The play is strong as a raging bull...a hungry tiger...This is a play to shudder at..."[26] There is no exaggeration in saying that hysteria moved that vast audience. Women were removed fainting, and men shouted as the curtain went up and down in response to repeated calls. It was an unprecedented night in the theater. (Moses and Gerson, *Letters* 385–386)

Indeed, Fitch was "deeply conscious of the fundamental truths of life, and he was eager to put strength into his dialog in order to offset the delicacy and feminine flashes which the public always considered Fitchean. 'The City' was his first, as it proved to be his last, effort in that direction." (Moses, *American Dramatist* 326).

This record of audience response to *The City*, along with the testosterone-loaded metaphors of strength that the critics employed, bears some analysis. The Broadway audience, which included a number of nervous Professional Managerial men, seemed hungry (even starved) for manly displays from the stage heroes and powerful, shocking scenes that made wives and girlfriends faint. Here there were no conventional matinee idols to attract "matinee girls" of all ages, nor were there last-minute rescues or intrusions that saved the characters from impropriety and bad taste. *The City* gave the audience an identifiable "nervous" hero, placed the hero in the depths of degradation heretofore unheard of on Broadway, and certainly unheard of from Fitch himself, and finally, allowed the hero to show the requisite strength to attain a moral (if not material) victory. One can practically hear the young George Rand Juniors of the audience, along with the middle-aged men who felt they had once been young George, shouting a rousing, manly cheer of "Bully for Fitch!" shortly before attending to their unconscious spouses and escorts.

Although Fitch struggled with, and perhaps at last attained, his own playwriting "manhood," critics at the time of his death gave him credit for doing almost as much for the American drama.[27] Although, as Moses admitted, by the 1920s Fitch's plays would already fall out of favor,[28] the claim is not entirely inaccurate. Nevertheless, it was not so much Fitch's final display of "masculinity" that paved the way for what the PMC would first acknowledge as "modern American drama," but rather his display of the male neurasthenic, and the strong females who were arguably more PMC than the men.

NEURASTHENICS CAUGHT ON KODAK

The Moth and the Flame, from 1898, represents Fitch's first major depiction of a fundamentally weak, excitable (i.e., nervous) male figure who, although in many ways well-intentioned, causes the key crises that the plucky Fitchean heroine must solve and/or overcome.[29] The heroine, Marion Wolton, has the earmarks of American fin-de-siècle modern womanhood—she's been to college (and studied Sociology) and works earnestly with settlement houses and the YMCA, or, as one of her less enlightened companions calls it, "that Christian thing-a-may-gig" (568). Marion's natural bent toward "saving" the unfortunate leads her to make an ill-considered love-choice in the wastrel Fletcher, who, it turns out, has not acknowledged his child to a woman he has not married. The unfortunate young woman, Jeanette, stops the wedding between Fletcher and Marion with the sort of dramatic confrontation Fitch and his audience reveled in: "No! You shall not write Bastard on the forehead of *my child*!" (576). The cowardly Fletcher reveals his true colors by striking Jeanette in the church, in front of God and everybody. In the rather calmer final act, Marion prevails upon Fletcher to marry Jeanette, and the man Marion should have been with all along, Douglas, appears to take on Marion's debts and, presumably, Marion herself.

While the play had a (then) respectable ten-week run in New York (cut short by the summer) and a happy touring future, the critical response proved interesting, particularly regarding the character of Fletcher. As Gerald Bordman comments: "One much voiced complaint...was that none of the characters truly enlisted sympathy. The most interesting figure was Fletcher, who seems genuinely willing to put his ugly past behind him and reverts to his baser self only when the woman whom he sees as his sole chance for salvation spurns him" (Bordman 1994, 424). This overview is confirmed by Edward A. Dithmar's examination of the play about a week after the opening:

> We are interested in their [the characters'] actions, but we do not feel heartily for them, nor do we ever even detest them. Perhaps we are all a little sorry for Fletcher when he loses his temper in the church, because that is such a "bad break" for a man of his kind. I think we feel sorry for him, too, when he starts for Europe and Asia just before the last curtain. (Dithmar, "Week at the Theatres")

What makes Fletcher so interesting as a character and the critical response to him of equal interest is that despite his "baser" actions, he is not (nor was he considered) a "villain."[30] The (limited) "pity" that is evoked in the wedding scene is not for the "meddlesome" (in Dithmar's words) fallen mother, but for the "bad break" that Fletcher receives in the process. The existence of the double standard regarding men who make impulsive, unfortunate mistakes and "fallen" women is evident,[31] but there is something else at work as well. The identification of Dithmar and others with Fletcher as a young man attempting to put his past indiscretions behind him and assume a new life, only to be trapped by fate and circumstances, evidences considerable commonality with later, "deeper," psychologically conflicted heroes of O'Neill—that is, of what audiences and experts considered "mature" and "modern" American drama.

Fitch was by no means finished with the neurasthenics. *The Climbers*, produced in New York in early 1901, provided the Broadway theatergoers with another "nervous" type, once again supplying the obstacle to the heroine's happiness.[32] Fitch gives a detailed description of the neurasthenic Sterling, the heroine's husband: he "is handsome and distinguished. His hair is grayer than his years may account for and his manner betrays a nervous system overtaxed and barely under control. At the moment that he enters he is evidently laboring under some especial, and only half-concealed, nervous strain" (Fitch, *Climbers* 512).[33] Sterling moved and acted, in other words, like a typical Mr. Nervous.

Fitch contrasts the fatally flawed husband with a more ideal male: Edward Warden, Blanche's best friend and soulmate. "He is good-looking, practical, a reasoning being, and self-controlled," Fitch writes. "He is a thorough American, with the fresh and strong ideals of his race, and with the feeling of romance alive in the bottom of his heart" (522–523). Once again, however, it is the less "practical, reasoning, and self-controlled" male who commands more interest. Sterling, a lawyer (fitting within a PMH) and, like a number of Fitch characters, an unsuccessful Wall Street speculator, pays for this lack of control by taking his own life—the price of nervousness run amok.

"Nervousness" would beset many of Fitch's male characters throughout his career. In *Her Own Way*, first presented in 1903, Fitch again presented a weak man whose rash actions precipitate a crisis, who openly displays his nerves: "his voice and body almost vibrating with nerve," the stage directions read (Fitch, *Her Own Way* 473). In contrast, the man worthy of the heroine has "no finicking about him, no nerves. Just a sane, healthy, fine fellow" (488–89). That he is also a bit of a dull fellow once again reflects Fitch's greater interest in, and facility for creating, not only a fairly complex heroine but also a fairly complex neurasthenic man.[34] Nevertheless, the condition of nervousness in Fitch's supporting male characters is not insignificant. Many of Fitch's nervous men were professionals, agitated due to business deals gone wrong. Sterling, for example, is a lawyer, trying unsuccessfully to emulate the "killings" of the stock market. Steven Carley, in *Her Own Way*, is another misguided speculator, although (with the heroine's help) he is able to give up his penchant for bad investments and become a respectable business manager, one who will buy or sell only on the word of his client. In turn,

Geoffrey, in Fitch's Clara Bloodgood vehicle *The Girl with the Green Eyes,* is described as "a young, good-looking man, but with a weak face"—his weakness manifests itself in a shameful, drunken marriage (Fitch, *Green Eyes* 18). And finally, Fitch's most "manly" hero, George Rand Jr. of *The City,* could be said to be his ultimate man of nervousness—he and his family are all too nervous to stay in Middleburg. Rand Jr.'s nervous energy is of such magnitude that only "The City" can contain it.

Fitch's depictions of nervousness were very much in line with the culture of the era. As Tom Lutz writes in his anecdotal study of nervousness and neurasthenia, there were "numerous texts...which link nervousness and success, nervousness and social mobility, as well as nervousness and divorce or any other disruption of the gender system" (Lutz 3). There was, in fact, a certain amount of cultural capital to be gained by suffering from the "disease" of nervousness: "Nervousness...was therefore a mark of distinction, of class, of status, of refinement. Neurasthenia struck brain-workers but no other kind of laborer" (6). Although nervousness never proved positive for Fitch's characters (or for Fitch himself), the possibility of identification among the nervous members of the audience was still quite possible and, perhaps, therapeutic. Just whose disease neurasthenia was is a matter for debate; while the moneyed elite feared modernity (and thus became nervous), neurasthenia was also linked with more progressive responses to cultural change.[35] The question arises: could not gentlemen (and gentlewomen) also be nervous? And the answer is that they certainly could, and they often were. The quality of nervousness tended to unite, rather than separate, the moneyed elite from the cultured elite, or the gentlemen from the PMC. One of the crowning achievements of the PMC would be how it dealt with neurasthenia—experts would find a way to control this particular field while at the same time appearing to level it. Nerves, in other words, would also come to be a matter for the experts.

At any rate, nervousness was inevitably making its mark on Broadway bodies and their audiences, and the strain of neurasthenia would keep physical and psychological experts busy for the next generation. With the vestiges of nineteenth-century notions of honor, morals, manners, and integrity, Fitch continued to insist on character. Nevertheless, Fitch was also keenly aware of more modern notions of personality—described by adjectives such as "stunning," "attractive," and "magnetic," his characters are frequently striving to "be Somebody."[36] What Fitch accomplished, finally, was to place on stage a modern psychological PMH that anticipated O'Neill.

These plays of nerves and neurasthenics stirred the beginnings of class consciousness of the emerging PMC. Audience members from both the moneyed elite (capitalist) classes and the PMC could most likely recognize themselves, their colleagues, and their business associates onstage, and this consciousness must have been less than pleasant. But this consciousness was indeed only a beginning, as the PMC itself was only in its infancy. Fitch's neurasthenic heroes straddled both the dominant (capitalist) and emerging (PMC) classes, so that a deep form of class consciousness was not yet possible. Class consciousness, both pleasant and painful, would emerge more clearly with the plays that featured college athletics as well as with some surprisingly sophisticated musicals.

4. Muckraking the Playing Field: Emerging PMC Class Consciousness ⁓

THE FRESHEST KIDS IN TOWN

In an era when the elite classes—both the "moneyed" elite and the "cultured" elite—dealt with social disorder, radical anarchists, immigrants, and other threatening issues, what Lears refers to as "Anglo-Saxon revitalization" became a goal of paramount importance. A natural destination for the "search for order" was the playing field. The college football field emerged as a key "realm of upper-class revitalization" (Lears, "American Advertising" 61). Although most team athletics fulfilled this function to greater or lesser degrees, football nevertheless provided the key "field" of manhood. As Harvey Green writes,

> By the 1890s...its [football's] allegedly controlled violence seemed to signify that men were steeling themselves for battle in the best possible way, whether that fight was to be against foreign (or domestic) adversaries armed with the traditional weapons of war or against others in the corporate boardrooms of the nation and the world. Football was a key to success, because, like the religious devotions of earlier eras and other cultures, it instilled discipline and team spirit. (Green 9)

College was the place where the athletic elite were trained for later comparable positions in business and society. In an extension of the prevalent social Darwinism,[1] only the fittest could endure, both on the and off field (Green 10).

78 Broadway and Corporate Capitalism

Another significant factor in the national interest in sport was, not surprisingly, Theodore Roosevelt. Roosevelt published *The Strenuous Life* in 1900, and the country was paying attention:

> The tremendous interest in sports and outdoor life which characterized this generation can be explained in part by the growth of wealth and leisure and in part by the desire to recapture something of the benefits of rural life which were disappearing for large numbers of Americans. A nation scarcely two decades removed from a fighting frontier was hardly ready to forgo the strenuous life, and Roosevelt's excoriation of the "over-civilized man" and the "life of slothful ease" fell on receptive ears. (Faulkner 281)

Nevertheless, enthusiasm for sport was already undergoing a change by the early twentieth century. As athletes and businessmen alike were striving to "shape up,"[2] sports was in the midst of a transition between two distinct embodiments—discipline on the one hand, and victory at all costs on the other. As Donald Mrozek explains,

> The rationale for sport that emphasized its rational organization and its encouragement of discipline reflected the values of an older middle class whose power was already in decline by the end of the nineteenth century. The new middle class, as Robert Wiebe has suggested,[3] accepted order as a kind of value in itself. And, to the extent that victory was viewed as proof of effective organization, this attitude contributed to a "win at all costs" attitude which split the practice of sport from its former social purposes. (Mrozek 19)

When college sports at last arrived on Broadway, all of these factors—teamwork, discipline, and the quest for success—came into play (and into the plays). Appropriately for Broadway, college was mostly, though not quite entirely, the stuff of fun and games. And when the PMC took the field, they did not necessarily emerge the victors.

The college "field" that invaded the Broadway "field" was not necessarily the college that current and future "professionals" knew. What Broadway seized upon was youthful energy, pretty girls, and, in the words of one of the characters of O'Neill's *The Iceman Cometh*, "rah-rah exaggeration" (O'Neill, *Iceman* 38). The "rah-rah" element of the collegiate world was well in sync with Broadway's quest for liveliness and excitement, and it made a suitable subject for not-too-subtle parody. Although a college or university education was a key element of self-identification for the PMC, it remained slightly exotic and perhaps slightly absurd to the most successful Broadway practitioners—and these practitioners assumed college environments would prove too exotic for the Broadway audience. By the same token, the PMC itself found its most common onstage embodiments as campus "grinds," that is, students who took studying much too seriously (and at the expense of the big game), or as comically pompous (and verbose) professors and college presidents. No doubt PMC audience members enjoyed the humor of these college plays and perhaps got caught up in the natural drama inherent in the inevitable big game. At the same time, however, they must have recognized that the onstage college had little relation or relevance to their actual university education that led to their present employment.

Another historical consideration deals with the colleges that were educating and forming the new PMC—these were not, by and large, the colleges that found their way to the Broadway stage. Democratic and practical ideals of American education led to the creation of land-grant colleges and technical institutions, giving more American men the opportunity to learn agricultural and mechanical arts (the "A&M" in "A&M" universities). While schools such as Yale, Harvard, and Dartmouth had created separate scientific institutions by the late 1840s and early 1850s, the passage of the Morrill Act in 1862 enabled each state to build an affordable university for students to concentrate on A&M. "By 1900," as Bruce E. Seely writes, "the great majority of American engineering students were enrolled in A&M schools" (Seely 19).[4]

Such background relates to the "college" plays under examination in several ways. Although throughout the rest of the country, college was becoming both increasingly accessible and increasingly important in terms of learning a trade (and earning credentials within the trade), this was not yet a phenomenon that appeared conspicuously in Broadway's field of vision. This was partly a geographical consideration; the colleges that were known for turning out the engineers and scientists who constituted the PMC were, for the most part, a considerable distance away. The nearest land-grant college to Broadway, for example, would have been Cornell in upstate Ithaca. Furthermore, the atmosphere of such colleges, with its emphasis on (and reputation for) practical studies, was not necessarily conducive to creating the stories of light-hearted frivolity that would dominate the Broadway campus. Also, the students who took advantage of the land-grant college system were primarily from the middle classes, who, at least when onstage, would serve only as foils for both the comic and serious-minded gentlemen who attended.[5] Finally, as evidenced in the plays of the period, as well as in the popular culture that would follow at least until the middle of the twentieth century, there existed a distinct prejudice against college education as opposed to practical, "real world" experience.[6] This prejudice would give birth to one of the most lasting stereotypes of the American stage—the recent college graduate who is usually good-hearted and well-meaning but is of no earthly use.

In the early years of the twentieth century, when audiences were presented with college life, love, and athletics, Broadway's attitude toward academia was cheerfully irreverent. The attitude toward athletics was irreverent as well, but fraught with complications, not the least of which was a reliance on the importance of teamwork, and on the playing field as a place where men became real men or else settled for being waterboys or mascots. While ambitious playwrights occasionally tried to impart serious messages in between the "boolah-boolah" scenes, audiences could be reasonably certain that scenes featuring the latest snappy slang and at least one rousing sporting match would not be left out. A good-natured graduate of Purdue would first clear the playing field(s) and set many of the rules to follow.

FAIR PLAY: *THE COLLEGE WIDOW, STRONGHEART,* AND *BROWN OF HARVARD*

George Ade's friends and producer did not think a play dealing with college athletics was a good idea—they were certain that only those who had gone to college would be interested. The wise money in 1904 said that there were not enough college graduates in the audience to make a "college play" viable onstage.

To an extent, census education summaries for the period justified this concern. In 1904, institutions of higher learning in the United States had a total enrollment of 264,000, with 31,500 earning BA degrees. (As a point of comparison, enrollment figures would reach 941,000 by 1925, with 97,300 BA degrees conferred.)[7] Nevertheless, Ade's friends might have known that college students had gained a reputation for enjoying themselves at the theater in a manner that might best be described as "rowdy." As Richard Butsch writes,

> Harvard students would arrive in hundreds and really "whoop it up." When Mae West performed in New Haven, Yale students purchased a block of seats down front but left them empty until her turn. Then they marched in, singing "Boola Boola." When she was canceled due to the boisterousness, the students wrecked the theater. Student crowds from the University of Michigan, Purdue, Notre Dame, Indiana, and Ohio State, in small-town Midwestern theaters often threw things at performers they disliked and harassed the female troupers as they left the theater.... The behavior of these privileged young men belied the image of rowdiness as a working-class trait. (Butsch 119)

Such collegiate displays, however, were more true of "small-time" vaudeville audiences than of Broadway (Butsch 118–119).

For his part, Ade thought the idea could work as a comedy. "Give the people natural types that they can recognize and have them say things that people can understand. Be careful not to hurt anyone's feelings. Try to amuse the public and not offend good taste," Ade declared (Kelly 187); to which he might have added the following: and make sure what happens on stage has almost nothing to do with American college life as any American collegian would recognize it.

George Ade did not take up the subject of college as an outsider, although, going by the play's script, one might assume he was writing with an outsider's point of view.[8] He graduated from Purdue in 1887 and would contribute to the university as well as to the Sigma Chi fraternity throughout his later years.[9] He was, nevertheless, an outsider in terms of the details of college football; he frankly admitted in his stage directions that the producer would need "a football man" to determine the proper equipment for the characters (Ade 70). The college atmosphere gave Ade plenty of opportunities to poke fun at particular college "types" and, more significantly in terms of the PMC, to question playfully the ultimate usefulness of a college education. Although the verisimilitude of Ade's onstage college atmosphere could be called into question, the fact remains that Ade was the first to put distinctly American college life and male college bodies on the Broadway stage.[10]

The setting is Atwater College, and the Atwater football team is trying to recruit Billy, a promising young athlete. Billy's father, a bottom-line businessman, has already made arrangements for Billy to go to a rival school. The coach convinces Jane, the college president's daughter and the "college widow" of the title, to convince Billy to join Atwater—the whole school knows that Jane is "the lady with the pull" (Ade 8).[11] Her plan succeeds, but complications arise when Billy and Jane really fall in love. Audiences most likely had little doubt that Atwater would win the big game and that the love crises would resolve themselves by the Act IV curtain. Nevertheless, Ade clearly tapped into something fresh and new for Broadway audiences of October 1904. What was new was Ade's conception of the "student body." Most of those who comprised the student bodies were gentlemen and sons of privilege, not taking their studies too seriously, but taking their sports and their manly friendships with the utmost seriousness. A key element of the gentlemanly fun was to poke fun at those who *did* take academia too seriously—a telling demonstration of where the budding onstage PMC stood in the pecking order.

In other words, the characters in *The College Widow* who most conspicuously inhabit a PMH are the ones that the audience is meant to laugh *at,* rather than *with*. One such character is the university president, Peter Witherspoon (AM, PhD, Dr.). Witherspoon speaks with an exaggerated locution that bears only slight relevance to the world around him. "Restrain yourselves, young gentlemen," he admonishes the high-spirited collegians upon his entrance (Ade 22).[12] Similarly, a graduate student with the telling name of Copernicus Talbot, who performs tutoring duties for the players, speaks in the same comically elevated manner. "I shall immediately collect my impedimenta," Talbot says to let the football player he's instructing know that he just needs to get his things together. Ade did not originate this sort of characterization by any means; foolish pedants appear in Shakespeare and Aristophanes. However, with colleges and universities gaining increasing visibility during this era, such characters as Witherspoon and Talbot would find their place in a long line of comic academics who would continue to appear in theatres throughout the twentieth century and beyond. Such characterizations embodied the opinion that a college education had little use or relation to the "real" world.[13]

This opinion is voiced directly by the hero's father, the railroad tycoon Bolton, who is arguably the play's voice of reason. Ade describes Bolton as "a bluff, brusque business man of the Middle West type. He wears a good tailor-made suit, derby hat or soft traveling hat, mustache or tuft of chin whiskers, but no side whiskers. He is of the West and not Wall Street" (Ade 19). Bolton, Ade makes clear, is no neurasthenic Wall Street speculator, subject to nervousness and the vagaries of the market. There is a strong indication of a regionalist bias (if a comic one)—the common sense of the Midwest trumps the mercurial East (Ade himself was raised in Indiana).

Bolton is introduced as Witherspoon's friend and "a captain of industry" (22). He later speaks directly about his brief college career, when confronted with a question in science class: "I'm a full-grown man and I don't propose to waste my time pickin' dandelions to pieces." Bolton then offers this summation of college in general: "Oh, colleges do some good—they keep a good many light-weights out of the railroad business. But there ain't any money in a college education" (Ade 27–28). The question of what there *is* in a college education becomes playfully complicated in Ade's conception. In the world of the play, there not only "ain't" any money in a college education, but little to no cultural capital as well.

The subject that receives the most kidding in *The College Widow* is the importance of athletics, particularly football, on college campuses. Witherspoon receives criticism throughout the play for making the athletes go to classes, even from the sensible Jane: "If we lose this game, I'll blame you! You compelled those poor boys to attend recitations when they should have been practicing!" The well-meaning but hapless Witherspoon can only cry in bewilderment, "What would John Calvin say to this?" (Ade 78).[14] By the climactic big game, however, even Witherspoon is caught up in the excitement: "This mania for athletics is a veritable cyclone—I am carried along with it, helpless but protesting" (Ade 107). A good many Americans could say the same thing. In the meantime, the comic conceit of players not taking classes, a conceit based greatly on fact, would prove a sturdy one in American comedy.

The other major signifier of young American manhood that surfaces in *The College Widow* is that of the fraternity. Stub, one of the Atwater teammates, and Billy, the tricked hero who has fallen in love, belong to the same fraternity (107–108). When Billy confronts Stub, it is with the special fraternity handshake that he is able to compel Stub to tell the truth. In the world of the play, it is the fraternity that has practically the ultimate authority. Both Billy and Stub must "play fair," just as the earlier gentlemen heroes had to do.

In the end, Billy gets the girl and, with one last chide from his father ("No wonder you've been a freshman for four years!"), takes his rightful place in the family railroad business (108). College would seem to have its advantages—primarily playing football and getting the girl. At any rate, graduation seems to be, at most, a secondary concern. For the characters in *The College Widow*, the chief value of college is as something of a way station on the road to maturity. There is no question of Billy bringing his college-trained expertise to improve his father's business—Billy, of course, has never made it out of freshman year. For the hero who finally wins "the college widow," the railroad business is his for the taking as soon as he finishes playing games and grows up.

This jaundiced view of college and academic life (and of the PMC) continued to pervade Broadway's efforts at staging the university. The "types" who appeared in Ade's show also populated college shows ranging from *Strongheart* and *Brown of Harvard* in the same decade, to *Leave It to Jane* (the musical *College Widow*) the following decade, as well as *Good News* in the 1920s, and popular college-themed songs such as "Freddy the Freshman."[15] It was largely due to Ade's lighthearted efforts that the American popular consciousness was given the college man with the fur coat playing the ukulele and carrying the pennant that read "State." And it was also largely due to the success of *The College Widow* that playwright William C. de Mille was inspired to take on a more serious theme, with an atmosphere that was already known to generate audience interest.

In some ways, de Mille's contribution to the college epic *Strongheart* is the most thematically ambitious.[16] *Strongheart* takes on not only the evils of college gambling but also the race issues involving the plight of the Native American, embodied by the hero Soangataha (known as "Strongheart").[17] While Soangataha is not the last of the Wampanoags, he is the son of a chief, with some of the heroic stature of the Edwin Forrest hero of the mid-nineteenth century.[18] de Mille first introduces some of Strongheart's teammates, as well as another representative of the (comic) PMC—Reade, "a small man and a typical grind" (de Mille 7). Reade fulfills his role as the too studious student who just does not get it. "He seems to be a very intelligent fellow," Reade comments early on regarding Strongheart. "They say he knows an awful lot of Pol. Econ." To which Strongheart's teammate scornfully replies, "Pol. Econ. be blowed. He knows an awful lot of football and *that's* what counts" (8, author's emphasis). If Political Economics are indeed to "be blowed," a good deal of the PMC's home field is to be blowed as well. Fair play and the world of gentlemen are still what counts. Once again, PMC audience members would have to resign themselves to enjoying the story, while being aware that real-life college and learning would be acknowledged only with an impatient or ironic gesture at best.

De Mille teases the entrance of the heroic savage on Strongheart's first appearance; his football colleagues kneel, with joshing cries of "Hail chief" and "Thy Braves Greet Thee" (de Mille 19). Strongheart himself treats his stature with tongue-in-cheek humor, as he greets his friends with "mock solemnity": "Gentlemen, this reception touches me deeply" (20). When a nervous college girl who does not know how to start a conversation with the affable Native American opens with a "Tell me—how—do you like America," Strongheart returns with "My people have always been very fond of the place" (30).[19]

As the play opens, Strongheart has met the challenges of being a leader on the Columbia football team, keeping up with his studies and earning the respect of the coach and his fellow players. He tells the girl he loves, Dorothy, of his duty to his people that he must fulfill upon graduation: "You made me know that the son of a chief must fit himself to govern wisely" (32).

"Fitting" oneself is indeed a major theme of the play, and Strongheart has tried to fit his body into the white collegiate world as much as possible, including mastering the language of both the moneyed (gentlemanly) elite as well as the cultured elite. As much as anything else, *Strongheart* concerns the hero's efforts to affect a different habitus—to become like his gentleman friends. He cannot, by virtue of his race, attain a gentlemanly habitus, but he is at least partially successful in attaining and appropriating a PMH. And for a while, in the world of the play, this appropriation is enough to earn considerable cultural capital at Columbia. As Bourdieu writes with regard to language,

> This production of instruments of production, such as rhetorical devices, genres, legitimate styles and manners and, more generally, all the formulations destined to be "authoritative" and to be cited as examples of "good usage," confers on those who engage in it a power over language and thereby over the ordinary users of language, as well as over their capital. (Bourdieu, "Sport" 57–58)

Strongheart, in fact, somewhat *over*learns the language—he never uses contractions except as he describes the big game in Act II, overcome by excitement (55).

Strongheart has mastered even the art of hegemonic intimidation, which is such a necessary component in football. To turn to Bourdieu again, "*intimidation,* a symbolic violence which is not aware of what it is (to the extent that it implies no *act of intimidation*) can only be exerted on a person predisposed (in his habitus) to feel it, whereas others will ignore it" (Bourdieu, *In Other Words* 51, author's emphasis). Thus, just as the team is subjected to the coach's salty halftime pep talk, full of exhortations to "kill" the other team (42–43), Strongheart knows that the nervous freshman Ross will keep his head in the game only if the coach properly bullies him and makes him angry: "He will play good football now," Strongheart says approvingly when Ross is ready to punch the coach (44). (Ross, one could say, has been successfully tailored—or Taylorized.) Strongheart, like a proficient PMC employee (both a member of the team and a team leader), excels in preserving and propagating the team ethos.

Nevertheless, for all of Strongheart's skills in negotiating his adopted college world, he finds the team turning on him as a result of a gambling scandal. Strongheart is innocent, of course, and he protects the honor of his friends Frank and Dick (also innocent, but the circumstantial evidence points to them). All friendships are off, however, when Strongheart admits that he loves Dorothy, Frank's sister. "For her I have adopted the manners and customs of your people," Strongheart protests bitterly (82).

Once the misunderstandings are solved and the guilty parties found, the friends realize how honorable Strongheart has been, but there can be no reconciliation. "Strongheart, you are one of the finest men I know, but you are not one of us," Frank explains sadly (82). Dick is more specific: "Something stronger than you or I has come between us. You're the finest man I know, but we cannot be friends" (93–94). In a last act of defiance, Strongheart determines to take Dorothy back with him to his tribe, where he will be chief, but the Indians will not have her ("She white woman. She stay here"). Strongheart and Dorothy realize that "the law of the races" is stronger than honor, friendship, and love (95, 98).

This is not to imply that de Mille had written a protest play or an impassioned plea for racial tolerance. Strongheart is meant to be a sympathetic character, certainly, and Dorothy protests that "the law of the races" is "a cruel law" (98). But de Mille gives the protest to the (emotional) female; Strongheart is heartbroken, but he accepts the final justice of the situation. In de Mille's world, and in the world of Broadway 1905, there were some men who, no matter how successfully they could appropriate a PMH, could never truly belong.[20]

Indeed, there are indications that de Mille and his actors took the race issue more seriously than did audiences and critics. In a qualified positive review from the *New York Times*, the critic admits that the play succeeds, but that "there is nothing complex or subtle about the play; its appeal is simple, direct, such as to attract the 'average theatergoer.'" Furthermore, regarding race issues specifically, the *Times* writer seems, if anything, rather bored: "W.C.D. Mine [*sic*], the author, has undertaken to present to the public a phase of the sometimes rather tiresome 'race problem'" (it is interesting that the critic feels both "average theatergoer" and "race problem" belong within quotation marks) (" 'Strongheart' Well Liked" 9). Following a serious summary of Strongheart's ultimate crisis ("Soangatha [sic] first gets a bitter glimpse of the line beyond which race feeling forbids him to step"), the critic feels free to indulge in stereotypes: "The girl finally agrees to marry him and take up her life among the wigwams and medicine men." After the reviewer notes the audience's approval of a gentlemanly display of fair play (when the opposing team's manager refuses to use stolen signals), he gives a final dismissal of de Mille's intent: "There never was an Indian like Soangatha [sic], but that's not Mr. Edson's [sic] fault. What the man was meant to be, that Edson made him" (" 'Well Liked" 9). As far as the *Times* was concerned, the idea of bringing an Indian into either the gentleman or the PMC class was a non-issue, since such a promising figure could have been only a playwright's (and an actor's) creation.

De Mille, in fact, was more in touch with the efforts of Indian assimilation than the *Times* critic. The Carlisle Indian Industrial School of Carlisle, PA, which de Mille references early in the play (de Mille 8), was probably best known for its powerhouse football team, as well as for its aggressive program of assimilation of Indian youths.[21] What was perhaps less well known was the bullying and destructive methods the white instructors used to force the Native American children to assimilate. Just as immigrant children were "Americanized" as much as possible, the "Indians" were made to leave their families, cut their hair, and wear the clothes of youngsters in an American military academy. The abuses at Carlisle constitute one of the more shameful chapters in American cultural history.[22] Although the cruelties of the institution might have escaped de Mille, the notion of attempting to assimilate the Native American must have been appealing on a dramatic level. To de Mille's credit it must be said that he treats these issues with a degree of skill and compassion.

The racial issues of *Strongheart* bring to partial light the race consciousness of the PMC. The fictional Strongheart goes to one of the most prestigious American universities of his own volition with the hope of providing aid to his people. A question arises: How "PMC" is Strongheart allowed to be? He can, and nearly does, acquire at least one major PMC credential—Strongheart is set to graduate from Columbia. As to the question of helping his tribe with his knowledge of the "manners and customs" of the white elite, Strongheart's future is left understandably vague. Most likely, to *Strongheart*'s initial audience, helping his tribe meant helping the Indians become more like "us." This, of course, was a doomed enterprise, since, as Strongheart has painfully discovered, no amount of study and assiduous appropriation could ever make him or any other Indian one of "us." In a context determined by white hegemony, Strongheart has already achieved the best position he could hope for. To paraphrase Mary Brewer, Strongheart is perceived by the dominant class as a "good" Indian, because his desire for white privileges makes him valuable in controlling potentially "bad" Indians.[23] He has earned the respect of his elite class friends (who can no longer be his friends) before being relegated to his permanently separate and hopelessly unequal reservation. And, in a very real sense, the *Times* critic was right: as played by white Robert Edeson in red make-up, there never was an Indian like Soangataha.

How difficult (if not impossible) it is for the outsider to belong to the crowd of "regular fellows" also figures strongly in Rida Johnson Young's *Brown of Harvard,* though the tone on the whole is generally lighter. This play also provides its share of merry young gentlemen-athletes, along with a "grind" who is not so easily dismissed.

Young, in her contribution to the "rah-rah" drama, cleverly integrated up-to-date references to college athletes and their studies (or lack of them) into an essentially old-fashioned melodrama.[24] The initial confrontation between Thorne, a poor but serious-minded Southerner who earns extra money tutoring, and "regular fellow" crew team member Madden sets up the key oppositions: Southern versus Northern, poor versus privileged, individual academic excellence versus team athletics, and not, incidentally, PMC versus gentlemen. Thorne, who is described as a "tall, ungainly Southerner—poorly dressed, strong, stern face," is never merely a figure of fun and ridicule in the course of the play (Young 5). Nevertheless, his efforts to teach the crew member some basic principles of astronomy are shut down at every turn by the fun-loving Madden. When Thorne launches into a definition of binary stars, Madden interrupts: "Now look here, old man, really, seriously, I don't care to know anything deep about the subject" (Young 5). Picking stars to pieces, to use the parlance from *The College Widow*, is no more useful in the long run to Madden than analyzing the dandelion was to the businessman Bolton. All Madden wants from Thorne is "a few handy catch-words" (5) to get him by. The perplexed and exasperated Thorne is not familiar with the term "catch-words," and although he eventually joins the crew team, he never fully "catches" on to the knack of becoming a regular fellow. Thorne's "ungainly" physicality is a further indication of his crippling self-consciousness—despite his intelligence, he lacks the tools to "fit himself" to his new society.

Tom Brown makes his star entrance moments later, with glib patter about a "bunch of dry-goods" (i.e., girls) and the "benzine buggy" (7).[25] Brown is a child of privilege and is perfectly content to be so, breezily writing letters to his father for more money in cases of overindulgence. Brown's greatest overindulgence, the audience quickly learns, is generosity—the (gentle)manly virtue/vice of helping out a pal. The hero takes the virtue a step further. He learns of Thorne's hardships in trying to take care of himself and his sister—Thorne has been reduced to living in a garret on nothing but oatmeal and water for three days. "By jingo," Tom comments approvingly, "there must be something pretty decent in a fellow like that." Brown then assists Thorne anonymously through a weekly allowance—anonymous because, as Tom explains, "You see, I don't want the reputation of being an Andrew Carnegie" (17). Nevertheless, by evoking Carnegie, Tom becomes an embodiment of the values of noblesse oblige and philanthropy—values closer to the moneyed than to the cultured, elite.[26]

Another friend whom Tom assists is the unfortunate Wilfred Kenyon, who is "not his own master" (1). Kenyon's misfortune is that he is born of "one of the oldest and best families of Cambridge," and he must somehow keep up appearances on his "mother's paltry income" (11). In terms reminiscent of one of Boucicault's most famous melodramas, Kenyon is one of the true "poor of Cambridge."[27]

Young evokes earlier melodramas in other details as well. Thorne's sister Marian, who is in love with Kenyon, insists on the wayward youth's basic goodness: "It is the drink that has done it, and the cards" (17). Along with the collegiate slang that permeates the script, Young retains the elevated elocution of the melodramatic heroes and heroines. When Kenyon is confronted with the onerous choice of sabotaging the school team to cinch an opposing bet, he declaims, "Betray my college—my own friends—Colton, I know I am of no account, weak and good-for-nothing, I know that, but, if I am capable of such treachery—such rottenness as you seen to think, then I want to die right now." Young finds room to comment on even this elevated language; after Kenyon's speech, the treacherous Colton replies with a laugh, "Oh, you talk like a Sunday School book" (41).

Issues of manliness and morality are pertinent as well, and in terms of manliness, "T.R." once again serves as an apt model. Tom advises an uncertain young man, "Don't be diplomatic, be Rooseveltian and you'll win out every time" (49). Later, when confronting his girlfriend, Tom cautions that "there's no use asking a man questions that he doesn't want to answer. Because he will only tell you fibs. The best thing to do is just to accept the brute in spite of all his faults" (53). When the college men meet to decide Tom's guilt or innocence, they engage in "a long session with pipes and drinks"—gentlemanly civilization in action (75). Tom also has timely words of wisdom for his friend Kenyon: "The rotten standards of our world have made it a worse thing for a so-called gentleman to steal money than to steal a woman's heart,—something... that all the money in the world can't buy back again" (79). *Brown of Harvard* accommodates the bluff manliness of President Roosevelt, the lack of men's honesty with women, and an aspect of "gentlemanliness" that perhaps might have been overlooked by the men in the audience—playing fair not just with one's fellow men, but with women as well.

Another important element inherent in *Brown of Harvard* is patriotism. Young, while successfully appropriating elements from previous "college" shows and earlier melodramas, also shrewdly utilized several pages from George M. Cohan's playbook. Indeed, not only does Harvard beat the English crew while the orchestra plays "The Star-Spangled Banner," but also one of the musical interludes features Cohan's "Yankee Doodle Dandy." As critics were quick to point out,

Young did not necessarily break new ground in her playwriting. She was nevertheless a proficient practitioner who proved to be just as capable as her male counterparts in successfully gauging the taste of the Broadway public.

Young also has her characters grapple directly, if perhaps with little conclusiveness, with issues of class. Madden is annoyed that Thorne has not stayed where he belongs: "Well, why didn't he stay home and work the farm? I'm tired of having my leg pulled for ambitious backwoodsmen who come here with fifty cents and a writing pad and expect to get through college on them" (16). Money (and the lack of it), for Madden, is a definite, and legitimate, limitation in terms of attaining a quality education. It is a point of view that playwright Young does not completely refute.

Thorne, in turn, has no use for his more privileged classmates: "of all the ungodly, purse-proud snobs, that crowd, led by Madden and Brown, are the worst!" While the team acknowledges his rowing ability, "they never let me feel that I am one of them" (34). Thorne then expresses his own doubt that he belongs: "I should never have gone in for rowing. A poor fellow such as I. We've no business, my sister and I, attempting to mix up with that fast rich set" (35). Thorne never masters the appropriation of "that crowd's" habitus; as Bourdieu notes, "Bodily hexis is political mythology realized, *em-bodied*, turned into a permanent disposition, a durable way of standing, speaking, walking, and thereby of feeling and thinking" (Bourdieu, *In Other Words* 69–70, author's emphasis). It is Thorne's misfortune that throughout the play, as he struggles with the mythologies of Harvard, the gentlemen-athletes who have made the campus their own, and his own mythology as a poor man trying to "make it" on his own terms, he cannot find a way to "mix up" with the rest of the rowing team. Thorne's body towers uncomfortably over those of his fellows, his movements are uncertain and ungraceful, and his ways of standing, speaking, and walking cannot possibly be durable. Such permanence and durability could come only with the confidence of knowing one's place in the political mythology, and how one is meant to preserve and contribute to it.

Thorne has to suffer a jibe even at his study habits: "Say, you've got to cut the study out if you expect to do anything in athletics. What did you come to college for, anyway?" (36). This would appear to present an opportunity for Young to dramatize the notion that being a regular fellow transcends class distinctions by having Thorne prove himself. That play, however, would be the story of something resembling a PMC triumph, something audiences would not see (or perhaps, be ready for) until the "business" plays of the 1910s. *Brown of Harvard* has other victories in mind.

The plot machinations enable Tom to win the big match against England, protect the weak (but repentant) Kenyon's honor, and win the girl. One issue he does not resolve, at least not onstage, is the class- (and PMC-) related problem of Thorne, who is left thinking that both Kenyon and Brown have sullied his sister's honor. "I'll wait," Thorne says upon his Malvolio-like exit, when he is promised that satisfaction will be forthcoming. Presumably, he is still waiting as the final curtain falls, since he never appears again (79). Thorne, much like Strongheart, is left alone, although his predicament is not so dire—certainly the situation is not so serious that Young (or, presumably, the audience) felt any pressing need to resolve it. Perhaps the Malvolio comparison is apt, as well: if Shakespeare's Puritan did indeed get his revenge with the closing of the theaters two generations or so after *Twelfth Night*'s first performance, Rida Johnson Young's PMC representative did not have to wait as long to score a series of triumphs. It would be a matter of a PMC hero finding his place in the political mythology, and finding a way to embody it—conscious choices leading to an unconscious ease of movement and speech.

The very seriousness with which Thorne is treated in *Brown of Harvard* most likely made his character one of the most painful in terms of PMC class consciousness. It was easy enough to laugh at goofy grinds named Copernicus, or small men obsessed with "Pol. Econ." trying to fit in among football players. In the case of Thorne, however, the audience saw a young man of a lower-than-gentleman class trying to get his education and make his way in the gentlemanly world of sport. Despite a sense of honor and considerable intelligence, Thorne is rejected, with any reconciliation or respect presumably to come after the curtain has already fallen. In terms of placing representatives of an emerging PMC onstage and earning respect, the college plays, all told, represented a considerable step back.

Running concurrently with the collegiate shows were a number of business plays—an understandable phenomenon as Broadway became increasingly aware of and interested in the world of American corporate capitalism. The business plays of the first decade of the twentieth century were not the PMC hero-driven business farces, because PMC characters were not front and center solving the problems of machinery. Nevertheless, these plays did deal directly with class consciousness.

SWEEPINGS FROM THE MUCKRAKES: *THE LION AND THE MOUSE*

In the introduction to this study, I quoted John Gassner's remark about the sweepings of the muckrakers landing on the Broadway stage. He might have had in mind Charles Klein's *The Lion and the Mouse*, considered by Bronson Howard himself as the logical, modern successor to his own *The Henrietta* in terms of staging modern American business.[28] Writers were indeed engaging with the world through the newspaper headlines, and if the results seldom turned out to be plays of long-lasting distinction, the dramatic "punch" of sensational journalism was not lost on the Broadway practitioner. As Montrose Moses writes, "The dramatist of that time was keenly alert to newspaper effectiveness. With astuteness, Klein read Ida Tarbell's *History of the Standard Oil Company*, and behold, there rose before him the main outlines of 'The Lion and the Mouse'! Edward Sheldon came across the details of an editorial on the political leader, and wrote 'The Boss'" (Moses, *Representative Plays* 353).

Tarbell's *History of the Standard Oil Company*, which first appeared in *McClure's Magazine* in November 1902, was the result of "five years of patient research into the devious transactions that had built up that great monopoly" (Barck and Blake 28–29) and became one of the outstanding "muckraking" classics of the era.[29] The muck Tarbell raked in her Standard Oil study was genuine; Klein used the muck to bring some contemporary grit to an essentially old-fashioned story of a plucky heroine beating the villain (in this case, a Rockefelleresque tycoon) at his own game, clearing her father's name and winning her young man, who happens to be the tycoon's son. Klein's setting and characters proved fresh in November 1905 when the play opened, the antagonists in particular bearing strong resemblances to people easily recognizable to the audience. Appreciative audiences were also "keenly alert to newspaper effectiveness."

As the play opens, the "careworn" and "pathetic" Judge Rossmore lives in exile in Massapequa, Long Island, having had the temerity to tangle with American corporate capitalism at its most ruthless.[30] "In my capacity as Judge of the Supreme Court," the Judge explains sadly, "I rendered decisions, several of which were adverse to the corporate interest of a number of rich men" (14–15). The leader of this capitalist cabal is John Burkett "Ready Money" Ryder, who, with his associates, drove the Judge from the bench under the shadow of the accusation of taking bribes. Ryder, of course, still possesses the incriminating papers that prove Judge Rossmore to be innocent.[31] The Judge's daughter Shirley, who writes (and muckrakes) professionally under the name of Sarah Green, sets out to insinuate herself into Ryder's household and his trust. She accomplishes this with comparative ease, considering that she has already written a book about Ryder with the title "The Great American Octopus" (37).[32]

Ryder is a hard-edged tycoon who extols the virtues and necessities of thinking: "Thinking is a harder game than any, and you must think or you won't know" (43). The capitalist owner could take on the mantle of both the mental worker as well as the PMC expert—in other words, Ryder appropriates a PMH for his own purposes. Shirley/Sarah counters with an argument of love for mankind: "suppose we all wanted to be the richest, the most powerful personage in the world...I think it would postpone the Era of the Brotherhood of Man indefinitely—don't you?" (48)

Fortunately for Shirley, Ryder's thinking abilities do not extend to hiding (or shredding) his incriminating papers, allowing the heroine to steal them and make sure they are sent to the proper authorities.

Her code of honor, however, forbids her to continue to dissemble, even to her enemy—"'Twas I who took the letters and sent them to Judge Stott," she confesses somewhat poetically (76). Ryder is duly impressed by Shirley's integrity, allowing for the happy ending.

Klein gives Shirley a fair amount of rhetoric denouncing Ryder and his way of doing business. Her speeches fall short of denouncing corporate capitalism per se, but she does denounce American business run amok: "The machinery of his money-making mind typifies the laws of perpetual unrest—it must go on—go on—relentlessly—resistlessly—making money—making money—and continuing to make money—it cannot stop until the machinery crumbles" (47). This idea of the machine gone out of control is an early or nascent PMC notion—it would fall to the PMC experts to control the machines so that they would not crumble. Therein lies the PMC class consciousness work of this particular business play—PMC audience members might recognize themselves as clerks caught up in "the laws of perpetual unrest," or as those who would be called upon to make sure that the Ready Money Ryders of the world do not abuse the machinery and cause a breakdown.

Nevertheless, the play's own machinery was not built to protest American corporate capitalism—the climax and denouement emphasize, once again, individual responsibility. The audience is not to blame American business any more than it was meant to blame "the City" in Fitch's last work—the soulless machinery of corporate capitalism could be ably embodied on the American stage in a single misguided tycoon.

Klein had achieved a critical and popular success, though critics at the time did indeed recognize the narrative inconsistencies and the allowances that audiences had to make. The *Times* reviewer summed up the difficulties that faced a playwright who wanted to tackle certain current events and yet remain "theatrical":

> The complex machinery of financial and governmental intrigue though possibly dramatic—not to say melodramatic at times—does not lend itself readily to ordinary theatrical purpose. When one remembers that a play to be of any popular value at all must contain some kind of sentimental interest, it is

Muckraking the Playing Field 97

readily understood that the difficulties are increased. ("An Absorbing Play of American Life" 9)

By the end of 1905, theatrical critics and practitioners were still speaking of elements of "sentiment" in terms of necessity. Playwrights had found a way to take the field of business and make the subject palatable to wives and matinee girls. Before long, Broadway audiences would find themselves applauding plays that placed business above sentiment.

The next business play also features a capitalist gone wrong—in this case, a rough-and-tumble Irishman who has ruthlessly worked his way to the top. The PMC characters in *The Boss* have to lead the workers on the right track for their own benefit.

STRIKERS, GENTLEMEN, AND TOUGHS: *THE BOSS*

Edward Sheldon's 1911 look at a colorful and ruthless labor boss fell just short of popular success, running 88 performances.[33] It is worthy of some examination, however, not only as an attempt to treat the labor situation seriously (with some comic overtones) on stage, but also as an attempt to stage the PMC in the capacity of actively preserving capitalist culture—in this case, not by managing the affairs of the capitalists directly, but rather by helping to organize labor in opposition to corrupt business practices. This was a provocative notion to present to a Broadway audience, and Sheldon found an interesting, if perhaps only partially successful, strategy to sell his pro-worker sentiments. It proved to be an interesting experiment in arousing PMC class consciousness, as *The Boss* most fully articulated one of the primary PMC agendas—keeping the business of business running. Perhaps, however, the Broadway audience as a whole was not ready to wholeheartedly accept any PMC-inspired ideas on how best to maintain corporate capitalism.

As Thomas Greenfield writes in *Work and the Work Ethic in American Drama, 1920–1970*,

> For all his proworker sympathies, Sheldon cannot bring himself to give proletarian characters their own voices, nor does he portray them as having control

over their own political activity. The union itself is not founded by the men but by an aristocrat, Griswold's son, who is avenging his family's defeat to Regan.... Even the proletarian riot in the final scene is made middle-class and thus, respectable. (Greenfield 34–35)

There are several elements of *The Boss* that support Greenfield's analysis. The audience is plunged into the dire straits of Griswold and Company—"Shindy" Mike Regan has taken over the company's wheat contracts. "Shindy" Mike, as his nickname indicates, is an "Irish tough of an ex-barkeep" (Sheldon 851), a huge blow to the aristocratic Griswolds.[34] Worse, father Griswold, in a fashion similar to Fitch's doomed Rand Sr. in *The City,* has engaged in not-quite-above-board dealings with the bank's money (Griswold is one the bank directors), placing him in potential legal danger if the company fails. Donald, Griswold's son, is certain that with more time, he could get Regan's men to strike: "Why, they're just like a powder magazine waiting for the match! All they need is a leader who's studied law and has a little nerve" (854). Although young Griswold is identified as an aristocrat, his place as a PMC-style figure is quickly established. Indeed, as Greenfield points out (Greenfield 35), "Shindy" Mike goes to his window to report to us the names of some of the community leaders who legitimize the strike: "There's Archibald Moughton, the vice-president of the First National...And the fellow climbing the fence—isn't that Grayson, senior member of Grayson and Grayson and company...Strikers, gentlemen and toughs, scoopers and big businessmen" (Sheldon 882). The onstage workers needed smart, thinking people to lead them, just as Frederick Winslow Taylor insisted in his book *Scientific Management,* which had been published the same year (1911). Sheldon took great pains to frame the strike not in terms of a riotous proletarian takeover, but as a logical corrective to a misguided and downright criminal misuse of corporate capitalist culture.

Perhaps of equal import in Sheldon's examination of corporate capitalism is the presence of the Fitchean, thinking heroine, Emily Griswold (Donald's sister), who has more influence on the plot, and on the eventually-to-be-reformed "Shindy" Mike, than does the PMC-style hero. She is described teasingly by her father as a "young scientific philanthropist" (852), and the description is accurate. She is a thinking girl, which intimidates most men, including her best guy pal Duncan—"For heaven's sake, stop *thinking* a moment, can't you?" he cries in exasperation (855, author's emphasis). A kindred spirit and a kind of younger sister to Fitch's Marion Wolton, she is concerned about the denizens of the slums, who would suffer the most if the banks fail, a concern that leads her to the highly charged, and highly improbable, "business" arrangement with "Shindy" Mike—Mike will leave the Griswold side of the business alone in exchange for marriage, a marriage that will end, Emily insists, "at the church door" (862). It is this unfulfilled marital (and sexual) tension that drives most of the play's drama.

Although it is onstage that Donald rallies the workers and is eventually almost fatally injured by one of Mike's men (without Mike's knowledge or approval), most of his PMC-style efforts happen offstage. *On*stage, Emily's eventual love and trust tame "Shindy" Mike into legality and respectability. This taming culminates in Emily's refitting of Mike's clothes—the wearing of aristocratic clothes, and indeed the fitting into upper-crust society, is a self-conscious problem for the former "barkeep," and Sheldon gains considerable comic mileage from Mike's discomfort. It is Emily who finally shows Mike how to wear his hat properly—"No—straight! Quite straight! It's always bothered me before," Emily admonishes in the happy ending (890). While the running of business was still largely in the hands of the aristocrats by the end of *The Boss*, the thinking woman would become an important partner to the thinking PMC man—often to the point of out-thinking the men entirely. The results would vary from the satisfyingly comic to the near tragic, for example, in George Kelly's later *Craig's Wife*—a stern 1920s jeremiad warning the striving PMC man against the dangers of the too-independent wife.

Despite Sheldon's flair for color and conflict, as well as his care to stage his strike as conservatively as possible, there was not a sufficiently sympathetic audience to bestow "hit" status on *The Boss*. For the *Times* critic, Sheldon's play contained "rather too much color to be entirely convincing" ("Holbrook Blinn Fine Figure in 'The Boss'")[35] It would require a national capitalist calamity and a new generation of theater-goers to wholeheartedly welcome and cheer an onstage "strike"—the fervent chant, with audience plants spurring on audience participation, that brought Odets's *Waiting for Lefty* to its close.

The American musical comedy also played an important role in PMC class consciousness during this period. Although, once again, the PMC characters portrayed were generally not the best and the brightest, a modest group of Princess musicals ensured that at least some of the class consciousness would be not only tuneful but pleasant as well.

5. A Size Thirteen Collar: Musicals and PMC Class Consciousness ∽

THE MUSICAL: PRE-POSTMORTEM

On September 7, 1902, the *New York Times* pronounced the musical comedy dead on arrival. According to the article, "the general opinion was that in the not far distant future the musical comedy and its kin will be found among the 'have beens' so far as concerns New York. Nearly all agree that the cycle is dead" ("Musical Comedies' Vogue Said to be On the Wane" 10).[1] If the reports of the musical's death were greatly exaggerated, the identity of musical comedy was rather up in the air. In the twentieth century's first decade, the musical comedy was beset by, in Gerald Bordman's words, "a blurring of definitions" (Bordman, *American Musical Comedy* 79). Audiences seeking musical entertainment on Broadway found themselves choosing between operettas, comic operas, musical comedies, musical plays, revues, and "French vaudevilles," nomenclature employed by producers more for the sake of novelty than accurate description (Bordman, *American Musical Comedy* 78–80). Roughly speaking, Cohan and Victor Herbert set the tone of the early years of the century, Viennese operetta (and many imitations thereof) ruled Broadway from 1907 to 1914,[2] and around 1915, the American musical would reach something close to maturity, at least temporarily, with the shows that would come to be named for the theatre where they were produced—"Princess" musicals.

Relating PMC class consciousness to watching the American musical of this period means, in general, looking past center stage and the spotlight.

Gentlemen, along with outlandish and exotic kings, princes, and sultans, were the men who carried the day. As in the college plays, PMC types were lurking around the edges while critics championed the occasional show fit for the elusive "intelligent playgoer." Most particularly, however, the Girls were the main focus, especially in the Ziegfeld shows. What sort of PMC cultural work was the musical doing during this period with regard to stirring class consciousness? Part of the answer lies in an acknowledgment of "summer widowers" in the audience. Still another aspect of the answer lies in a playful and jaundiced view of a new American "-ism"—imperialism. The musical version of imperialism would also give onstage PMC characters some employment. And, in the second decade of the twentieth century, a seemingly modest series of musicals would start to put PMC people in the spotlight as regular people (who happened to burst into song periodically). In the meantime, no discussion of musicals would be complete without dealing with Ziegfeld and his "girls."

Experts and historians have identified the appeal in a number of ways. Robert C. Allen, in his book *Horrible Prettiness,* referred to "male scopic pleasure." For Laura Mulvey, the appropriate term was "to-be-looked-at-ness."[3] Perhaps Ziegfeld himself summed it up best: "Bring on the girls." Treating the Girls as objects of desire is perhaps a tired (and certainly narrow) way to look at the Ziegfeld phenomenon. Nevertheless, the relationship between the *Follies* and the emerging PMC was, in many ways, mutually nurturing. Not the least important element of this nurturing atmosphere was a direct acknowledgment and definition of the *Follies* audience. For *Follies* shows, in New York at least, from 1907 until 1931, were summer shows—not for the "tired businessman and his family," but rather for the businessman who had to stay in the City while the family summered on Long Island and elsewhere. Ziegfeld recognized the emerging phenomenon of the "summer widower" and found a way to entertain him.[4] The summer widowers, largely PMC-types, came through with enough positive response to spawn a new generation of young managers who welcomed the opportunity to help glorify the American Girl.

Perhaps more pertinently, the "Ziegfeld Girl," positioned in contrast to "low" chorus girls and threatening "New Women," was something of a PMC creation—a recognizable and reliable brand name created not only by the unique genius of Ziegfeld, but also by shrewd marketing and advertising techniques. These advertising techniques not only took full advantage of prevailing notions of patriotism, desire, and respectability; the Follies Girl advertising machine indeed *created* the ideal embodiment of these notions. As Linda Mizejewski writes, the "liminal status of the chorus girl in relation to bourgeois respectability was the key to Ziegfeld's articulation and promotion of his Follies Girl" (Mizejewski 16–17). Thus, the Follies Girl also became a model for young women the way present-day fashion models influence the fashion and body images of girls and women of today. If a girl wanted to emulate the Follies style, for example, she could wear the Knox Hats that Ina Claire, "leading woman for the Ziegfeld Follies at the New Amsterdam Theatre," wore for ads that ran in popular magazines of 1915 (Holme 52). Respectability was important to the upwardly mobile bachelor as well. As Mizejewski explains, "A specified body, designated as white and heterosexual, was conflated with other desires; the body-we-should-want (as male desire, as female ideal) enacts the other things 'we' should want: the society wedding, Anglo blondness, tourism, the Panama Canal" (12).

"There are chorus girls and chorus girls," as one Ziegfeld press release put the matter (Mizejewski 90). As this study is to a large degree concerned with class emergence and class distinction, Ziegfeld and his Girls play a significant role. One of Ziegfeld's great triumphs was to take the foundation of "to-be-looked-at-ness" and create spectacles that "the best people" were looking at—the very act of looking endowed the viewer with "class." Summer widowers and bachelors alike gained cultural capital by indulging in "scopic pleasure." Ziegfeld and his public relations department accomplished this cultural coup by assiduously utilizing "the discourse of corporate advertising," a discourse that depended upon brand names and guarantees. The Ziegfeld "brand" became a "guarantee" of the highest quality in feminine pulchritude, dressed in the highest quality fashions—up to and including intimate articles of clothing that the audience would never see. It was through this attention to fashion that Ziegfeld could successfully conflate the provocative bodies (to-be-looked-at), the department store presentation (for consumer emulation and purchase), and the "artistic" (for moneyed and cultural elite identification). The formula not only became hugely successful in its own time but also left its mark on shows, movies, and fashion alike for years to come (Mizejewski 90–93).

Critics eventually fell in line, giving their own stamp of respectability to the *Follies* and the Girls. Such respectability took time and persistence to earn. The *New York Times* review of the 1907 *Follies* (not yet the *Ziegfeld Follies*) laconically noted that it was "conceived and produced by F. Ziegfeld, Jr. A large audience enjoyed it" ("Follies of 1907"). It was four years later that Ziegfeld officially included his name in the title, thus creating one of the era's most recognizable brands. "The audience voted that Mr. Ziegfeld has come close to outdoing himself. Of course the show was mostly girls and glitter, music and rapid action, but the crowd liked it," the *Times* reported on the 1911 edition ("Girls and Glitter"). The critic-expert, in this case, is still somewhat defensive and apologetic regarding the "girls and glitter" factor, but not for much longer.

By 1915, the *New York Times* was treating the impending opening as a major, and classy, event: "It is the ninth edition of the entertainment Flo Ziegfeld brings to town every Summer, and which has become so established an institution that it is doubtless one of the things they have in mind who every once in a while announce, with all the gusto of discovery, that New York is the greatest of the country's Summer resorts" ("1915 Follies Here Tomorrow"). Musical historian Ethan Mordden corroborates the date of 1915 as significant: besides the appearance of such celebrated performers as Bert Williams, W.C. Fields, Ed Wynn Mae Murray, and Ann Pennington, "the 1915 edition introduced Joseph Urban, the Austrian designer whose bold color schemes and stylistic approaches, lit with advanced Continental technology, made the *Follies* the best-looking show in town" (Mordden 38).

As Linda Mizejewski points out, the *New York Times* considered the *Follies* "eminently respectable" by the 1920s, noting that "the best people" attended the shows. In turn, as *Times* critic Brooks Atkinson stated in another article, such respectability "rescued" the chorus girl because Ziegfeld and the *Follies* endow chorus girls "with the style and the poise of good breeding that make for illusion as they decorate the stage" (qtd. in Mizejewski 89).[5] Ziegfeld and his marketing people had meticulously laid the foundation for this respectability throughout the *Follies* years.[6]

With regard to the shows themselves, as Mordden notes, pinning them to a discernable formula was something of a challenge; journalists could say little beyond "the famous good Ziegfeld taste...Yet...Ziegfeld kept his *Follies* trimmed on very certain lines." These were, roughly, (1) Sex is suave, (2) Song and dance may be competent, but comedy must be unique, (3) Tap is nice but ballet is swank, and (4) A show is for looking, and one had better see sights (Mordden 39). The summer widowers could and did certainly look—they could afford the price of a ticket, if not the fine Ziegfeld fashions to clothe their wives. For the PMC, covetousness proved to be a powerful bond to capitalism, and envy went a long way toward guaranteeing loyalty. "To-be-looked-at-ness," in this case, proved to be important in terms of PMC class consciousness as well, as PMC men were all too conscious of the difference between "to-be-looked-at-ness" and "to-be-touched-ness," not to mention "to-be-owned-ness."

That the "girls" would play a dominant role in the relationship between the PMC and the musical is not necessarily surprising. What is somewhat of a surprise, however, is how little, comparatively, the onstage musical men contributed to the work of the PMC, at least until 1910. Nevertheless, one outlandish onstage sultan did his fair share to arouse class consciousness—if, once again, a rather painful consciousness.

THE PROVIDENCES OF GOD: *THE SULTAN OF SULU*

How the rebellion of the Philippines in February 1899 found its way to Broadway provides an interesting case study in the history of American musical comedy. Following the treaty in which the United States paid Spain $20 million for Guam, Puerto Rico, and the Philippines in December 1898, there was considerable controversy regarding whether or not the United States should indeed take the Philippines. President McKinley, asking God for guidance, received His answer: "There was nothing left for us to do but to take them all and to educate the Filipinos, and uplift and civilize and Christianize them, and by God's grace do the very best we could by them, as our fellow men for whom Christ also died" (Zinn 312–313).

"The Filipinos," as Howard Zinn acerbically observed, "did not get the same message from God." *Insurrectos* leader Emilio Aguinaldo led the fight against the United States, a rebellion that took three years for 70,000 U.S. troops to eventually put down (313). Reports proliferated regarding U.S. brutality, including decimating villages and killing women and children, for the larger purpose of gaining, in Postmaster General Charles Emory Smith's words, "a market for our surplus." This idea did indeed have its appeal for big business and for a number of the trade unions, who reasoned that greater markets could prevent another depression (314–317).

Nevertheless, a significant group of business people, including antilabor aristocrats (such as Andrew Carnegie), intellectuals (most notably Harvard philosopher William James), as well as working-class men and women, was instrumental in educating the public about the particular horrors of the Philippine campaign and the evils of imperialism in general. This was the Anti-Imperialist League, formed in 1898, which led the campaign against the treaty for annexation of the Philippines. It was a powerful, if ultimately unsuccessful campaign, as the treaty did indeed pass by one vote (Zinn 314–317). Mark Twain, commenting on the Philippine war, voiced and summed up a great deal of the bitterness that the war brought to the surface:

> We have pacified some thousands of the islanders and buried them; destroyed their fields; burned their villages, and turned their widows and orphans out-of-doors; furnished heartbreak by exile to some dozens of disagreeable patriots; subjugated the remaining ten millions by Benevolent Assimilation, which is the pious new name of the musket; we have acquired property in the three hundred concubines and other slaves of our business partner, the Sultan of Sulu, and hoisted our protecting flag over that swag.
>
> And so, by these Providences of God—and the phrase is the government's, not mine—we are a World Power. (qtd. in Zinn 316)

The Anti-Imperialist League could indeed count among its members and supporters a significant number of PMC types (i.e., the intellectuals, philosophers, and many of the business people). Nevertheless, supporters of the war included PMC, some labor unions, and many of the working class as well. The war was an issue that divided all the classes, and its issues created arguments that were both highly intellectual and emotional. It was not an issue that one might expect to be treated on the frivolous Broadway stage of the turn of the century. Nevertheless, Broadway audiences did indeed receive a comic (and frivolous) glimpse of *The Sultan of Sulu* in December 1902.

George Ade, providing book and lyrics, at once gave Broadway audiences "a very funny story of absurdities," in the words of the *Times* ("'The Sultan of Sulu' at Wallack's" 9). Critics also realized that Ade had provided Broadway with something more intellectually stimulating than the norm. The occasion was significant enough for the *Times*' John Corbin, writing shortly after the opening, to wax not only rhapsodic but also evangelical:

> As a rule musical comedies are so bad, so very bad, that...it is only a question of which is worse than others. When they pitch their tents on Broadway you can't see the Intelligent Playgoer (a somewhat fabulous person, to be sure) for the dust he kicks up in getting away from them...here at last is a piece that is not only laughable throughout, but reasonably, intelligently, philosophically laughable. In a word, it is satire—satire that is as timely as it is pointed...And, brothers, do you realize what it means that a musical comedy not only has a plot, a logical, coherent—an almost consecutive plot, but that this plot arises from the dramatic struggle between the two opposing forces involved, just as the precise canon of the most meticulous dramaturgy requires? (Corbin 34)

The show found a way to tweak American mores and, in a sense, a way to tweak PMC positions. The experts and order-keepers in the exotic island scenario were naval officers and a comely judge advocate, who, in turn, had a thing or two to learn from the exotic sultan.

In the case of *Sultan,* the officers are Lt. Handy and Col. Budd, aided and abetted by Judge Advocate Pamela Francis Jackson, who has arrived to oversee the "benevolent assimilation" of the sultan's Philippine island. As, in Corbin's words, "the dramatic embodiment of the Constitution," it is Pamela's duty to jail the sultan for multiple alimonies. (It does not help matters that the sultan has been wooing the judge advocate for much of the first act.) In something of a *Presidentus ex machina,* a dispatch arrives from Washington stating that since the Constitution follows the flag on Mondays, Wednesdays, and Fridays, the sultan, having been assimilated on an "off" day, is allowed to rule as he sees fit. As the titular sultan sings to the befuddled U.S. representatives in the song "The Smiling Isle," their island has no college—therefore, no dissipated youth whose only education is in "chorus girls and cigarettes." As for class and labor relations, the Sulus have those issues well under control: there are "no janitors to sass us/No bell boys to harass us," and, consequently, no strikes (Bordman, *American Musical Theatre,* 3rd ed. 217).

The song hit the burgeoning PMC where it lived—college, a sassy (and harassing) working class, and strikes. As in the college shows, PMC types were either left waiting or on the wrong end of the clever badinage. The PMC audience members, in the meantime, no doubt enjoyed the show along with the rest of the Broadway crowd. Once again, however, there was most likely that twinge of painful class consciousness in seeing educated managerial types portrayed as silly and incompetent—no match for an "uncivilized" sultan.

With great faith in intelligent playgoers, Corbin declared that "the success of the piece, and it is nightly crowding the huge auditorium of Wallack's, is due to the satirical vigor of the story…and to the popular delight in Mr. Ade's slanguage" (Corbin 34).[7] *The Sultan of Sulu* was not only successful on its own, but it also inspired a distinct trend— Americans versus natives, and Yankees in exotic environments. As Gerald Bordman noted, the theme of Americans visiting exotic potentates became quite the rage for the next several years. From roughly 1903 to 1905, Broadway audiences were treated to *The Runaway* (an American general becomes king of the Island of Table d'hote), *The Isle of Spice* (a Chicago import), *The Yankee Consul,* and *The Duke of Duluth*, all musicals "in the *Sultan of Sulu* tradition," and all but the last quite popular (Bordman, *American Musical Theatre,* 3rd ed. 221, 224, 230, 246, 594). Such vehicles, however, tended to owe their success less to "satirical vigor" and more to the imitation of a popular formula.

Nevertheless, with regard once again to Ronald Wainscott's quote in the introduction to this study, there is ample evidence that if the musicals of the era did not directly confront the vicissitudes of the modern world, there was at least a playful acknowledgment of that world. It seemed that no vicissitude was so grave that some clever Broadway practitioners could not put it to music and lyrics. Adding in the glorified bodies of the chorus girls and the graceful bodies of the dance experts, Broadway could generally dance to those vicissitudes as well. This would prove particularly true in the following decade and through World War I.

MUSICALS GROW UP FOR A MOMENT: THE PRINCESS SHOWS

Regarding the years 1914–1921 and the musical, Gerald Bordman writes, "The seasons from mid-1914 to mid-1921 were possibly the most exciting in the history of the American Musical Theatre. These seven years saw the birth of the American Musical as it was to be known for at least the next half century" (Bordman 2001, 343). Music gained a new popular terminology—the language of jazz. The critical experts floundered in their attempts to keep up with the music; the terms "jazz" and "rag" were used frequently and just as often, mistakenly. For many critics, "jazz" could be interchangeable with "fast," "noisy," "cacophonous," or even "new." Furthermore, composers began to challenge the producer over who sets the tone of a show. The formation in 1914 of the American Society of Composers, Authors, and Publishers (ASCAP) eventually gave the composers a greater degree of independence (Bordman 1992, 298). In a sense, musical hegemony began to shift from the producer to the musical *expert*—in this case, the composers. This power shift created the difference, in other words, between a "Ziegfeld" show or a "Shubert" show and an Irving Berlin or a Jerome Kern show between 1910 and 1920, and Gershwin, Cole Porter, and Rodgers and Hart shows of the succeeding decades. A small clutch of shows staged from 1910 to 1920, performed at the small Princess Theatre, illustrates one of the most exciting and satisfying developments in the musical, and in the roles of new experts.

Very Good Eddie, which opened on December 23, 1915, began to establish the Princess "formula" as critics, audiences, and later musical-comedy lovers came to understand and embrace it. The book, by Guy Bolton and Philip Bartholomae (taken from Bartholomae's play *Over Night*), deals with newlyweds, misunderstandings, and switched identities on the Hudson River Day Line and at the Rip Van Winkle Inn in upstate New York. As P.G. Wodehouse and Guy Bolton describe the show in their book *Bring On the Girls*,

> It was a farce-comedy which would have been strong enough to stand on its own feet without the help of music, the first of its kind to rely on situation and character laughs instead of the clowning and Weberfieldian cross talk with which the large-scale musicals filled in between the romantic scenes. It was, in fact, intimate. It had no star part, the interest being distributed among a number of characters... (Wodehouse and Bolton 7)

In other words, rather than a clown or a vaudeville team (such as Weber and Fields) dominating the evening with their popular and expected routines, *Very Good Eddie* sought to tell a story—a silly, farcical story, to be sure, but nonetheless a fairly plausible one, with people who might conceivably exist in the real world, and in the audience. Wodehouse and Bolton might also have added that the "interest" was "distributed" equally between the typical romantic lead (Oscar Shaw, in this case) and the "character" comedian—Ernest Truex, at the beginning of a long and distinguished career as a character actor. Truex's physicality was an important part of the success of *Eddie*—short and unprepossessing, he embodied the "everyday" man as potential hero. Indeed, Eddie uses his body for most of the show to cower, hide, and generally let himself be dominated by the other characters as well as the machinations of plot.

The musical sets the tone of recognizable, hard-working (but not the manual labor kind) young people escaping Manhattan for a brief summer holiday in the opening number, "The Simple Life": "The simple life for us/We've come aboard this bus/To swap a pitiful city/Full of fashion and fuss."[8] Class consciousness for the PMC playgoer, for a change, becomes pleasant and tuneful. The kind of modest vacation that the characters take—from Manhattan to upstate New York—would be in line with the kind of getaway in which an up-and-coming middle-class couple could indulge. Included in such a middle class would be many members of the PMC. The romantic hero, Dick Rivers, has just seen Elsie the ingénue, a budding singer under the care of Madame

Matroppo: "I've fallen in love at first sight." It is Dick's plan to woo Elsie away from the stage, and he is determined to succeed: "When it comes to sticking, I've got Mr. Postage Stamp licked" (Bolton and Greene 6).

Dick is a college friend of Eddie Kettle, the "Eddie" of the title.[9] In the context of the play, although not a great deal is made of the characters' college careers (or even where they attended), going to university is not necessarily a sign that these young men are inherently useless nitwits or gentleman layabouts. The shift in attitude about college is not a huge one by any means, but the absence of references to college being useless might not have gone unnoticed by the PMC audience. As for Eddie himself, he is a little man already henpecked by his new bride and seems resigned to be, to paraphrase one of his key songs, a worm in a world of robins. The stage directions describe Eddie as "very small very winning [sic] and in no way effeminate. He has tried to raise a moustache. He speaks with a lisp.... Eddie looks very important and serious" (16).

The fairly brief stage description of Eddie raises and confronts a number of significant issues. The audience meets Eddie in the act of trying, and failing, to live up to a specific set of "manly" expectations. He cannot quite speak properly, and he is unable to "raise a moustache"—probably an attempt to offset a boyish or "baby" face. These characteristics mark Eddie as a figure of fun, and the audience certainly gets plenty of opportunities to laugh at the many indignities that befall Eddie throughout the course of the evening. Perhaps the most devastating humiliation comes early on when the Steward calls, "Say, boss." "Are you speaking to me?" Eddie asks. "No," the Steward replies, gesturing toward Eddie's wife, "I was speaking to *her*" (20, authors' emphasis). Nevertheless, the stage directions equally emphasize those elements of Eddie that *are* manly—namely, that he is not effeminate. While Eddie remains a figure of fun, the potential of manly self-fulfillment exists, as it must in order for Eddie to gain full audience sympathy. The audience must root for Eddie to gain control of his situation, his life, and, not least of all, his wife. Again, recognition for the PMC members of the audience was undoubtedly a large part of their enjoyment. While the PMC did not hold a monopoly on being henpecked, the men (those Eddie's age as well as those who were more middle-aged) could appreciate seeing on stage an example of a woman who "wears the pants," and who is constantly pushing her husband into social, business, and familial situations for which he is ill-equipped.

Both Eddie and Dick become caught up in an appropriately farcical round of misunderstandings as both Eddie's wife and Percy Darling (who also went to college with Eddie and Dick) miss the boat that will take them to the inn upstate. Eddie and Elsie Darling (not the Elsie that Dick has designs for, which adds to the confusion) must pose as husband and wife to avoid scandal. As Dick maneuvers his way around the overprotective Madame Matroppo to get to his Elsie (while misunderstanding Eddie's marital situation), Eddie gradually realizes that to steer his way through the escalating complications, he has to make decisions with greater commitment and confidence.

Eddie, for his part, is all too aware of his shortcomings. This self-awareness is also crucial to his ability to win over the audience. In the song, "Size Thirteen Collar," Eddie ruefully reflects on his place in the world, as well as on his inability to put on a "brave front." What Eddie wants is fairly simple—he "should like to go out one night with the boys" (Bartholomae, et al. 2–38). More to the point, he would like to *be* one of the boys; Eddie is a self-described "peaceful little person" who has been pretty much stepped on by the rest of the human race, as he thinks, because of his small and unimposing stature. If only his collar were a size 19 (with corresponding size 11 shoes), why, he could lead a band of pirates—or, at least, "smoke and drink and swear and chew" (2–37–38). Audiences, perhaps in particular PMC audiences, could relate to such "manly" fantasies on multiple levels, while at the same time laughing knowingly at Eddie's ideas of what "real men" do when they get together. First, there was the immediate recognition that what Eddie needed to succeed was confidence, an important plank in the building of the PMC mythos. The key to success for future PMC heroes, as well as for such embryonic PMC heroes as Eddie, was that leading-man looks and an imposing appearance (or a size 19 collar) were not as important as a Can-Do attitude. Second, the idea of breaking loose from the confining business uniform and indulging in more "primitive" behavior—smoking, swearing, drinking, and chewing (tobacco), for example—also held its not inconsiderable appeal for the "tired businessmen" in the audience.

By the play's end, Eddie has discovered that a "size 19" mentality can come from a smallish body. While Dick wins the girl, it is Eddie who gets the triumphant curtain moment as he at last gains the fortitude to order his wife to sit down: "I'm going to wear the breeches and be master in my own house hereafter," he announces (2–91). This display of manhood and control prompts the titular approving response from the inn clerk, with grammatical comma added: "Very good, Eddie!"[10]

The show itself ran almost a year and toured successfully. Bordman emphasizes the importance of the show in relation to the American Musical Comedy: "More than any other piece it formed the mold...Its people were everyday people—neither cartooned clowns nor cardboard lovers. Its situations were plausible—however unlikely. Its easily singable songs helped the story flow but were lovely and natural away from the stage" (Bordman, *American Musical Theatre* 2nd ed. 312). More to the point, its people, particularly Eddie, shared the concerns that the "business" heroes dealt with during the same period. Furthermore, the critical experts, rather than pronouncing and prophesying the death of the musical, began to embrace an incontestably American product (this despite the English background of some of its key practitioners, including Bolton and later, Wodehouse) as something of equal or greater value than Gilbert and Sullivan and the Viennese operettas.

The acclaim proved even greater for the "Princess" effort of February 1917, *Oh, Boy!* "You might call this a musical comedy that is as good as they make them if it were not palpably so much better," the *Times* reviewer raved. The critic further playfully suggested a new title based on the earlier hit—"Even Better Eddie" ("New Princess Play").[11] The *Sun* reviewer was even more effusive: "If there be such things as masterpieces of musical comedy, one reached the Princess last night" (Bordman, *American Musical Theatre* 3rd ed. 366). Once again, the plot involved separated couples and outlandish misunderstandings, most notably a hard-boiled actress on the run from police masquerading as the romantic hero's Quaker aunt. Critics and audiences appeared to agree that Bolton, and particularly Jerome Kern and P.G. Wodehouse as composer and lyricist, had given Broadway a cause to celebrate. "Till the Clouds Roll By" became the most notable song of the show, and it remains a favorite for fans of the prolific Kern. But what "class" work did the play do for Broadway and its audiences?

As it happens, to return to the Ehrenreichs's terminology, class distinctions in *Oh, Boy!* are particularly "fuzzy." Bolton, Wodehouse, and Kern introduce the audience to tasteful bachelor suites on Long Island and in upper-crust country clubs. The hero's buddy, Jim Marvin, has just "led the polo team to victory"—it would appear that we are well immersed in the world of gentlemen not too far removed from their boola-boola college days.[12] Many of the characters from *The College Widow, Strongheart,* and *Brown of Harvard* would have been at home in this atmosphere following graduation. George, the mild-mannered hero who does not like going out, has a valet and a new wife. Like Eddie and his friends, George also went to college, and there is a similar vagueness as to what, if anything, George does. George also shares with Eddie a certain amount of deference to his wife. He has a Quaker aunt who is in charge of his money—again, more of a moneyed class than PMC feature. Furthermore, not only does George's friend Jim play a mean game of polo but also has a collegiate smart-aleck habit of shortening random words, as in "You're welk" (for "You're welcome") and "Don't be redic" (for "Don't be ridiculous"). Jim is the "wild" friend who is always in the midst of a party and planning the next one—in the show, he casually throws one in George's apartment without bothering to ask permission. One of the "conflicts" of the plot is that Jim is always trying to get George to join the party, with George constantly refusing.

Nevertheless, when Jim agrees to help and befriend the comic heroine, Jacky—an actress who has (fairly) innocently gotten mixed up in a potentially scandalous situation with a rich older gentleman (who, it turns out, is George's father-in-law, a judge)—they sing a comic song of domestic bliss, "Nesting Time in Flatbush." The lyrics denote the joys of settling in the suburbs: "We will take a little flat/With welcome on the mat/Where there's room to swing a cat" (Bolton and Wodehouse 2–24). One might fairly ask, as New York *Times* critic Alvin Klein did regarding a 1983 *Oh, Boy!* revival, "Why, then, do Jim, the polo champion who smiles ceaselessly and lops off word endings because 'it's just a hab' and Jackie [*sic*], an actress who is being pursued by a policeman she punched out at a party raid, sing 'Nesting Time in Flatbush?'" (Klein, "Theatre in Review; *Oh, Boy!* Is Delightfully Silly"). Jacky and Jim, in other words, are singing about a distinctly middle class aspiration—attaining a nice "nest" in the suburb of Flatbush.[13] This was not a question that particularly plagued the New York critics in 1917, nor, presumably, its audiences. One could fairly make the case that such questions of internal character and story logic with regard to songs would not be a significant factor in the musical comedy until the musical plays of Rodgers and Hammerstein, beginning with *Oklahoma!* in 1943. Broadly speaking, the biggest priority in a musical was still putting over a good song (along with making sure the star had the best songs, a criterion that still exists to a large extent). There was, however, another factor at work in the case of "Nesting Time in Flatbush."

It is with this apparently careless lapse in class consistency and logic among the characters that class consciousness comes to the fore. Audiences, including the PMC contingent, knew the initial territory of *Oh, Boy!* quite well—rich people (gentlemen) getting themselves involved in silly predicaments that would work themselves out by roughly 11 a.m. What the PMC audience received with the "Flatbush" song was most likely a pleasant surprise of recognition—a hint of "regular" people (hard-working, business-oriented, possiblly PMC types) wanting that most regular of young couple necessities, the "starter" home, and dealing with the same issues of space and size that up-and-coming couples were likely to deal with. That the class identification most likely began and ended with this particular song was not a primary concern—the authors had put it there in recognition of a significant segment of their audience, irrespective of internal story and character logic. The same might be said for a song appearing later in the show, "Flubby-dub the Caveman," who "was never trampled in the crush/Every evening in the uptown rush" (2–47). Presumably, bachelors who had their own spacious apartments on Long Island and did not have to worry about money would also not have to worry about rush hour, but, again, many members of the audience *did* have to worry about it. At any rate, the happy audiences who enjoyed *Oh, Boy!* certainly left their worries outside the Princess Theatre doors.

The next Bolton-Wodehouse-Kern collaboration appeared later the same year, in August 1917. Aside from having its own merits, the show is also worth examining for its source material: George Ade's *The College Widow*. The show was *Leave It to Jane*, and it also proved successful with a five-month Broadway run.[14] The *Times* reviewer pronounced the evening "gay and tasteful," and, in a paragraph devoted to the lovely chorus, kidded the juxtaposition between genuine university atmosphere and the university of the American Musical:

> Ah, the chorus! Learning rests lightly on the massive intellect of co-eds at this fresh water college. Digging Greek roots has not sullied the fair white symmetry of their hands, and abnormal psychology has left their hearts unclouded by any Freudian emotional complex. And how they do manage to dress on an undergraduate income! Radcliffe and Barnard have much to learn in the matter of Domestic Economy from this fresh water Atwater. ("'Leave It to Jane'")

Of note here is the reference to Freud, whose theories were entering mainstream thought and parlance. Applications of and references to Freudian analysis had become something of an intellectual touchstone—terminology that an "expert" would know about and utilize. An ability to apply and invoke Freud would become almost indispensable in appropriating a PMH.

Bolton, Wodehouse, and Kern made a further significant adjustment to Ade's original. The businessman Bolton (not to be confused with the libretto-writer) in *The College Widow* delivered many of his choicest barbs at college and collegians. Thirteen years later, the businessman has a different story to tell, and profoundly different aspirations for his son, the musical's hero: "I had to quit [college] before I could graduate, because my money ran out. But I always swore that, if ever I had a son, *he* should do what I wasn't able to" (author's emphasis).[15] A college education was now an admirable goal, a credit to the person who is able to earn it—not merely a place to keep the lightweights out of the railroad business. This was a key validation of one of the most important PMC signifiers—the college diploma.

Other character changes are more subtle, but still significant. Witherspoon, the college president, is still something of a fogy, but rather less ridiculous in his locutions and his attitudes. Nevertheless, he does regard modern dance with the disdain of a number of religious leaders of the day—an attitude that much of the audience would have read about in the papers: "You will call me an old fogy, but I maintain that the ballroom dance is an immodest performance" (1–2–1). Not surprisingly, it remains for his daughter Jane, the heroine, to educate Witherspoon about the modern college world: "Athletics are so *necessary* to a college. They *advertise* it" (1–17, author's emphasis). And even Witherspoon himself acknowledges that it pays to advertise, even if he disagrees with the methods: "There are worthier advertisements," he responds, a bit huffily. "But none half so *quick*," Jane counters (1–17, author's emphasis). Advertising and speed defined the playing field of 1917 at least as much as athletics. As Jane admonishes the hero and soon-to-be boyfriend Billy, "You really *must* think quicker" (1–2–21, author's emphasis). Indeed one must, not only to keep up with Jane, "the girl with brain," but also to keep up with an America that was moving to the rhythm of quicker machinery, where the PMC were the experts. If there is a definitive answer to the question "When do PMC characters get respect?", the seeds of the answer most likely lie in this special cluster of Princess musicals.

For the PMC at this time, the major positive components of class consciousness were college (and the accompanying diploma), the awareness of having a particular place in the world of American corporate capitalism, and the insistence on having the autonomy to work with a large degree of independence to ensure that the machines, whether literal, bureaucratic, or governmental, were running smoothly. The negative components included an awareness of not always being able to afford to live like the capitalist class in terms of living space, clothes (for the wife or girlfriend as well as himself), and entertainment. There was also an awareness that many capitalists had no use for college graduates—as self-made men, some of the most successful capitalists (Carnegie, for example) did not trust those with a diploma. Plays and musicals were starting to acknowledge the presence of a PMC, if not in glowingly positive terms, at least no longer as jokes. The best years of the PMC on Broadway were yet to come, and if the PMC were to embrace those best years fully, they would have to prove themselves not only onstage, but also on the dance floor. Fortunately, expert help was on the way.

SHOWING A CLASS HOW TO MOVE: THE CASTLES

In his essay "Célibat et condition paysanne," Bourdieu examined and described the country dances of his native village, referring to them as "occasions of a clash of civilizations—between rural and urban life. The difficulties of cultural adaptation experienced by the traditional peasants are manifested in their awkward physical movements" (Robbins 28). While there are no traditional peasants to be found in this section of our study, the PMC did their utmost to dance out their "difficulties of cultural adaptation" on the ballroom floor. Those who would assume a dancing PMH needed the help and support of experts, and such experts were quite plentiful in the second decade of the twentieth century.

Experts—PMC experts in particular—were needed in the field of dance for a deeper reason as well. The perceived war against capitalist culture was waged on many fronts, including the dance floor, often to the tune and rhythm of ragtime. Susan C. Cook explains, "As ragtime became increasingly popular, it literally came to embody, through its music and movement, the purported freedoms and vitality of the modern age. For many, however, the new music, movement, and social informality represented not the enticement of freedom but a threat to social order" (Cook 133). As any PMC expert worth his salt knew, the right experts had to be deployed for the right job. More than any other dancing masters of the period, the right experts, in this case, were the Castles.

Elisabeth Marbury, in her introduction to *Modern Dancing* by Vernon and Irene Castle (billed as Mr. and Mrs. Vernon Castle), offers a defense of dancing circa 1914: The book "shows that dancing, properly executed, is neither vulgar nor immodest, but, on the contrary, the personification of refinement, grace, and modesty" (Marbury 18). Marbury, who was also the Castles' manager, goes further to place dance and the Castles on the side of medical experts and social reformers: "Social reformers will join with the medical profession in the view that dancing is not only a rejuvenator of good health and spirits, but a means of preserving youth, prolonging life, and acquiring grace, elegance, and beauty" (18). To understand this defensive stance, we need to understand what "dance" and its experts were up against.

A *New York Times* article from January 1914 addressed an issue upon which Catholic, Protestant, and Jewish leaders could agree: as the headline noted, "Pastors Approve Ban on the Tango" ("Pastors Approve Ban" 5). The need for thrills, a leave-taking of common sense, and social degeneracy were all to blame, the various pastors and priests felt. The Rev. Dr. Charles A. Eaton, pastor of the Madison Avenue Baptist Church, evoked the term "craze" in its most pejorative sense: "It is a craze, a form of nervous degeneracy. It has been stimulated, first, by unwholesome social conditions, and second, by commercialism…They are consumed by an itch for social advance, and they think the only way to get into society is to dance in" ("Pastors Approve Ban" 5). Indeed, the "dance craze" was another neurasthenic manifestation—the "uneasy confrontation of civilized manliness and primitive masculinity" (Cook 135). Had Clyde Fitch lived a bit longer, he might well have put his neurasthenic characters through their paces on the dance floor, caught in the throes of an over-stimulated Turkey Trot.

Dr. Christian F. Riesner of Grace Methodist Episcopal Church gave his concurring opinion: "Human beings are constituted that they require thrills…Home life is as dry as a sponge without it. Business is a grind without a thrill" ("Pastors Approve Ban"). For the religious leaders and other anti-dance advocates, there were familiar arguments against the "craze." Morality and decorum were sacrificed at the altars of thrills and social climbing, and dancing was at best a salacious outlet for "nervous degeneracy"—all issues, in other words, that touched the PMC. The moral and social arguments that threatened the world of dance became, as so many other issues during this period, a matter for the expert. The Castles entered the scene by way of a Castle Walk, but there were also other experts who came to the aid of the dancing PMC.

By November 1914, the *Times* announced, "under the patronage of Mrs. Reginald Vanderbilt, Mrs. Berry Wall, Mrs. Oliver Harriman, and other members of the American Dance Club of Paris, a new idea in ballroom dancing has come overseas to New York" ("New Dances" SM2). According to the article, the "opera tango" and the "opera waltz," by emphasizing "evenness" of movement that would "do away with the dance of the acrobat," would seize the ballroom floor at Delmonico's, the Holland House, the Astor, and the Majestic ("New Dances"). While, once again, we encounter the fuzzy delineation between the elite gentlemen (and gentlewomen) and the PMC, we can appreciate the chief target of the dance experts—acrobatics, hopping, and "snake dances" that sacrificed grace for sheer energy (and sex).[16]

Marbury, for her part, made it clear that there was no room for such shenanigans at Castle House: "The One Step as taught at Castle House eliminates all hoppings, all contortions of the body, all flouncing of the elbows, all twisting of the arms, and, above everything else, all fantastic dips. The One Step bears no relation or resemblance to the once popular Turkey Trot, Bunny Hug, or Grizzly Bear" (Marbury 20). And what was chiefly to blame for the most sordid dances? One of the chief culprits, according to Ms. Marbury, was the musical comedy. As she explains: "A working man and girl go to a musical comedy. From their stuff seats high up under the roof they look down upon the dancers on the stage.... The man on the stage flings his partner about with Apache wildness; she clutches him around the neck and is swung off her feet.... 'Society' does not do those dances" (26–27).

Fortunately for those who wanted to do "society" dances and who also went to Broadway musicals, Vernon and Irene Castle made notable appearances in Irving Berlin's revue *Watch Your Step*, which premiered in December 1914.[17] The show enabled Vernon Castle to kid the dancing craze and the role of teachers with the song "I'm a Dancing Teacher Now."[18] Irene (again billed as Mrs. Vernon Castle) appeared in the show as herself, in something of a contradiction to her and her husband's book, leading the chorus through "Show Us How to Do the Fox Trot."—"You'll have to watch your step," Mrs. Castle warns.[19]

In their book, the reader watches the Castles' steps, with detailed instructions geared toward "our tired business men" and their partners (Castle 32). The pair assured readers that "athletic prowess" was less important than "the lithe grace of a well-poised body and a sense of rhythm" (38). Vernon Castle, for his part, embodies this grace, but not in a way one might expect. It is not exactly, for example, a Fred Astaire sort of grace.[20] In a photo illustrating the tango, Castle does his steps in the requisite evening dress, with slouching posture and his hands in his pockets (Castles 36). Castle is not only holding something back; he is also holding something *in*. The overtly sexual element is contained.²¹ There is repression as well as reserve, in an interesting counterpoint to some of the more energetic and freeing sentiments the Castles provide in their prose. "We are flinging off our lethargy," the Castles proclaim, "our feeling of having time for nothing outside of business, and are beginning to take our place among the nations who enjoy life" (38). Furthermore, they even suggest something primal and atavistic in the dance: "People can say what they like about rag-time...but when a good orchestra plays a 'rag' one has simply *got* to move" (43, author's emphasis). Nevertheless, as Bourdieu wrote, "there is no way out of the game of culture," not even by way of ragtime (Bourdieu, *Distinction* 12). Even if one has simply got to move, one also has simply got to move *right*. According to the Castle House Suggestions for Correct Dancing, moving right meant, among other things, dropping "the Turkey Trot, the Grizzly Bear, the Bunny Hug, etc. These dances are ugly, ungraceful, and out of fashion" (Castles 177).

For all his hard work and popularity, however, Vernon Castle had particular difficulty negotiating the perceived cultural divide between "manliness" and "dancing." Cutting remarks from the press regarding Castle's effeminacy significantly decreased only with his suitably "manly" service and untimely death as a flyer in the Great War.²² There was, as Cook points out, a lingering suspicion of "lounge lizards" and "under-sexed butterflies"—smooth ballroom dancers "whose dancing skill and popularity with upper-class women who might financially support them rendered them unnatural and unmanly" (Cook 138). That Castle himself was painfully aware of this perception is borne out by the reminiscences of wife Irene: "He had never been a man's man in the public eye...That may have been part of his motive for wanting to go to war in the first place, to silence the very critics who might blame him for not going" (qtd. in Golden 140). In obituaries and tributes, Vernon Castle gained a retroactive stamp of "real manhood" that validated the Castles' work for any doubters. The *New York City Sun,* employing animal metaphors similar to those the press used in hailing Clyde Fitch's last play, proclaimed Vernon Castle "the butterfly who grew into an eagle" (qtd. in Golden 197).²³

This tension between the celebration of freedom and the containment of "primitive" sexuality in the dance during this period is, arguably, a uniquely American phenomenon—and further, a uniquely PMC phenomenon. German dance historian Curt Sachs, commenting on American popular dance of the period from a relatively short distance of 20 years, noted that "our standardized civilization extracted from these foreign dances everything in them that is primitive, forceful, and ecstatic" (Sachs 446). Sachs elaborates,

> But the rapid transformation which the *tango* and all the other American dances have undergone, the quick abandonment of the waving of arms and the shaking of shoulders, illustrates the universal socializing principle—civilization demands close movement. The final result of dance importation today is not, as one might think, the rejuvenation of intense emotion, but rather the rejection of all expanded movement and the preservation of those qualities only which lead inevitably toward closeness and restraint. Grotesque and exaggerated movement is discarded. The quiet glide replaces the old turning, and the restrained sliding step, the affected toe step.... The dances of our modern ballroom are extremely quiet and reserved. (Sachs 446–447)

This rejection of "grotesque and exaggerated movement," along with the outcries of the era's moral guardians, guided the Castles' moves. When Vernon Castle directed his readers regarding hand position, he offered a few choices: "The hands may be either kept behind your back, on your hips, or in your pockets; look at yourself in a mirror and decide which position suits you best" (Castles 104). The lack of touching in the dance is an interesting element in the Castle instruction and bears further examination.

The hold in couples dancing had long been a part of the history of patterned dance movement. The waltz, for example, "established the close hold whereby the man held the woman at the waist in semi-embrace," as Lewis Erenberg illustrates (149). The hold was simultaneously close, for the purpose of the man guiding his female partner, and also distant and formal. "Given the correct hold," Erenberg continues, "the waltz expressed a look but do not touch approach to one's partner, a distance between sexes under the guise of ideal, bodiless love contained in the face of one's partner." As waltzing and other ballroom dances were generally done in unison in large groups, the dance was not so much about the intimacy of the couple as it was about the conformity of the couple with the group and the community (150).

By the time the Castles reached their peak in the 1910s, a plethora of new dances had jumped and trotted into and out of popularity (Erenberg 150). Black and Latin cultures in particular contributed dance and music wherein bodies responded to the rhythm with a great deal of personal enjoyment, and the Castles were well aware of this contribution (one has simply *got* to move, as Vernon himself put it). The Castles, through their own efforts and through the positive publicity they reaped in the pre-World War I years, became the upholders of white capitalist culture by taming, downplaying, and repressing those elements of dance that were too threatening and "vulgar" (i.e., too Black, Latin, or lower-class) to the white audience, and too sexual (i.e., too Black, Latin, or lower-class) for the rabbis, ministers, and priests. "Nigger" dances needed refinement, and the "look-but-do-not-touch" approach that could once be suggested even with a close hold in the early nineteenth century now needed to be quite literal.[24] As Jane C. Desmond writes: "In most cases we will find that dance forms originating in lower-class or nondominant populations presented a trajectory of 'upward mobility' in which the dances are 'refined,' 'polished,' and often desexualized" (Desmond 34). The popular dance of the 1910s entailed a complex set of negotiations, and the PMC required all the expert instruction it could get.

The taming, or PMC-ing, of Negro dancing is significant in this era. As Lynne Fauley Emery writes, descriptions of Negro dances dating from the end of the nineteenth century generally contributed to and confirmed white images of savage, wild Negroes and their uninhibited movements (Emery 163). As white ballroom dancing appropriated the names and the basic moves of the Negro dances, the shifts and evolutions reflected the prevailing white attitudes. For example, when the Cake-Walk gained popularity as the century turned, the dancers in the white ballrooms literalized a subversive, satirical movement. As Emery points out, the Cake-Walk was "a kind of shuffling movement which evolved into a smooth walking step with the body held erect. The backward sway was added, and as the dance became more of a satire on the dance of the white plantation owners, the movement became a prancing strut" (208). When the whites danced the Cake-Walk, the dance became an imitation of an imitation: "The whites [were] now imitating the blacks, who were already satirizing the whites" (Emery 216, ftn. 25).

Other black dances, including Ballin' the Jack, which gained national popularity in 1913 following the *Darktown Follies* in Harlem's Lafayette Theatre, also featured swaying, shuffling movements, with an accompanying serpentine hip rotation. These dances upset not just the white clergy—Negro church leaders too opposed such dances and just as adamantly (Emery 214–220). Such were the moves that needed to be contained and restrained—"whitewashed," in a sense. In the "clash of civilizations" that played itself out on the dance floor, "civilization," or the white hegemonic vision of civilization, spelled out with necessary instruction by the experts, would ever emerge triumphant. The instruction, it might be said, had its influence beyond dancing, as the Broadway PMC hero was at last ready to look in the mirror, decide on his best position, and seize the spotlight.

Along with examining the Victorian habitus and emerging PMC class consciousness, it is necessary to examine and chart emerging PMC class habitus as well. Two of the biggest forces in terms of shaping this new habitus were an obsessive, egomaniacal efficiency expert and a Yankee Doodle Dandy.

6. System and Farce: Emerging PMC Habitus ❧

> *What this office needs is system, and I'm going to have it. System, get me, system!*
> —Edward Peple's "A Pair of Sixes" (1914)

COHAN AS SUPER MODEL—POSITIVE AND NEGATIVE

A website dedicated to George M. Cohan refers to him as "America's First Mega-Star."[1] As over-the-top as that description reads, it is hard to overestimate Cohan's contribution to Broadway during the early years of the twentieth century. Through a savvy combination of showmanship and hard work, he became the most successful individual on the New York stage. What Cohan accomplished wittingly is impressive and a matter of historical record; what he managed to do *un*wittingly contributes a great deal to the discussion of class formation and embodiment. In the service of providing entertainment, Cohan often found himself in the center of audiences, critics, and theatre professionals choosing sides and drawing lines. Cohan did not have his own habitus, for a habitus can belong only to a class of people. Nor did he singlehandedly establish a new class habitus. Cohan did, however, challenge the habitus of the Victorian gentleman through singing, dancing, writing, and a great deal of cheerful cockiness.

Cohan's natural brashness, sincere sense of patriotism, and genuine love of theatre led him to create and personify a new American musical comedy, and a new American musical comedy hero. The brashness was often abrasive, and the patriotism was not infrequently jingoistic, but the desire to entertain ensured Cohan a consistently appreciative audience from the time he became his own Broadway writer-director-composer at the age of twenty-two (following years of vaudeville with his family as the Four Cohans) through the end of the 1920s.

Cohan's appreciative audience strikes at the heart of the problem that the Broadway critic-experts had with entertainment (the audience itself seemed to have no problem). As noted in chapter 2, social historian Richard Butsch writes of the "legitimate" audience as divided into two major categories: "affluent" and "cultured" (Butsch 122). These distinctions jibe roughly with Fitch's informal labeling of the audience who attended the "first-class" theatres as "plush" or "unupholstered." Jack Poggi makes the following supporting distinctions:

> The "first-class" audience represented a fair cross section of society, including the rich and the fairly well-to-do in the orchestra and balconies, and some people with less income in the galleries; despite differences in background, they all seemed to like the same kinds of plays. In their tastes the "first-class" audience were not very different from the many people who saw the same productions later on the road. (Poggi 265–266)

These distinctions were an articulation of "the dynamic intersection of structure and action, society and the individual" that defines "habitus" (Postone 4). Aided and abetted by the growing authority of the theatrical critic, the PMC was delineating its parameters through both positive and negative models. And, largely because such parameters are seldom if ever wholly consistent, Cohan was a model who was simultaneously positive and negative—neither "cultured" nor "affluent" himself at first, but he would eventually gain considerable affluence and become embraced by arbiters of culture. Irrespective of what many critic-experts felt was "good" for American theatre and what audiences "should" be seeing, audiences found Cohan and enjoyed his product.[2] Even when New York audiences attended Cohan's shows in comparatively modest numbers, Cohan nevertheless permeated and helped redefine American popular culture.[3]

In many ways, critical respect for Cohan increased as his popular successes decreased toward the end of his career in the 1930s. (Critics praised his performance in O'Neill's *Ah, Wilderness!* as his finest, which both pleased and rankled him.)[4] For better and worse, Cohan lived to see himself become a part of theatrical history and legend. But critical comment during his rise and heyday revealed the arbiters of theatrical taste grappling in frank confusion with Cohan's vitality and success. Channing Pollock, writing in *The Green Book Album* in December 1910, offers a pertinent example: "I have admired...Mr. Cohan's industry, his versatility, his undeniable cleverness, but...I have resented his blatancy, his reliance upon noise and speed, his sympathy with all that is least praiseworthy in Forty-second Street, and his self-appointed championship of the American flag" (Pollock, "Get-Rich-Quick Wallingford" 96–97). The dichotomy Pollock presents is informative: industry, versatility, and cleverness appear as values to be admired and encouraged; speed and noise, "blatancy," and overdone patriotism are shunned. Blatancy constituted another challenge to the Victorian gentleman habitus.

A bigger issue was "manners." As we have seen, theatre audiences were expected to display good manners, and onstage heroes nearly always did the same (as did most of the villains). Even Sherlock Holmes remained impeccably polite as he shot up. Cohan, impertinent on and off stage, was often at best a puzzlement to contemporaneous critics, and at worst, a massive affront. The *Theatre Magazine* critic who reviewed the 1906 *George Washington, Jr.* posed the problem this way: "His ideas are good but his manners atrocious. He is thoroughly flippant and common, not vulgar, but the spirit of juvenescent enthusiasm is so assertive that the actor has it all his own way" (qtd. in McCabe 73).

If *Theatre Magazine* found Cohan to be a naughty (but not vulgar) juvenile, *Life*'s drama editor James Metcalfe saw in him a threat to the intelligence, health, and well-being of the American theatre possibly as great as the Syndicate itself. He derides audiences and Cohan with equal vigor as he sums up Cohan's "ideal of American young manhood":

> He makes him a vulgar, cheap, blatant, ill-mannered, flashily dressed, insolent, smart Aleck, who for some reason unexplainable on any basis of common sense, good taste, or even ordinary decency, appeals to the imagination and apparent approval of large American audiences. As a living character in any American town or village, it is hardly to be conceived that he would not be

driven out as a public nuisance and a pernicious example to the youth of the community. The rounds of applause which greet the efforts of this offensive personality must convey to the minds of ignorant boys a depraving ideal for their inspiration and imitation. (Metcalfe, "George Washington, Jr." 94–96; also qtd. in McCabe 76–78)

By way of conclusion, Metcalfe urged his readers to see Cohan's show: "There could be no stronger appeal for the betterment of the American stage—no fiercer commentary on the debased condition of the intelligence of a large part of the theatre-going public" (Metcalfe, "George Washington, Jr." 96, also qtd. in McCabe 78). For the audience, according to Metcalfe, there were clearly choices to be made: good manners or insolent, smart-alecky wisecracks; blatancy or subtlety; flashy or "careful" dress; cheap vulgarity or "class."

To the probable exasperation of Metcalfe and many of the critics of the day, audiences did not necessarily receive Cohan and his work in terms of such choices. What Cohan brought to Broadway was a moral code that had been absent, particularly from the musical comedy: "be honest and fair, be pals with good men and worshipful of women, don't worry about money, cultivate confidence, and take pride in your people" (Mordden 27). It was the morality of an America where an upstart immigrant could succeed on his own terms through integrity, fair play, talent, and confidence. And here, as much as in any other place, was where arbiters of taste and society's guardians began to draw lines. The confidence of a gentleman was one thing, the confidence of an "upstart" was quite another. Nevertheless, in terms of the Broadway musical comedy (if less so regarding "straight" plays, at least beyond the era under study), Cohan's vision and morality would prove durable. As Ethan Mordden explains,

> Cohan...defined the urban, upstart, immigrant, egalitarian character that was to see...[the musical] through its golden age. The Cohan musical is a New York show, and that is what musical comedy is: fast town, hip characters, innocents getting wise...The notion of an Eddie Cantor or a Bert Lahr as the hero of a book musical is implausible without the prior arrangement of the immigrant upstarts. (Mordden 29)[5]

The limits of the era's stage photography add to the difficulty of "seeing" what Metcalfe and others were writing about, and Cohan was ideally adaptable to neither recording nor film, although he tried both.[6] There are some tantalizing clues, nonetheless. As to height, Cohan was on the shorter side of normal at five feet, six inches, and at his trimmest, between 135 and 140 pounds. Apparently both on and off stage, his habit was to keep the left side of his mouth twisted down (McCabe 52).[7] A 1901 photograph of *The Governor's Son* provides a hint of Cohan's physical impudence—we see him perched on a small sofa, perhaps having just sprung into position, apparently trying to calm the female chorus, who are staged in various poses of shock and dismay. Cohan's suit appears, at least from a distance, to be dark and conservative, but there is the sense that in this scene, at least, his character has crossed the bounds of propriety in a space for ladies only.[8]

A 1904 shot of Cohan as Little Johnny Jones gives the viewer a better look at the man in performance mode. The suit and shoes are dark, with the coat and pants wrinkling up as Cohan leans back, feet in mid-air, upon a pedestal of some kind. He wears a derby hat cocked jauntily (insolently?) to one side, and his mouth is open as if singing from the side of his mouth, confirming typical descriptions of his singing. With the eyebrows raised, the mouth slightly twisted, the insouciant position of the hat, and the arms apparently careless but firmly in control, there does indeed resonate from this photo something that might best be described in modern terms as "attitude." If the face is communicating anything to the audience, it might be something along the lines of "This is easy for me—I can impress you without even trying." Some of this attitude was, no doubt, a function of the character, as written and personified by Cohan; however, audiences (and critics) already surmised by 1904 that such distinctions were pretty much irrelevant.

Cohan himself describes coming up with his unique dance style more or less on the spot in the mid-1890s while still in vaudeville with his family, apparently due to a misunderstanding regarding the music:

> Every time I threw my head back, my hair (which I wore exceptionally long at the time) would fly up and then down over my face, and I'd brush it away and

do another throw back and up and down the hair would go again. I faked a couple of funny walks to fit in the spots where I had to eliminate certain steps on account of the slow tempo, and each of the walks got hearty laughs and rounds of applause. I finished with an eccentric walking step, throwing my head back with the hair flying all over my face and made an exit with the end of the strain instead of ending with the old-fashioned "break."

For twenty solid years I did this same dance to the same music, and this was the stunt which not only revolutionized American buck dancing, but also set the "hoofers" to doing away with jig sand, and letting their hair grow long enough to fall over their eyes.

The "Cohan style" they used to call it. (Cohan 143–144)

Cohan enjoyed playing up the notion that nobody liked his shows but the public, and playing the "little guy" who confounded the educated experts (i.e., the critics).[9] As he writes in his autobiography, "'A swaggering, impudent, noisy vaudevillian, entirely out of place in first-class theatres,' was the opinion of one of New York's foremost dramatic experts" (Cohan 199). If Cohan took some defiant pleasure in quoting his detractors, he nevertheless was not without fans in the press as well. The following review of *George Washington Jr.* from the *New York Evening Post Mail* of February 12, 1906, provides some insight into what made a Cohan show unique as well as the range of his appeal:

> That's one secret of the value of the production: it appeals with equal strength to all parts of the auditorium. On Saturday night after the second act I noticed the "gallery gods" and the pretty girls in pinks and blues in the boxes calling for "Author!" with the same amount of vim.
>
> I tried very hard to find a dull spot in "George Washington, Jr." and I gave it up in sheer delight. It's a short performance from 8:20 until 10:40—but there's more meat and ginger in its three swift acts than in all the other musical shows that have marched upon Manhattan for many a blue moon.
>
> I might as well add that he has blossomed into a Harry Lehr or Creighton Webb, considered sartorially.[10]
>
> Cohan holds to the theory, abandoned by most other present-day light opera makers, that "a plot carried through until the final curtain will be welcomed by a much-abused public....A story is there—definite, well sustained and running up to climaxes." (Untitled ["George Washington, Jr."], *New York Evening Post Mail*)[11]

The unidentified reviewer touches on some interesting aspects of Cohan's technique and his audience. He could appeal to Fitch's both "plush" and "unupholstered" crowds alike. By 1906, the term "gallery gods" was undergoing an evolution in meaning. As Richard Butsch explains,

> In the second half of the nineteenth century, teen-age boys had replaced the prostitutes, laborers, and blacks of the Jacksonian gallery. But the boys soon left increasingly "legitimate" theaters for cheaper admissions to vaudeville and then movie theaters. By 1910 the boys were replaced by gallery goddesses and earnest devotees of drama unable to afford orchestra seats. The new galleryites were middle-class and mostly women. They were canonized as the true lovers of drama. (Butsch 126–127)

Nevertheless, it would be a mistake to assume that there were hard-and-fast divisions between the Broadway audience and the vaudeville audience.[12] With popularity came imitation, as Cohan brought his vaudeville instincts to Broadway:

> Mr. Cohan as an impersonator of himself—to distinguish among the manifold emanations of his being—has been imitated to weariness by the youth of the stage. He was once as much the fashion with the younger men of it as Miss Billie Burke now is among the younger women...Have not our youth...sought to walk as jerkily as Mr. Cohan or to twist their mouths even as he twists his? (unidentified and undated article in *Boston Transcript*, qtd. in Morehouse 103)[13]

Imitation and parody were two forms of entertainment that linked vaudeville and Broadway, and their audiences, in the early part of the century. Indeed, Fitch and Cohan, two key subjects of this study, provided fodder for the vaudevillians and their fans. Weber and Fields kidded that Fitch plays under such titles as *The Stickiness of Gelatine* and *Barbara Fidgety* (for *The Stubbornness of Geraldine* and *Barbara Frietchie*, respectively).[14] To a large degree, the Broadway audience was also the vaudeville audience, since for parodies and imitations to be effective, the audience would need at least some familiarity with the Broadway prototypes. The catholicity of audience taste, as well as the "downstairs" audience with "upstairs" hearts (and vice versa), was a theme of Broadway critics and pundits, and Cohan's shows generated a fair amount of speculation as to audience identity. Peter Clark Macfarlane, writing an undated contemporaneous *Everybody's Magazine* article, posited the following observation regarding the failure of Cohan's play *Popularity* and his subsequent successes:

> In "Popularity," the hero was an impossible upstart of whom the public would have none. Cohan's heroes had all been of this smart-Aleck type. Cohan himself...seemed to lack refinement....The people who laughed with Cohan were not quite the same people who were pleased by John Drew or moved by Mrs. Fiske or delighted by Maude Adams.
>
> No doubt Cohan saw all this. Perhaps the failure of "Popularity"...struck in and tutored somewhat those personal tastes which, according to his critics, stood sadly in need of schooling. Anyway, from about this time forward...his performances showed here and there eliminations that marked an awakening sense of those eternal fitnesses which are the essence of good taste. (qtd. in Morehouse 83–84)

Cohan himself would most likely have referred to such an observation as "bunk," and, indeed, the theory does not ring true historically. If anyone was doing the tutoring in personal tastes, it was George M.; he certainly never saw a pressing need to change his walk, look, or manners. In reference to *Popularity* in his autobiography, Cohan merely said that its failure made him "mad," and that he was determined to turn it into a success, which he did by turning the play into the musical *The Man Who Owned Broadway*.[15] To say the least, dialog between Cohan, critics, and audience remained rich and lively throughout this era. Historian Arthur Hornblow tried to "explain" Cohan, easily fixing the physicality but still having noticeable difficulty pinpointing Cohan's audience:

> For the explanation of George M. Cohan's almost phenomenal success one must not turn to his plays, for they are entirely inconsequential...To a large part of our public Cohan represents the restless American spirit, the cheeky, go-aheadedness of the hustling Yankee. All the time he is on the stage he is in motion. His derby hat, worn jauntily on one side of his head, his face screwed

up into a perpetual grin, his legs never still for a moment, coming on with a skip that soon develops into a hilarious dance, singing his own songs with nasal drawl and forever waving the flag, George M. Cohan delights millions of theatre-goers of a certain class and to-day boasts of a following that for numbers might well be envied by a Kean or a Booth. (Hornblow 346–347)

Macfarlane's and Hornblow's theses provide intriguing and troubling issues—"not *quite* the same people who were pleased by John Drew"? "Theatre-goers of a *certain* class"? What is there to say, then, about Cohan's audience? To identify the points on the graph where Cohan (flashily dressed son of immigrants, up-to-the-minute slang), Broadway (WASP, reserved, with gentlemanly rules of "fair play"), and the audience ("tired businessmen," society wives, and matinee girls, lower middle class "new gods" in the gallery, and "intellectual" critics) meet is more than a little challenging. If we try to fit the contemporaneous commentary together neatly, we find no inconsiderable contradictions. On the one hand, Cohan appealed to "innocent," unthinking audiences with "chewing-gum taste" who did not appreciate "real" entertainment. On the other, his fans included "true" drama lovers who applauded Cohan's innovations as well as his personality as a performer. One could fairly say that the audience was largely the vaudeville audience that enjoyed the kinds of entertainment Cohan and his family provided in the previous decade. Or, the fans were the standby "tired businessmen" and their wives. Cohan himself liked to say he appealed to the plumber and his wife, whom one would most likely find in the gallery (or, increasingly, at the movies).[16] And, possibly, as many of his contemporaneous commentators suspected, his ideal audience had "gallery" hearts, irrespective of the physical location of their seats.

Nevertheless, it is possible to paint a historical portrait of Cohan's ideal audience, for the contradictions are not as great as they might appear at first glance. A key to Cohan's position on the Broadway field lies in a casual comment in the *Boston Transcript* article quoted earlier— the fact that "younger men" frequently imitated and sought to emulate Cohan. For roughly his first ten years on Broadway, Cohan was something of a rock star—or a James Dean or a Marlon Brando—a model for young men who admire outcasts and rebels and those who irritate the "establishment." This view is borne out by Adolph Klauber, writing for the *Times* in September 1912:

> Mr. Cohan has not always been as discriminating in his taste as might have been wished. In fact, it was often urged in the past, and not without some truth, that Mr. George M. Cohan was a bad influence in our theatre. In his earlier musical comedies he capitalized on the flip insolence which is a characteristic of certain phases of American youth. Like the funny "Kids" of various Sunday supplement cartoons, Mr. Cohan provided in his plays not only a type which was easily recognizable, but one which by its very attractiveness on the stage provided an incentive to imitation. Fresh youths found in his popularity an excuse for their freshness; others, not so fresh, wished and endeavored to become more like the Cohan hero of the footlights. (Klauber, "The New George M. Cohan")

If we return to our PMC audience member, we might well have found him at a Cohan show, particularly if he was a younger member of that emerging class—a man who might well have wished to be Cohan and drive away his nerves with a snappy, fresh attitude and some clever songs and dances. Indeed, a middle-aged man of nerves might have felt the same way.

The critics, having established themselves as experts, found much to admire in Cohan, including his industriousness, his inventiveness, most likely his sense of fair play, and certainly his success. More problematically, there was also much about Cohan that created distress—the bad manners, the flashiness, the slang, and the immigrant impudence. How did one solve a problem such as George M.? Cohan was, in effect, a problem to be solved by the emerging theatrical PMC. In the meantime, the audience members belonging to this emerging class saw someone challenge (with all due "blatancy") the habitus of the Victorian gentleman. For many in the audience, Cohan was someone worth imitating, if only for personal amusement. Again, this admiration and imitation in and of itself did not establish a new habitus, but such admiration did perhaps introduce the idea that a different way of behaving and moving was possible. And the possibilities were exciting.

Critics did, in fact, make their peace with Cohan as musical performer and writer in the decade following 1910. Although it is true that composers such as Irving Berlin and Jerome Kern had stolen a good deal of Cohan's musical thunder, the Yankee Doodle Dandy still found time and favor in delineating the difference between a "musical comedy" and a "revue."[17] Cohan, whose watchword had always been speed, did away with lavish and opulent sets in his revue *Hello Broadway*. He made scene changes visible to the audience—one sketch beginning as another ended, an innovation to the Broadway theatergoers. The revue format allowed Cohan to return somewhat to his vaudeville roots, affectionately kid the New York stage and other American institutions, and, in the most famous running gag of the evening, settle for good and all whether or not a revue needed a plot. Throughout the evening, characters search for a box that supposedly contains the show's plot. At last they find the box—empty. "There never was a plot," Cohan himself explains.

The *Dramatic Mirror* heralded the arrival of the modern revue in terms that reflected the conflagration in Europe: "The revue...is invading New York with the force and dispatch of the German Army....The musical revue seems to be what the public wants, judging from the attendance at 'Watch Your Step' and 'Hello, Broadway'" (Bordman, *American Musical Theater* 2nd ed. 304). It also seemed to be what the critics wanted from Cohan. "It is a large and lively entertainment, packed to the brim with noise and color and fun," the *Times* wrote. In the Weber and Fields tradition, the show spent a good amount of time poking "genial derision...at other theatrical offerings of the season," including those produced by Cohan himself. ("It pays to advertise," the *Times* noted, invoking the title of a notable Cohan-produced hit.) The show also reinforced the old vaudeville-Broadway audience connection: "Many of its jokes would be lost on the man from home or the gentleman from Mississippi. But they are immensely funny to Broadway," the *Times* noted ("'Hello Broadway' is Vastly Amusing"). If the musical was indeed set to leave Cohan behind, the entertainer had found a welcoming niche in the world of revue. Only by placing himself on the wrong side of the actors' strike of 1919 did Cohan begin to tarnish his long, loving, and profitable relationship with Broadway. In the meantime, critic-experts had begun to make their peace with Cohan; he was no longer the unruly, rebellious (immigrant) upstart, but rather the consummate, comfortable, and comforting Broadway professional.[18] Cohan's style of revue creation and management proved compatible with the PMC (and with those who appropriated a PMH) in two ways: (1) his style of production was recognizably efficient in terms of greatly reducing (and often completely eliminating) wait time for audiences between sketches and songs, and (2) by poking genial fun at Broadway products, Cohan was effectively propagating and preserving Broadway culture. Efficiency, the former quality, was already by this time a key PMC watchword.

Cohan would continue making extremely important contributions to Broadway and to the emerging PMC habitus, particularly through the business farces that he produced and often cowrote (or "Cohanized"). These business farces were, in many respects, the somewhat illegitimate offspring of Frederick Winslow Taylor and his concept of Scientific Management, which reached the business mainstream almost as soon as it was published in 1911.

F.W. TAYLOR: A SCIENTIFIC CALL FOR PMC

Broadway found the ideal response to big business, scientific management, and those who had to hustle to keep up with the machinery and to keep the machinery going. This ideal response was farce—loud, frenetic, and peopled with bodies seemingly in constant motion. The flowery speech of melodrama gave way to the rapid-fire bursts of heroes and their buddies who had no time to spend posing and declaiming. The American drama was still perhaps frivolous, but its most memorable products were drawn from a uniquely American phenomenon—American corporate capitalism. And, as is often the case with the best farces, much of the original source material was meant and offered in deadly earnest.

According to Teddy Roosevelt, "The conservation of our national resources is only preliminary to the larger question of national efficiency" (qtd. in Taylor 5). For the twentieth century's most celebrated (and criticized) efficiency expert, it was an appropriate quote to begin an explanation of the principles of Scientific Management. Indeed, Frederick Winslow Taylor did use the quote to introduce his 1911 book

The Principles of Scientific Management, and with the implied validation from T.R., American corporate capitalism would find its clearest set of rules as well as its strongest call for a PMC.[19]

The apparently natural antagonism between employers and employees was, like so many other problems and challenges of the period, a matter for the experts, and "the system" that Taylor devised seemed to be the ultimate word in expertise. As Taylor himself wrote, with a veneer of simple common sense, regarding the issues between owners and workers: "As engineers and managers, we are more intimately acquainted with these facts than any other class in the community, and are therefore best fitted to lead in a movement...by educating not only the workmen but the whole of the country" (Taylor 18).

The first order of business was to differentiate between mental and menial work, and Taylor accomplished this with his characteristic blunt clarity:

> Now one of the very first requirements for a man who is fit to handle pig iron as a regular occupation is that he shall be so stupid and so phlegmatic that he more nearly resembles in his mental make-up the ox than any other type. The man who is mentally alert and intelligent is for this very reason entirely unsuited to what would, for him, be the grinding monotony of work of this character. (Taylor 59)

Through a series of step-by-step instructions, examples, and seriocomic vignettes involving lovably "slow" workers such as the little German Schmidt, outfitted by Taylor with a thick skull and a thicker vaudeville accent, Taylor illustrated what the worker presumably wanted, and how he needed the experts to help him achieve it (41–46).

Uplifting tales of how Scientific Management improved lives and businesses competed with rival images of dehumanization and impersonalization. Taylor, his own best storyteller, calmly and patiently addressed businesses and universities on how the virtues of his system provided a triple-win situation—happy and better-paid workers, all too stupid to realize that they are being more productive; skilled and educated managers who gently but firmly guide the oxen-like labor force; and the business owners who show greater profits. Nor was Taylor a voice alone or apart—Scientific Management became a buzzword, a catchphrase, and, for many between 1910 and 1920 (and indeed, well beyond), an apparent godsend. Taylor's seemingly scientific common sense, combined with Dickensian narratives of poverty and degradation, and the effective use of supporting photographs, made terrific copy. In the ultimate search for order that drove the era under study, Taylorism and Scientific Management seemed to be something truly special—possibly the prime examples of, in Martha Banta's words, "how a culture is shaped by those who convinced themselves that they had finally accomplished what Emerson says we all set out to do in our rage for control—to discover 'a true theory' that will explain all phenomena'" (Banta ix).[20]

Nevertheless, not everyone willingly accepted the notion of men either as animals or as parts of the machine. In Taylor's lifetime, he faced a congressional committee that included many labor representatives, eager and able to confront Taylor's presumptions about how the labor force thought and felt.[21] Taylor's brand of efficiency was later tweaked in print by John Dos Passos, who made the visual point by cramming assembly-line verbs together into one congested nonsense word (Dos Passos 3:55; also qtd. in Banta 4–5). Perhaps the most immediately recognizable attack on efficiency's effect on the worker remains Chaplin's *Modern Times*—the little (though at least temporarily employed) Tramp sucked into the huge gears of the industrial machine, force-fed a two-minute meal to minimize lunch breaks, and finally so conditioned to tightening screws that he cannot keep his wrenches off a large lady with a bounteous pair of...buttons.[22]

As for Broadway, the atmosphere was simultaneously too irreverent to take Taylorism seriously and too good-natured for a negative response beyond the mildest satire. As Broadway continued to evolve and modify its more and more frequent confrontations with American corporate capitalism, PMC types—who provided straight lines for the clowns in the musicals and were the butt of (usually, but not always) good-natured jokes by the heroes of the sporting dramas—were achieving greater status. In order to negotiate the comically convoluted (though often with melodramatic overtones) world of American business, the hero needed to either have the trusted help of an expert or become an expert himself. Clyde Fitch often gave those jobs to his strong heroines. Between 1910 and 1920, the PMC characters rose from the ranks of grinds and neurasthenics to become heroic. They were heroic in farces, true, but heroic nonetheless. And particularly, in terms of habitus, the PMC characters began to embody their own way of behaving, speaking, and moving. An early example of this kind of farce pre-dates Scientific Management, and its hero's Can-Do behavior is not as assured as his counterparts' would be roughly 10 years later. In the case of *Brewster's Millions*, the hero had no choice but to turn himself into a business expert and then do everything wrong or backward, in order to succeed.

LOSING AND MAKING A FORTUNE: *BREWSTER'S MILLIONS*

On the last evening of 1906, Broadway audiences first witnessed the character of Montgomery "Monty" Brewster accepting the proposition of a lifetime: spend a million dollars in the course of a year and wind up completely penniless, in order to gain the ultimate prize of seven million dollars.[23] The stipulations of the will left by Brewster's uncle are clear, rendered in the uncle's own no-nonsense cadences: "No indiscriminate giving away of funds. Don't be stingy, though. I hate a stingy man. No more than ordinary dissipations, but I hate a saint. No excessive donations to charity, let him spend his money freely but get his money's worth" (28).

This passage from Winchell Smith and Byron Ongley's *Brewster's Millions* (dramatized from George Barr McCutcheon's novel) provides one of the clearest definitions of a "regular fellow" one could hope to find. A regular fellow was not a sap with his money, nor was he a tightwad. He indulged in a few "ordinary dissipations"—total abstinence was by no means healthy or regular. Charity was fine, but there was no merit in giving more than was reasonable. And a regular fellow expected and invariably received his money's worth. If Cohan prided himself on his ability to "Cohanize" a property, then in some respects *Brewster's Millions* went Cohan one better. The morality that Cohan brought to the American musical was now effectively tailored to fit the WASP moneyed classes at whom most of Cohan's characters had been thumbing their noses. The capitalists and the PMC not only *could* be regular fellows, they also would define precisely what being "regular" meant as well as the appropriate penalties for deviating from such regularity.

Brewster's transformation upon taking the challenge is nearly instantaneous; even as he completes the decision process, he begins "speaking more quickly and with nervous energy" (29–30). In order to spearhead the operation of "Frenzied Finance" (59), Brewster must attain a wide variety of PMC money management skills—he must spend recklessly and excessively while somehow making his purchases appear at least somewhat reasonable. As he becomes a mental worker, Brewster begins to feel the rigors of constant thinking: "It's all very well for the ordinary businessman to think. He thinks of something to do, does it and that ends it. But I have to think of what other people will think; and think what they think I think; and think what they think I think I think" (67). Brewster just manages to ride through the series of catastrophes that bring him more money as his time to go broke runs short—he is obliged to battle the vicissitudes of unwanted good luck as well as the damaging "help" from his well-meaning friends.

Brewster's thought processes, although set up in this case for a joke, become a significant part of both the emerging PMH and the emerging American drama. Part of the PMC habitus is a quickness of speech matching a quickness of thought and mental ability—a direct contrast to the deliberate musicality and correctness of diction favored by the Victorian gentlemen.[24] Brewster, new to the process, is still learning to be as fast as he needs to be, and thus his hard work does not constitute a full embodiment. Nevertheless, Brewster finds himself moving and speaking more quickly, in the headlong rush of Mr. Can-Do—but more out of desperately trying to keep up with the plot than controlling it, as future Mr. Can-Dos would accomplish. Also, O'Neill would become more and more interested in the spoken thought processes of his characters, and in how to give these processes free rein through various kinds of experimental dialog—most notably the "asides" of *Strange Interlude,* his greatest success (during his lifetime).

Brewster gains some particularly valuable expert help when he most needs it. One of Brewster's friends has paid back a substantial debt, just minutes before the fateful deadline. As luck would have it, the inopportune windfall exactly matches the executor's fee, bringing Brewster's balance to a happy-ending zero as the curtain falls (112). Brewster gets the girl, too, of course, but if business intrigue could not quite dominate a melodrama, it was just right for driving the machinery of farce. The story proved exceedingly durable, enjoying a long initial Broadway run as well as several movie incarnations.[25] Notably, the feel-good fantasy of the regular fellow becoming fabulously wealthy (and still regular) could not have been consummated without the hero's (inexpert) appropriation of a PMH, and the deus ex machina entrance of a PMC representative. The PMC were beginning to exhibit and define their importance on the Broadway stage.

Here George M. Cohan once again proves invaluable as a contributor and an instigator to the PMC-ing of Broadway—in this case, chiefly as producer (with longtime partner Sam Harris) and "Cohanizer," that is, as both credited and uncredited writer. The morality of Cohan's plays would undergo a subtle shift; loyalty to a pal was still important, but the ultimate message was to seize on success—whatever will "go" or "work" is what counts, and if the "gab" that the hero gives to the public in the world of the play is not entirely plausible (or honest), as long as he can fix the situation in the end, everybody benefits.

Shrewdly, Cohan no longer saw fit to always embody the young upstart himself, even though age was not really an issue. Cohan's spiritual stand-in was roughly Cohan's age and in some ways a good deal less impressive as a physical figure. Character comedian Grant Mitchell—forty-ish, short, portly, and possessed of a distinctly receding hairline—had done yeoman's work on Broadway roughly since the century had turned, earning the occasional positive nod from the critics. Rising through the ranks in a Cohan-driven trilogy, Mitchell would become something of a star and, more to the point, the ultimate incarnation of the PMC on Broadway.

GRANT MITCHELL—PMC POSTER BOY

Humbugging Prelude: *Get-Rich-Quick Wallingford*

"When Mr. P.T. Barnum uttered his famous remark that the American public likes being humbugged," the *New York Times* critic noted on September 20, 1910, "he might have added with equal truth that the one thing it likes even better is seeing the other fellow humbugged" ("Very Funny Satire of Common Failing" 11).[26] The *Times* was referring to *Get-Rich-Quick Wallingford,* which would run a year on Broadway and give George M. Cohan a chance to prove that he could, with George Randolph Chester's original stories as inspiration, indeed, write a successful "straight" play without music.

As for the humbugging and the humbugged, the con men who drive the plot are J. Rufus Wallingford and his partner, Horace "Blackie" Daw. Together, they have hit upon the scheme of selling shares in a bogus firm that will manufacture covered carpet tacks. They proceed to bilk the mayor and all the richest citizens of the medium-sized town in which they find themselves, under the pretence of building a covered carpet tack factory. "And then," in the words of Channing Pollock, "a wonderful thing happens. The covered carpet tack turns out to be a valuable idea" (Pollock, "Get-Rich-Quick Wallingford" 96–97). The lies become truth, and Wallingford finds true love ("of course, there is a love interest," the *New York Times* critic notes in its review, "Very Funny Satire") and legitimate entry into the world of American business and manufacture. The *Times*, in its (almost) unqualified positive review, acknowledges both the fun and the possible moral dubiousness of the situation: "it wouldn't do for you to have time to sit back and figure out just what a pair of crooked scoundrels are getting your sympathy and your laughter, both of which, if you can forget our moral sense for the moment, you unhesitatingly hand out" ("Very Funny Satire").

In this play, the first of the Cohan-Grant Mitchell "trilogy" under discussion, Mitchell was not the lead. He played the aptly named Edward Lamb, the hotel clerk who fronts Wallingford and Daw with nearly all of his life savings. While Hale Hamilton, as Wallingford, and Edward Ellis, as Daw, took the bulk of the performing honors, the *New York Times* acknowledged Mitchell as contributing one of several "capital little sketches" to the evening and further highlighted one of Mitchell's key onstage moments: "And so when the bright young man in the play who is looking for a good investment and is assured of his 75 per cent. [*sic*], and asked if he would like to get it, answers, 'Yes, ALL I can get,' the house recognizes and enjoys a very common failing" ("Very Funny Satire"). In this case, Mitchell himself is not Mr. Can-Do—the characters of Wallingford and Daw do all the fast-talking and hustling. It should also be noted that the con men become capitalists by the end of the play; *Wallingford* was not the full-bodied embrace of PMC class position that Cohan and Mitchell would bring about several years later. Mitchell's rather quiet role of Edward Lamb, and the play that contained him, is something of a PMC warm-up.

What the house also "recognized and enjoyed" was the pleasure of seeing the ingratiating heroes "make it," even at the occasional expense of truth, and audiences for the next year seemed to have little or no difficulty forgetting their "moral sense for the moment." In the words of the play's hotel proprietor, "What we need is young blood, new ideas, a lot of get-up-and-go fellows that'll start things" (16).[27] The "we" extended to Broadway audiences as well. Indeed, Blackie is not being entirely ironic when he tells the town that Wallingford represents "integrity and true American spirit" (24). This adjusted morality and "integrity" would serve the next two plays as well as Cohan and Mitchell particularly well.

Mitchell on the Rise: *It Pays to Advertise*

According to Montrose Moses, when "realism joined hands with incongruity…we began to get the modern farce…it really does not matter if the logic of the situation is consistent, or the ethics of the case tenable" (Moses, *American Dramatist* 329). In *It Pays to Advertise,* cowriters Roi Cooper Megrue and Walter Hackett hit upon the ideal business atmosphere where realism, incongruity, inconsistent logic, and untenable ethics seemed perfectly at home—the world of advertising.

In the same introduction to *It Pays*, Moses sums up the play's point: "advertising will make everything go in the world…you can fool the public all the time by 'gab'" (329). He also touches on the continued and evolving importance of "nervousness": "The nervous quality to such plays was probably the forerunner of the nervous quality the Expressionists have attempted to measure for us in such dramas as 'The Adding Machine' and 'Processional'" (330). In turn, the nervous men in the Fitchean parlors were succeeded by nervous American hustlers. The key difference, besides the fact that Fitch's "nervous" plays were not farces, was that the hustlers did not make the audience nervous, whereas Fitch's (often suicidal) neurasthenics most likely did. That character comedian Grant Mitchell came to become one of the premier interpreters of such hustlers seemed especially appropriate, since he had spent considerable time early in his career in comic supporting roles in Fitch's plays.[28]

Mitchell's character in *It Pays* does not begin as the paragon of American advertising—at his entrance, Rodney Martin, son to "Soap King" Cyrus Martin, embodies the rich man's son who has recently graduated from Harvard and is, therefore, naturally useless.[29] The authors provide a detailed description: "RODNEY MARTIN…is a young man of twenty-four with a certain quaint frank charm, in spite of his funny little mustache, English morning coat, spats and white carnation. He is by no means brainless, but simply undeveloped by reason of the kind of life he has lead under appallingly frictionless conditions" (Megrue and Hackett 336). Friction will meet Rodney in a variety of ways throughout the evening's two-hour traffic.

In the course of this "farcical fact in three acts," Rodney must prove to his father that he can make it on his own. To do so, Rodney decides to beat his father at his own business—he goes into the soap business. While Rodney might lack business acumen (as well as soap), he is smart enough to engage former press agent Ambrose Peale, who knows the most important element of the soap or any business—the power of advertising. In the world of the play, it is the fast-talking Peale who serves as the recruitment officer for the PMC, and Rodney proves an apt and willing recruit. As Peale "sells" the idea to Rodney, he bombards Rodney and the audience with a list of slogans that in 1914 would have been well known to the audience (and some of them are still familiar):

> If I say His Master's Voice, you know that advertises a phonograph. You're on to what soap "It Floats" refers to. There's a Reason—Uneeda—Quaker Oats—Phoebe Show—Children Cry For It—Sapolio—Grape Nuts—Peruna—The Road of Anthracite—Spearmint—Pierce Arrow—57 Varieties—Kodak—White Seal—Gold Dust Twins—He Won't Be Happy Till He Gets It—Bull Durham—Pianola—Cuticura—Melachrino—Clysmic—Goodyear—Steinway—Thermos—Coca-Cola—The Watch that Made the Dollar Famous. I suppose you don't know what any of them mean? (344)

Peale finds a way to bring in even the venerable Teddy Roosevelt into the discussion—"he's the best advertiser in the world" (344).

For Rodney and Peale, the first big step is to come up with a comparable slogan. "The Soap that Made Pittsburg Clean," Rodney suggests.[30] "Too long, and no good anyway, Pittsburg isn't clean," Peale replies dismissively. They ultimately come up with the winning slogan: "The Thirteen Soap—Unlucky for Dirt" (346).

With the requisite supply of mix-ups and complications, Rodney is able to sell the trademark to his father and get the girl (in this case, the elder Martin's former secretary). He succeeds because he sinks all the available money into advertising—by the end of the play, everyone is familiar with "Unlucky for Dirt," providing Rodney and Peale's concern with a valuable commodity. The name is more important than the (nonexistent) soap. In the process, Rodney becomes as expert as Peale in the realities of advertising. Just as Peale regaled the young hero with slogans, Rodney is able to recite a wealth of advertising statistics to his father—for example, that Ivory Soap spent some $450,000 on magazine advertising in 1913 (367–368). By this point, Rodney has learned to speak and move with a quickness comparable to Peale's. As to the veracity of these statistics, the authors carefully note at the outset that "the advertising statistics used in the play are facts, not farce" (334).

Not least among the facts of the play was its enormous success—399 performances, and hats-in-the-air notices for all concerned, including producers George M. Cohan and Sam Harris, as well as now-rising star Grant Mitchell. Channing Pollock, writing for *The Green Book Magazine,* enthused, "*It Pays to Advertise* is one of the real delights of the season!...The casting of mild-mannered Grant Mitchell, remembered for his hotel clerk in [*Get-Rich-Quick*] *Wallingford*...was an inspiration. Most managers would have entrusted Rodney to a leading man, instead of a character comedian, and so have lost half the humor of the play" (Pollock, "It Pays"). Most PMC audience members probably did not see themselves as "leading man" types and were most likely all the more pleased to see Mitchell, who looked like one of their own, succeed.

Significantly, Pollock's description of the moral world of *It Pays* bears similarity to the *Times*' account of *Wallingford*: "The whole piece is cheerfully, rollickingly, irresponsibly implausible, and yet, curiously enough, stimulates that little warm feeling around the heart that comes to the most sophisticated of us when pluck wins and virtue is rewarded" (Pollock, "It Pays"). This conflation of "pluck" and "virtue" forms a significant plank in the emerging American Broadway farcical platform— that pluck, in fact, is in itself not only *a* virtue, but *the* virtue. Presenting a brave front, even when there is little or nothing behind, became not lying or deceit, but *pluck*.

In the end, as Walter Lippman was quick to point out, "'It Pays to Advertise' is in itself an advertisement—an advertisement of advertising, and of the big national advertisers" (qtd. in Moses, *American Dramatist* 330). It was also an advertisement for Cohan, the partnership of Cohan and Harris, as well as for Mitchell. Perhaps most of all, it was an advertisement for the first mature onstage embodiment of the PMC—the expert on American business and on human nature. Like "Very Good" Eddie, Grant Mitchell's characters did not necessarily need a size thirteen collar to seize control of both the stage and American corporate capitalism—all that was needed was a size thirteen "gift of gab." By the time Cohan was ready to give Mitchell his next important role in *A Tailor-Made Man,* Mitchell was ready to take the lead and run with it.

PMC Apotheosis: *A Tailor-Made Man*

Mitchell's third outing for the Cohan-Harris concern was one of the most aptly titled plays of the decade (along with, perhaps, *It Pays to Advertise*). It proved to be Mitchell's PMC graduation, the culmination of a logical career progression from a patsy, callow youth who wises up and becomes an expert, to the hero who has the answers from the beginning. Harry James Smith's adaptation of a Hungarian play "The Well-fitting Dress Coat," rewritten "with the dynamic help of George M. Cohan" (Edith Smith 6), was indeed tailor-made for its audience, its star, and for the times.[31] Mitchell, playing the ambitious (and heroically named) John Paul Bart, a tailor's assistant in his early 30s (Mitchell was playing ten years younger while appearing ten years older—again, perhaps, to the delight of the middle-aged PMC members of the audience), demonstrated for the audience that belief in oneself, the right opportunity, and a brave front were all that one needed to make it in the business world. Clyde Fitch's once impartially heartless City could be tamed by the right expert.[32]

That John Paul Bart, despite (or because of) a propensity for stretching (or disregarding) the truth if the situation demanded, was intended to be a thoroughly admirable figure is made clear by the stage directions upon his entrance: "He is a clean-cut, likable young chap, very human and thoroughly sincere. His belief in himself is not mere self-conceit, but a real and fine thing. His clothes are shabby, but even so they have 'an air'" (Smith 16). Had Cohan himself played such a role some ten years earlier (which, indeed, he frequently did), the "mere self-conceit" might well have dominated.[33] With the proven-reliable Mitchell in the role, the playwright and the production team could proceed with confidence that, as a later stage direction notes, "we who know him...are eager for his success" (Smith 42).

The quick-thinking John Paul seizes the opportunity presented by a fine suit left behind by a frivolous gentleman on the night of a party to be attended by some of New York's finest, including Abraham Nathan, "the President of the American Oceanic Shipbuilding Corporation, the biggest proposition of its kind in the Western Hemisphere" (29). By wearing the suit and passing off some pithy pro-capitalist theories set forth by the stuffy Dr. Sonntag (who is engaged to Tanya, the ingénue), John Paul cleverly disarms all possible obstacles and opponents in the party scene of Act II, clearing the way for his new employment as star executive for Mr. Nathan. John Paul defuses a potential strike, but the jealous Dr. Sonntag (jealous, that is, because Tanya loves John Paul) exposes his origins and his initial "borrowing" of the suit. Or, more accurately, John Paul exposes himself to the press first to bring the third act to a close. By the end of the play, John Paul regains his position with Mr. Nathan and wins the girl.

The farcical plot, fairly ingeniously worked out by Smith (with, apparently, some degree of "Cohanizing"), gave Mitchell ample opportunity to score numerous points for the PMC team. There is still a variation of the humorless "grind" from the collegiate plays—in this case, Dr. Sonntag, the German-accented academic who writes of the necessity for wealth to be concentrated, once the reader (or listener) gets past the blocked metaphors: "Riches are the basis and symbol of that power which keeps the wheels of the social organism functionally reciprocal" (Smith 25). Sonntag's great misfortune, according to John Paul, is that he is "dull"—he lacks the personality to "sell" these great ideas. As John Paul puts it, "a man with a breezy, human personality, agreeable manners, and the right degree of self-confidence—like me, for instance—why, with those ideas I could lift the world off its axis" (26). John Paul's use of the term "personality" is significant; now the PMC hero is firmly entrenched in the culture of personality.

More simply stated, Sonntag's idea is to give the workers more of a stake in the success of the enterprise—working harder and more efficiently would then translate to more money for the worker (and, of course, for the owner). Once again, it not only pays to advertise, but also that without the "breezy" skill of the born advertiser, no one could ever implement the great and necessary ideas of the world. Frederick Winslow Taylor could have explained Sonntag's principles in a folksy and accessible manner; in Taylor's absence, the Tailor/Taylor-made man would do nicely.

John Paul, meanwhile, has studied the upper-class habitus assiduously and correctly assumes (for the world of the play, at least) that an alert student can learn this habitus and appropriate it as his own: "At first it seemed to me I could never acquire that unconscious, easy bearing that marks those fellows, but I kept at it and now I can turn the trick as well as the best of them" (22–23). Once again, the playwright gives Bart a particularly apt turn of phrase—"unconscious, easy bearing" is quite appropriate in terms of habitus. As it happens, however, John Paul's success is not the result of his appropriating an upper-class or "gentlemanly" habitus, although his convincing "embodiment" of the expensive dress suit does indeed gain him his necessary entry to the fancy party—again, John Paul illustrates the virtue of putting on a "brave front." His success lies in proving his worth as an excellent mental worker—the logic of Sherlock Holmes might be missing, but John Paul more than compensates with energy and persuasiveness. The speech is still fast, the movement is still quick and forward-leaning, but the speed is of a man in total control, much like a star pupil of Vernon and Irene Castle on the dance floor.

To secure his future employment, John Paul marries the stolid pro-capitalist ideas of the stuffy, Teutonic Dr. Sonntag to the breezy glibness of the American businessman who knows it pays to advertise. In other words, we see in John Paul Bart a PMC mental expert in full PMC-mode performing the key function of the Professional Managerial Class—that is, preserving, in no uncertain terms, capitalist culture. Here John Paul expostulates at the party, denouncing labor agitators and rousing the (gentlemanly) troops to action: "Look about you, my friends! The agitators are appealing to the blind and insensate ambition of the masses—caring nothing for consequences, ready to inaugurate a Reign of Terror. And shall we, my friends, we who are the natural protectors and guardians of the social order, shall we submit? Are we to abandon the ship to the pirates of Society?" (69). The shrewd Abraham Nathan (Jewish, playwright Smith informs us in a stage direction, but nevertheless "courtly," "large-minded and sincere"[34]) immediately pegs John Paul's speech as "wonderful Cockadoodalum," which John Paul freely admits to be true. Irrespective of the "cockadoodalum" content, in John Paul's words, "it'll *go*! It'll *work;* It'll *do it* for you!" (70, author's emphasis). "It" works on Nathan as John Paul begins the third act working at a high level of authority for Nathan's firm. And "it" proceeds to work on the dissatisfied labor representatives. John Paul is the firm's only hope to hold off an impending strike, and in several long speeches that would have done Frederick Winslow Taylor proud, he convinces the labor leaders through common sense that labor and management want the same things and should, therefore, be on the same side: "we can hardly see the simplest fact of all, which is that we belong *together;* that *you* can't do without *us* and *we* can't do without *you*" (89). John Paul gets more specific, appealing to his opponent who was once a skilled mechanic. While John Paul is not as blatantly patronizing as Taylor was in his fanciful encounters with Schmidt the pig-iron hauler, the strategy is similar:

> Mechanic? Good! You're given a piece of work which averages say, twenty hours, at a regular wage of forty cents per hour. Well, if you finish that job in the average time you get a bonus of twenty per cent. And again: if you finish that job in half the time—you could, couldn't you, Mr. Russell, many a time?.... Well, now, here's the inducement. You still get the same bonus and there you are with ten hours to the good, ready to tackle a second job on the same schedule. How does that strike you?.... I mean...that every unusual effort you make is capitalized into profit for you. *You give more—you get more!* (90–91, author's emphasis)

With the realization that "there's stuff in every man if you can only bring it out" (90), the labor leaders agree to call off the strike. John Paul Bart saves the organization from a misguided proletariat. As the business owner Nathan sums up: "in this country a man is valued by what he gets to, not what he started from" (117). Nor, Nathan might have added, is a man necessarily judged by *how* he gets to "what he gets to." By the end, John Paul earns the love of the girl, and, if not quite the thanks of a grateful nation, the thanks of the leaders of capitalist culture.

Critics heard the gospel of John Paul Bart, and for the most part, there was rejoicing. *The New York Dramatic Mirror* found the play happy proof that "a man can rise to almost any height providing he has the gift of consummate self-assurance" and further went on to praise Mitchell specifically: "Grant Mitchell's grave and casual manner made him a perfect representative of the adventurer and he delivered his lines with a skill that never suggested their length" ("A Tailor-Made Man" 272). (Indeed, Cohan himself could never have pulled off "grave and casual.") The *Times,* in turn, gave Mitchell his graduation honors: "In the title role, Grant Mitchell gave the crowning performance in a career that has shown a steady, even advance. As always, the character was solidly based on psychology, the thought ever underlying the action... Therein lay its power of convincing, and its sterling humor" ("'A Tailor-Made Man' Is Amusing Comedy"). Mitchell's star, like John Paul Bart's, had risen to its zenith, and a PMC mentality, morality, and habitus were all securely in place on the Main Stem. Significantly, John Paul Bart rises to a PMC position, not a capitalist one—he never takes over the company, although the play certainly allows for that eventual possibility. Bart's upper-management-level position is, in itself, the attained goal. Mr. Can-Do had done it on his own terms. The "PMC-ing" of Broadway had taken its greatest, hustling step forward, and there would certainly be no hustling back.

Restrained and graceful dance moves, along with a bearing of control and authority (being listened to and having orders obeyed), a visible ability to think quickly by use of gesture, speed of movement, and speed of speech were the major components of PMC class habitus. PMC habitus and class consciousness had altered what had been the major attributes of Victorian gentleman class consciousness and habitus. The PMC accomplished this feat through acknowledging the problem of nerves, and implementing different forms of Broadway entertainment to deal with the problem—through musicals, through business dramas, through dance, and through farce. By 1920, and into the 1920s, the PMC would find another, more lasting strategy—dealing with nerves through talking, and developing what audiences around the world would accept and applaud as modern American drama.

7. Conclusion: Business as Usual

CLARENCE: LEADING THE U.S. SAFELY INTO THE 1920S

Following the Great War, Broadway began to turn some of its attention to soldiers' homecoming. One of the earliest "homecoming" plays gave longtime star Alfred Lunt his first starring role and gave a PMC hero another important job to do—stabilize his postwar community, and by implication, the larger American community. The author was Booth Tarkington, and the play—a comedy, in this case, not a farce—was called *Clarence*.

Responding to Tarkington's tale of an out-of-step ex-soldier searching for employment, critic Alexander Woollcott told audiences that the play should be seen no less than once a week (Wainscott, *Emergence of Modern American Theatre* 17). Tarkington's description of Clarence upon his entry gave Broadway audiences an introduction to a far different sort of PMC hero than the ones embodied by the increasingly cocksure characterizations of Grant Mitchell:

> He is very sallow, his hair is in some disorder; he stoops, not only at the shoulders, but from the waist, sagging forward, and, for a time, to the left side; then, for a time, to the right; his legs "give" slightly at the knees, and he limps, somewhat vaguely. He wears the faded old shabby khaki uniform of a private of the Quartermaster's department, and this uniform was a bad misfit for him when it was new. A large pair of spectacles shield his blinking eyes...and altogether he is an unimposing figure. (17)[1]

A picture of the first act of *Clarence* reveals that Alfred Lunt, in his star-making performance, matches Tarkington's description to the letter (Tarkington 32–33).

Clarence's search for identity as well as for gainful employment enabled Tarkington to touch on the employment problems of the returning veteran. The unemployment rate when the United States entered the war was 4.6 percent. At the war's end, the rate was down to 1.4 percent, but it soon rose to 5.2 percent. By way of comparison, a postwar recession in 1924 would bring the unemployment rate up to 11.7 percent (*Historical Statistics* 2–31, 2–82).

While Clarence has been wounded, we learn that he has, in fact, been wounded during target practice in Texas—he never made it overseas. More importantly, Clarence is a displaced entomologist; before the war he studied insects. By the conclusion, "Clarence regains dignity and control.... He is not only fully integrated into the now healthier social unit—much stabler because of his contributions—but he is reunited with the larger society by being rewarded with his prewar entomology job and, not insignificantly, the love of the heroine" (Wainscott, *Modern American Theatre* 18). We see Clarence regaining his "dignity and control," dominating the stage in a gray suit and playing the saxophone as the gentlemen on stage (dressed in black) look on in amazement and confusion (Tarkington 80–81). Clarence, in other words, is ready to take his tailor-made place in society, and he will guide his community gently but firmly to postwar stability and prosperity.

As PMC characters were gaining increasing "dignity and control" onstage in the business farces, Broadway was ready for serious American theatre—plays and productions of a kind that American theatre experts could point to as proof that Broadway would soon set the bar for excellence in world theatre. This accepted maturation of American drama required the discovery and promotion of the final theatre practitioner in this study—playwright Eugene O'Neill.

As 1920 came to an end, O'Neill, along with supportive critics and growing audiences, was defining modern American drama. To a large degree, this definition would be brought about by the arrival to America of the father of modern psychoanalysis.

FREUD AND THE PMC

Clark University, in Worcester, Massachusetts, hosted Sigmund Freud and Carl Jung in the summer of 1909. Their lectures were part of a twentieth anniversary celebration of the university's status as the second graduate school in the United States.[2] It was this series of lectures that introduced psychoanalysis into the mainstream. American physicians learned and disseminated the material, publishing some hundred articles on the subject between 1912 and 1914, and another seventy through 1917. Psychoanalysis had, by this time, found its way into women's magazines, including *Good Housekeeping*, in 1915 (Pfister 63).

American corporate capitalism was quick to "capitalize" on psychoanalysis as well. The concept and practice of "industrial psychology" was, after the Great War, set into place, which had far-reaching consequences for business, the PMC, and the American drama (Pfister 242, ftn. 25).[3] The strategy of the American corporate capitalists was twofold: to convince the workforce that personal neuroses, rather than outside forces, were the basis of workplace problems, and to channel "neurotic energy" into corporate success. As Pfister summarizes: "Freud, superseding Frederick Taylor and Henry Ford, is embraced as the prophet of efficiency" (65). Similarly, neurosis, superseding neurasthenia, is embraced as the gold standard of psychological as well as cultural capital (Pfister 7).

The theatrical critics had been making some of their own judgments on Freudian references as well. Some of these were playful, as in the review of *Leave It to Jane* mentioned in chapter 5. Other notices commented on the "psychological" truth of the performers, as the *Times* critic had done in his praise of Grant Mitchell's performance in *A Tailor-Made Man*.[4] The Broadway stage, in essence, was more than ready for a playwright who could somehow stage "pop psychology for a professional-managerial class that was in the process of constructing and internalizing a new ideology of psychological selfhood" (Pfister 14). Enter O'Neill.

O'NEILL AND PSYCHOLOGICAL CAPITAL

One could conceivably accept the concept of the "graduation" of American drama by 1923, the year Oliver M. Sayler published *Our*

American Theatre. Sayler writes,

> Eugene O'Neill, the American playwright. The point needs argument, proof, as much as that the skyscraper is our contribution to architecture. But the reasons are interesting, suggestive. First, there is our innate national desire to personify ideas and movements in human guise—Edison, our native ingenuity; Ford, business efficiency; Rockefeller, enormous wealth; Roosevelt, the strenuous life. Therefore, O'Neill, the personal symbol of our awakening American drama.... O'Neill is the sole engrossing talent thus far given to and accepted by the theatre of the world. (Sayler 27–28)

By 1920, O'Neill was well on his way to establishing himself as "the American playwright." He would win the Pulitzer Prize that year for *Beyond the Horizon*—in Sayler's words, the story of "the tragic consequences of misplaced vocations" (28). David Sievers elaborates: "Although no Freudian terminology is used, *Beyond the Horizon* is a sketchy outline of Freudian figures which O'Neill was later to fill in. Failure of self-realization, he seems to say, is man's greatest tragedy" (Sievers 100).

Indeed, while *Beyond the Horizon* does not initially put any PMC characters onstage (although one major character would evolve into a PMC type), the key themes—"misplaced vocations" and the "failure of self-realization"—address PMC concerns. Robert Mayo, with "a touch of the poet about him," longs for a seafaring life that will yield some sort of secret of Beauty that lies "beyond the horizon."[5] Older brother Andrew is content and, it appears, one with the land and with the Mayo farm. It is Robert's love for Ruth (and hers for him) that proves the destructive, rather than nurturing, force in all three lives. Because Andrew too loved Ruth, it is he who drives himself off to sea—with "old salt" Uncle Dick (217)—rather than Robert (who was going partly because he felt his own love for Ruth would be forever unrequited). Robert, in turn, stays to work on the family farm—work for which he has neither the skill, the strength, nor the calling.

The Mayo men are warned by their father that "you're runnin' against your own nature, and you're goin' to be a'mighty sorry for it if you do" (232). Robert asks at the end of the first act, "Why did this have to happen to us? It's damnable!" This is followed by the telling stage direction: "He looks about him wildly, as if his vengeance were seeking the responsible fate" (237). That life itself is man's great antagonist is an ongoing strand in O'Neill's work. As Raymond Williams writes in *Modern Tragedy*, "The isolated persons clash and destroy each other, not simply because their particular relationships are wrong, but because life as such is inevitably against them" (Williams 116). Nevertheless, the striking element of this early, acclaimed O'Neill tragedy is not so much that the antagonist is Life or Fate, but that the greatest enemies are inefficiency and attempting to do the Wrong Kind of Work.

This emphasis on the dangers of inefficiency becomes clearer in the second act. The opening description of the farmhouse tells us that there is "evidence of carelessness, of inefficiency, of an industry gone to seed" (239). Ruth's invalid mother, Mrs. Atkins, is revealed as one of the play's chief villains due to her general physical uselessness: "She has developed the selfish, irritable nature of the chronic invalid" (240). Robert has mismanaged the family farm as well as the Atkins farm in the course of three years—"he's getting' worse 'stead of better," as Mrs. Atkins sourly (and astutely) notes (241). They hope that Andrew, due back shortly from his three-year voyage, will be able to "fix everything when he comes" (246). Meanwhile, three years of unhappy existence have produced for Robert and Ruth a small child and a great mutual hatred and resentment.

Andrew, for his part, has changed as well. He has been successful, but something has been lost, as O'Neill notes in his description: "The old easy-going good nature seems to have been partly lost in a breezy, business-like briskness of voice and gesture. There is an authoritative note in his speech as though he were accustomed to give orders and have them obeyed as a matter of course" (261). Andrew has turned himself into a business expert, complete with accompanying "breezy" personality and talk of business possibilities in Buenos Aires. His rhetoric is similar in many ways to the "tailor-made man," as in this speech to the increasingly despondent Ruth, who has hoped Andrew would stay: "I tell you, Ruth, I'm going to make good right from the minute I land, if working hard and a determination to get on can do it; and I *know* they can!" (270, author's emphasis). Nevertheless, Andrew, too, has turned away from his true vocation—farming. Andrew jumps at the chance of getting away to Buenos Aires, leaving Robert and Ruth (and their young daughter) in a greater state of despondency than before.

By the play's third and final act, the farm room now "presents an appearance of decay, of dissolution" after another five years have passed. Robert and Ruth's daughter has died, and Robert has become mortally ill. Robert reaches the height of his despair: "I could curse God from the bottom of my soul—if there was a God!" (281).[6] Despite his black moods, Robert still entertains dreams of a new start in the city, away from the curse of the farm. Ruth, apparently deadened beyond emotion, nevertheless placates Robert by agreeing to go—excessive anger and emotion from Robert generally brings on violent and frightening coughing spells.

As Andrew returns with a specialist for Robert, he, too, has changed, now resembling one of Fitch's nervous professionals: "His face seems to have grown highstrung, hardened by the look of decisiveness which comes from being constantly under a strain where judgments on the spur of the moment are compelled to be accurate" (288). By now, Andrew is also "dressed in an expensive business suit and appears stouter" (288). And, like many of Fitch's hapless neurasthenics, Andrew has dabbled too heavily in speculation, as he explains to a now barely responsive Ruth: "I made money hand over fist as long as I stuck to legitimate trading; but I wasn't content with that. I wanted it to come easier, so like all the rest of the idiots, I tried speculation. Oh, I won all right! Several times I've been almost a millionaire—on paper—and then come down to earth again with a bump. Finally the strain was too much" (292).

Eventually, Robert, aware of his imminent death, goes outside for one last look at the horizon while Andrew "clenches his fists in an impotent rage against Fate" (305). As Robert dies, crying "The sun!" (305),[7] Ruth and Andrew are left to try to help each other, despite absence of mutual love or hope.

Critics at the time seemed to be in agreement regarding the nature of man's greatest tragedy. The *New York Dramatic Mirror* critic noted: "It is a play written with imagination and dramatic feeling. There is a pitilessly ironic undertone to its symbolism" (Reid 10). Alexander Woollcott, writing for *The Times,* described *Beyond the Horizon* as "vital and moving," drawing "breathless and enthusiastic audiences" (Woollcott 9). O'Neill rated a glowing "personality portrait" in *Theatre Magazine* a month after *Beyond the Horizon*: "O'Neill has found himself, master of the theatre as his medium and of individuals as his material" (Coleman 264, 302). By the time *The Emperor Jones* took the stage later in the year, O'Neill was earning the unofficial title of The American Playwright, as this notice from *Shadowland* confirms: "Since the relentless power of his *Beyond the Horizon* impressed us last season, following upon the heels of a number of vastly promising one-act plays, we looked upon Eugene O'Neill as the one significant new force in our theater" ("The Emperor Jones," 66–67). It would seem that O'Neill, American drama, and the PMC had just about "arrived."

OTHER CURES FOR NERVES: A LOOK AT THE 1920S

One way of summing up the era under study is to observe that Broadway expended much of its considerable ingenuity and resources in the service of that clichéd figure, the "tired businessman," and his nerves. Popular psychology of the early 1920s embraced the audience full of men of nerves who had been written about at least since the 1890s. Smith Ely Jelliffe and Louise Brink wrote in 1922:

> The drama, through its artistic setting as well as through its emotional character, its closeness to the actual events of life and to the impulses which move beneath these, is particularly fitted to serve humanity, whether it appears in its serious or its lighter moods. It stands in all times and no less in these later more sophisticated times for a safe and ready avenue of release of otherwise overcharged emotions, the outlet for which is neglected or too severely restrained. (Jelliffe & Brink 1)

Different practitioners tackled the problem from a variety of angles and a wide range of attitudes. For Fitch, nerves were a matter of personal responsibility and will power. Ziegfeld would dazzle the nerves into submission with his Follies and his Girls. The Castles and Cohan set out to dance nerves away; while Cohan the writer/producer (and "Cohanizer"), and those who successfully adapted his farcical formulas, got audiences to laugh them away for a while. O'Neill's great contribution to the Main Stem was introducing the possibility of *talking* the nerves away. As Bruce McConachie points out in reference to *Desire under the Elms*, for O'Neill's characters, "the play acts like a long therapeutic session: complexes, repressions, and neuroses are recognized and exorcised through a dramatic version of the 'talking cure,' as Freudian psychoanalysis has been called" (McConachie, "Case Study" 360). Even Broadway's most enduring "cures" proved temporary, however; the modern world was here, and the anxiety and neuroses that accompanied it would not dissipate any time soon, or perhaps ever.

By 1920, the core components of PMC class consciousness, as well as habitus, were in place. The PMC role on Broadway as well as the popular acceptance of that role would continue to develop throughout the decade. While O'Neill emerged as the major star and representative of playwright as PMC, the business farces, sex farces, and musicals would figure prominently in this development as well.

The business of business still provided plenty of fodder for playwrights and entertainment for audiences. Harold Clurman, in introducing *Famous American Plays of the 1930s*, had this to say about the 1920s theatre and business: "It was the artistic pleasure of the twenties to deride, curse, bemoan the havoc, spiritual blindness and absurdity of America's materialistic functionalism with its concomitant acquisitiveness and worship of success" (Clurman 9). There is truth in this observation, particularly with regard to the end of the decade (such as Sophie Treadwell's *Machinal* and the plays of John Howard Lawson), but there were a good many other plays during the decade that celebrated the havoc and the experts who guided the havoc into controlled chaos. As Ronald Wainscott notes, "From 1919 to mid-decade entrepreneurship and big business were unequivocally glorified" (Wainscott, *Cambridge* 176).

Clever con artists in the style of *Get-Rich-Quick Wallingford* continued to please audiences while celebrating a comic business expertise (Wainscott, "Commercialism" 176–177). Guy Bolton, a key member of the Princess musicals team, came up with the business farce *Polly Preferred*, which premiered in January 1923 and had a successful six-month run.[8] The plot involves Bob, a salesman who sees "possibilities" in life, and Polly Pierpoint, the chorus girl who becomes Bob's principal possibility.[9] Bob hits upon the idea to sell shares in Polly as a commodity: "I'm going to incorporate you 'Polly Pierpont' and sell shares in you!" (1–18). Bob and Polly fool two moneyed potential speculators, James and Kennedy, into a movie venture, even though they have "no equipment—no studio—no scenario—nothing" (1–18). But, as had been previously established by the business farces of the 1910s, "personality—charm—magnetism" (1–3–23), along with the ability to advertise, was all one needed to succeed. And indeed, after a year, Polly is enchanting the nation in her new motion picture, "Joan of Arkansas," and she and Bob end the evening on a romantic note. As Wainscott observes, the incorporation of a performer, although currently common practice, was a novel idea in 1923 (1993, 177). Once again, experts in salesmanship and business practices led the way. John Corbin of the *New York Times* summed the evening up appropriately: "Guy Bolton has applied the 'It Pays to Advertise' idea to the movies," resulting in "a genuinely deserved success." (Corbin, "The Play" 13:3).

Opening at nearly the same time, and running almost exactly as long as *Polly Preferred,* was a rambunctious farce by Aaron Hoffman that fulfilled PMC functions on a number of levels. *Give and Take*, set in a California canning factory, follows the efforts of Jack, a "pleasant but very earnest" young man just out of college, to bring "Industrial Democracy" to his father's plant (Hoffman 5–7).[10] Marion, the company's loyal secretary (who will end up with Jack by the final curtain), accuses Jack of Bolshevikism with some barbed anti-worker commentary: "You belong out there in the shops with your abused, downtrodden workingmen. The poor things—everyone [sic] of them with his own home, his own car, money in the bank—work all year round—and at better wages than they ever got in their lives" (6). The "very earnest" Jack, appropriately enough, delivers a very earnest speech about his intentions, with rhetoric similar to that of *The Tailor-Made Man*:

> I am going to do away with discontent. I'm going to establish harmony, the get together spirit between capital and labor, the principle of give and take—the golden rule—between employer and employee, and let me tell you unless we want to end in one grand smash up—that's what we've got to come to, not only in this plant, but all over the entire country. (6)

Jack is ready with a constitution in hand with the intention of freeing the "wage slaves" (9), and the set-up would appear to be for the overeager college graduate to learn a lesson in business reality.

Jack's father, John Bauer, is described as being a now-familiar type: a "very nervous, irritable, typical—almost neurasthenic business man, very quick" (11). Bauer has good reason to be nervous, irritable, and almost neurasthenic; the bank is calling in the mortgage on the plant. "Money's tight," the banker, Mr. Drum, repeats throughout the play (tight as a drum, one imagines). It is Bauer, in response to the threat of a strike, who delivers the most impassioned pro-capital speech, which certainly must have proved satisfying for the capitalist gentlemen in the audience:

> You ask me where all the money goes? I'll tell you. Most of it goes in wages, to the slaves. There are twenty million slaves in this country, going to the ball games, to the movies, riding around in their flivvers, putting money in the bank. The figures show that there are twenty million bank accounts at an average of five hundred dollars a piece. Those accounts belong to the laboring class. Twenty million times five hundred dollars—that's ten billion dollars. That's what the slaves have got in the bank. And the richest man in the world is Rockefeller and he's only got a billion, and you fellows... have got ten times more than him—and you call *me* a capitalist. (23, author's emphasis)

Bauer, most likely after waiting for the audience laughter and applause to die down, lets his vitriol take him even further: "Now suppose capital would go on strike?... Why can't it? It can. Suppose the rich men all got together and said 'We don't care about the future. We don't care about the country. We only care about ourselves. Let's go on strike'" (24).

Jack, however, proves himself a Taylor-made man in the most productive sense. "Under the present conditions," he explains with the patience of Frederick Winslow, "the workingman is giving the least that he can in return for the most he can get" (27). Furthermore, Jack also shares Taylor's feelings about the workers' general level of intelligence: "Those men must be taught. We must have a school room" (34). In order to avoid the impending strike, Bauer agrees to Jack's conditions, and there remains the possibility that Jack's Tayloresque plans will be made to look foolish.

At the opening of Act II, the company has indeed become "a public laughing stock," bogged down by too many constitutional meetings and the fact that "everybody is a boss" (47, 50). No work is getting done, and nothing is produced. Nevertheless, in an intriguing turn-around, industrial democracy saves Bauer and the company—the workers unite to buy back the note from the bank. A savior also emerges in the person of Thomas W. Craig of Chicago, who intends to use the factory to supply his fleet of "Motor Grocery Stores" (62). Craig is a fan of industrial democracy, and by the end of the play, Bauer has become a convert as well: "Look at Wilson—just because he had the same idea as my boy—because he tried to bring all the nations together in the spirit of 'Give and Take'—look what they did to him—but he won't give up his great idea and neither will I" (86). With this tribute to former president Wilson and the League of Nations—perhaps the era's ultimate professional managerial attempt to organize the civilized world—the play's PMC philosophy falls firmly into place. For just a few years earlier, President Wilson, looking much like the embodiment of the campus grind or the comic college president (which, comic or otherwise, he had been at Princeton), "publicly acknowledged the importance of the PMC" by bringing a group of experts with him to the Paris Peace Conference (Ehrenreichs 26).

Although the protagonists need a wealthy capitalist to bail them out, the tenets of industrial democracy in support of capitalism carry the final rhetorical victory in the world of the play. Onstage, playwright Hoffman engineered an opportunity for PMC-inspired Jack to negotiate successfully between labor and capital, thus preserving the capitalist culture of the factory.[11] In terms of the audience, Hoffman was further able to give both the capitalist and PMC audience members—the Bauers and the Jacks—their money's worth.

Along with the farces that spoofed and celebrated business, the 1920s saw many other farces that dealt more directly with sex. As Brooks Atkinson put it, "people who went to the Broadway theater were willing to laugh at the facts of life" (Atkinson 80). Avery Hopwood was one of the most prolific artisans in the field of "risqué" boulevard entertainment, with a career that stretched from Fitch's time (and Fitch was an admirer of Hopwood's early plays) until his death in 1928, apparently drowning in the ocean under the influence of alcohol. Arguably, Hopwood's most lasting contribution to Broadway and to posterity was introducing the term "gold digger" in his 1919 play *The Gold Diggers* (Atkinson 80–82). *The Gold Diggers* was one of Hopwood's biggest hits, running some nine months, but Hopwood's popularity proved reliable throughout his career, with such largely forgotten bedroom/sex farces as *Fair and Warmer* (1915), *Ladies' Night (in a Turkish Bath)* (1920), *Getting Gertie's Garter* (1921), and *Why Men Leave Home* (1922). [12]

Such farces were far removed from the more commonly recognized thread of 1920s theatre, the notion that American theatre could be artistic, "highbrow," and "good for you." It is true enough that *Beyond the Horizon* "signaled momentous change in serious American drama" (Wainscott, *Cambridge* 70). It might well be true that "O'Neill had won an epochal battle for all of us. He gave to his contemporaries and to future generations new perspectives for the theatre," as Emory Lewis summarizes in *Stages: The Fifty-Year Childhood of the American Theatre* (37). Certainly this was and is the accepted history that the PMC theatre experts (including O'Neill) helped propagate. Nevertheless, in terms of the 1920s (as opposed to future generations), and in terms of entertainment value, Hopwood and other farce practitioners arguably meant more to their "tired businessman" audiences. Growing audiences admired, thought about, and discussed O'Neill; they *laughed* at farces of the business and bedroom variety.

Critics were resigned to the sex farces—ready to applaud them if they were funny, dismiss them if they were derivative, and chide them if they became too suggestive. Therefore, critical responses were as typical as the farces themselves, for example, Alexander Woollcott on Otto Harbach's *No More Blondes,* from January 1920: "Of a farce of such familiar complications there is little to report on the morning after, except to answer one burning question. Is it funny?" For Woollcott, the answer was yes (Woollcott 22:1). When Woollcott weighed in later that year on Hopwood's *Ladies' Night*, which dealt with a man mistakenly entering a Turkish bath on ladies' night, he was less congenial: "certain managers and playwrights...both seem bent on seeing how far they can go without being arrested" (Woollcott 10:1). And, there was the run-of-the-mill product, as evidenced by the dismissal of Wilson Collison's *A Bachelor's Night* by the unnamed *Times* critic who found "nothing to mark it particularly apart from the run of similar pieces that have gone before, and are likely to go again" ("'A Bachelor's Night' Dull" 20:1). The critic was quite right. Similar pieces would go again.

As for musicals and spectacles, Ziegfeld was still going strong throughout the 1920s, as the best comics of the day set off the iconic Ziegfeld Girls. Ziegfeld would also give Broadway its most important musical experiment of the 1920s, *Showboat*, complete with a serious story and black and white choruses in the same show (although not onstage at the same time). Cohan, who never joined Actors' Equity, still had his fans, though his creativity was starting to fail him. If he grew derivative, however, at least he was stealing from himself.

Nevertheless, Broadway in the 1920s provided more than enough "highbrow" and "good-for-you" theatre to justify the subsequent historical consideration that mature American drama had not only survived its tentative beginnings but was thriving. As Dorothy Chansky points out, "The American belief that theatre is spiritually and emotionally fulfilling, socially elevating, of civic importance, a site for assaying social change, and an enriching locus of cultural capital originated in the early decades of the twentieth century" (Chansky 2).

The most famous examples of 1920s plays have been greatly anthologized and discussed, gaining a considerably longer shelf life than the most popular plays of the first two decades of the twentieth century.[13] O'Neill was a key and probably *the* key contributor to the 1920s American drama, but there were many other playwrights who made their own marks. Maxwell Anderson, with Laurence Stallings, gave Broadway its first strong antiwar play, *What Price Glory*, with a frankness in language that illuminated at least one of the differences between 1909 and 1924. Fifteen years, a world war, and a more worldly PMC audience (joining the ever-present gentlemen and ladies, who themselves could show a greater tolerance for adult language) allowed the actors to let loose with multiple "God-damns" throughout the evening with apparently no fainting or shrieking reported. Sidney Howard's characters in *They Knew What They Wanted* could display a mature attitude toward an unplanned out-of-wedlock pregnancy to ensure a happy ending. George Kelly took a shot at suburbia and suburban wives in *Craig's Wife*—a cautionary tale for PMC men whose smart wives assume too much control (a girl could and should have "brain," as Jane did in *Leave It to Jane*, but she needed to know and mind her place). Philip Barry and S.N. Behrman provided high comedy, featuring a witty upper class (with occasional help from PMC types) that could speak reams of sprightly, intelligent dialog. Elmer Rice contributed enduring examples of American expressionism with *The Adding Machine,* and American slice-of-life naturalism with *Street Scene.* Examples are plentiful—enough, perhaps, to overshadow the many more plays that failed, as is the case with any decade. But the general consensus among the theatre experts, both contemporaneous and, as of this writing, current, was that O'Neill was the leader.

What was missing for O'Neill, at least temporarily, was general popular acceptance. The experts had proclaimed him America's first theatrical genius, and he had enjoyed some box office success, but America as a whole had not quite accepted that it now had a theatrical genius. This would be the one factor that would put the PMC over the top in terms of Broadway dominance. PMC heroes could carry a farce. PMC experts convinced other PMC experts that O'Neill had recreated American drama. With *Strange Interlude* in 1928, O'Neill had his monster popular hit. His third Pulitzer Prize (the second had been for *Anna Christie*) was practically superfluous after a year's run on Broadway, two road companies, and being banned in the Boston controversy (because of Nina's abortion, as well as the baby having born outside of marriage)[14]—in short, enough scandal to tantalize, enough psychoanalytic rhetoric to intellectualize, and enough length (complete with dinner break) and artistic asides to polarize.

Strange Interlude serves as a fitting summation of the PMC-ing of Broadway. O'Neill presents the gamut of PMC bodily types in his epic examination of thwarted love and suppressed desires. In novelistic fashion, O'Neill's major male characters, all in thrall to the troubled and troubling Nina Leeds, evolve from Mr. Nervous neurotics, to Mr. Can-Do business types, and back again, all under the fog of neurosis. Indeed, even the inanimate objects cannot escape neurosis: "The table has become neurotic," O'Neill's stage directions tell us (O'Neill, *Strange Interlude* 115).[15] Thus, Nina's simple, childlike husband Evans, failing in the world of advertising (it did not always pay to advertise), is discovered as "his eyes shift about, [and] his shoulders are collapsed submissively" (116). Later, as he becomes increasingly successful, "he has grown executive and used to command, [and] he automatically takes charge wherever he is" (259–260). Evans's transformation is similar to Andrew's in *Beyond the Horizon,* and Evans's physical appearance is reminiscent of the onstage Grant Mitchell—stout, balding, and frequently in motion. O'Neill's tailor-made man, however, succumbs to a stroke. Similarly, Marsden, the mother-fixated lifelong bachelor who is also drawn into the heroine's orbit, makes an entrance as "his tall, thin body stoops as if a part of its sustaining will had been removed" (125).

O'Neill also includes a number of up-to-date Freudian references for his in-the-know audience. "A lot to account for, Herr Freud!" Marsden thinks (aloud) fairly early on, "'O Oedipus, O my king!'" (62). Further, the play stages a father substitution drama between Nina and Marsden, which features Marsden even modulating his speech to sound like Professor Leeds, ending with Nina girlishly cuddled in Marsden's lap—a lot to account for, indeed.

The combination of critical acclaim and scandal proved potent for the Broadway box office as well as for the road companies of the production. In a *Times* article reporting the first anniversary of *Strange Interlude*'s New York run, the reporter noted that the play had "stirred up quite a fuss." Enough of a fuss, in fact, that a complaint was lodged with the district attorney—the production "was subsequently exonerated."[16] As the Broadway production reached its one-year anniversary, the touring company consistently sold out, including playing "to capacity for a week in Columbus, Ohio" ("One Year of 'Strange Interlude'" X1). In a *Times* article following the awarding of the Pulitzer Prize, Brooks Atkinson noted, "In book form it [the play] has been selling in numbers enviable in the barter of printed plays. It has drawn such critical enthusiasm—superlatives and panegyrics—that the excerpt printed on the jacket blinded the credulous reader's eye" (Atkinson, "Laurels" 105).

In other words, by the end of the 1920s, if someone said he felt as if he were in an O'Neill play, everyone would know what he meant. O'Neill was a firm fixture in the popular culture. The PMC were in the driver's seat, managing the road with easy authority.

POSTSCRIPT: THE RETURN OF THE TAILOR-MADE MAN

Toward the end of October 1929, Grant Mitchell returned to Broadway to recreate his signature role of John Paul Bart in a revival of *The Tailor-Made Man*. Critics were welcoming and warmly receptive. The *New York Times,* while quibbling about the somewhat creaky construction, declared the production to be a "revival full of laughs." Mitchell, twelve years older, and now in his mid-fifties (perhaps even more gratifying to older PMC audience members), still apparently gave the role the relentless energy required: "Grant Mitchell is a dozen 'go-getters' (before the name was invented) and a dozen political candidates rolled into one," the *Times* critic noted ("Revival Full of Laughs" 33). While the show most likely would not have made the splash that the original had, Mitchell and company might well have had reasonable and justifiable confidence in a respectable run.

The eighth (and final) performance came within just a day or two of the crash of the stock market. While the crash was enough to put a stop to the fictional John Paul Bart, the real-life tailor-made men would face their biggest challenge: preserving capitalist culture in the face of the greatest failure of American capitalism. The PMC and Broadway would have to adapt to survive—the story of another era.

Notes

The notes use the following abbreviation throughout:
NYPL for the New York Public Library of Performing Arts at Lincoln Center.

1. INTRODUCTION: A MATTER FOR EXPERTS

1. The motto of South End Press, the Boston company that publishes *Between Labor and Capital*, from which the Ehrenreichs' essay is taken, is "Read. Write. Revolt."
2. Wiebe, antedating the Ehrenreichs, does not use the term "PMC," but he references "a new middle class," which was common alternative parlance regarding the professional workers under consideration. See Robert H. Wiebe, *The Search for Order: 1877–1920* (New York: Hill and Wang, 1967) 111.
3. The new experts led various reforms throughout the Progressive Period, but such reforms need to be placed within the broader perspective of preserving capitalist culture. As Howard Zinn explains, "What was clear in this period to blacks, to feminists, to labor organizers and socialists, was that they could not count on the national government. True, this was the 'Progressive Period,' the start of the Age of Reform; but it was a reluctant reform, aimed at quieting the popular risings, not making fundamental changes." See Howard Zinn, *A People's History of the United States, 1492–Present* (New York: Harper Collins, 2003) 349.
4. Drieser captures the mindset of such professionals in *Sister Carrie*, writing about the salesman Drouet:

    Drouet... only craved the best, as his mind conceived it, and... Rector's, with its polished marble walls and floor, its profusion of lights, its show of china and silverware, and, above all, its reputation as a resort for actors and professional men, seemed to him the proper place for a successful man to go. He loved fine clothes, good eating, and particularly the company and acquaintanceship of successful men... He would be able to flash a roll of greenbacks too some day. As it was, he could eat where *they* did. (author's emphasis)

    See Theodore Drieser, *Sister Carrie* (Cambridge, MA: Robert Bentley, 1971) 44–45. This is not to say that dreams of conspicuous consumption constituted

PMC values or habitus in particular. However, no doubt many striving professionals, including those that could be considered "PMC," wanted "the best" once they could begin to afford it.
5. See Frederick Winslow Taylor, *The Principles of Scientific Management* (New York: Harper and Brothers, 1911).
6. The notion of actor as scientist probably begins more properly with the ideas of Delsarte, imported to the U.S. at the end of the nineteenth century by Steele Mackaye. In his attempt to discover how real people move and speak in various situations, Delsarte accumulated data through long-term and long-range study of people of all ages and stations, in moments of great stress as well as in ordinary situations. See Ted Shawn, *Every Little Movement: A Book about François Delsarte* (Princeton, NJ: Princeton Book Co., 1976) 16. While Delsartean teaching gained considerable capital as part of a burgeoning American "health" culture, and proved influential in American modern dance (particularly the Denishawn schools), its direct influence on the Broadway stage and American acting in general proved limited. See also James McTeague, *Before Stanislavsky: American Professional Acting Schools and Acting Theory, 1875–1925* (Metuchen, NJ: Scarecrow Press, 1993).
7. Woodruff, in fact, claimed to be 27 at the time. See James Metcalfe, "Brown of Harvard." *Life* Magazine, 8 Mar. 1906. In *Selected Theatre Criticism, Volume 1: 1900–1919*. Ed. Anthony Slide (Metuchen, NJ: Scarecrow Press, 1985) 36.
8. Abraham Erlanger, Marc Klaw, Charles Frohman, Al Hayman, Samuel Nixon (Nirdlinger), and J. Fred Zimmerman, who formed the (in)famous Syndicate, or "Theatrical Trust," in 1896.
9. See especially Bruce McConachie, *Melodramatic Formations: American Theatre & Society 1820–1870* (Iowa City: University of Iowa Press, 1992), as well as David Grimsted, *Melodrama Unveiled: American Theater and Culture, 1800–1850* (Chicago: University of Chicago Press, 1968).

2. THE GROWTH OF BROADWAY, THE EMERGENCE OF THE PMC

1. See, for example, *The Cambridge History of American Theatre, Vol. II: 1870–1945.* Ed. Don B. Wilmeth and Christopher Bigsby (New York: Cambridge University Press, 1999).
2. "The weakness of the Syndicate's position from the standpoint of business morals and ethics, lies in the fact that it was both principal and agent. It competed against its clients and as a result it could not give them its best services. This is undoubtedly a breach of faith, and there is no defense against it."

See Alfred L. Bernheim, *The Business of the Theatre: An Economic History of the American Theatre, 1750–1932* (1932; rpt. New York: Benjamin Blom, 1964) 60.
3. Program, *Little Johnny Jones* [1907?], http://digital.nypl.org/lpa/lpa_milleimage.cfm?bibid=666&topic='Programs'; Progamme, Princess Theatre, Feb. 26, 1906, *Brown of Harvard*, NYPL.
4. Ibid.
5. For an account of one of the era's most colorful press agents, A. Toxen Worm, who worked for the Shuberts, see, Brooks McNamara *The Shuberts of Broadway: A History Drawn from the Collection of the Shubert Archive* (New York: Oxford University Press, 1990).
6. Program, Princess Theatre, *Brown of Harvard*, 26 Feb. 1906, NYPL.
7. The financial and social elite who contributed to the theatre included John Jacob Astor, J. Pierpont Morgan, Cornelius Vanderbilt, and Otto Kahn. As Brooks Atkinson notes, the New Theatre was meant to "represent the taste of discriminating people," but "nothing worked. The public was not interested. The New Theater, which was fifteen blocks north of the Broadway district, had the reputation of being for millionaires and highbrows but not for people who enjoyed theater." See Brooks Atkinson, *Broadway* (New York: MacMillan Publishing Co., 1974.) 126–127. See also Garff B. Wilson, *Three Hundred Years of American Drama and Theatre from Ye Bare and ye Cubb to Chorus Line* (Englewood Cliffs, NJ: Prentice-Hall, 1982) 196.
8. See E. Digby Baltzell, *The Protestant Establishment: Aristocracy and Caste in America* (New York: Random House, 1964): "When, in any society, there is an upper class which protects its privileges and prestige but *does not continue* (1) to contribute leadership or (2) to assimilate new elite members, primarily because of their *racial* or *ethnic origins,* I shall refer to the process of caste. If an upper class degenerates into a caste...the traditional authority of an establishment is in grave danger of disintegrating, while society becomes a field for careerists seeking success and affluence" (8, author's emphasis).
9. See Matt Wray, *Not Quite White: White Trash and the Boundaries of Whiteness* (Durham, NC: Duke University Press, 2006): "I define *white* as a social category, not a racial category...Reconceptualizing whiteness as a flexible set of social and symbolic boundaries that give shape, meaning, and power to the social category *white* focuses the attention of whiteness studies exactly where it belongs—on the processes and agents that generate symbolic boundaries and grant them social power" (139).
10. See *Historical Statistics of the United States: Earliest Times to the Present.* Vol. 2. Ed. Susan B. Carter et al. (New York: Cambridge University Press, 2006) 2–182, 2–183. The numbers, for example, of Black college instructors,

lawyers, judges, and mechanical engineers, while small compared to national totals, were still not insignificant.
11. The boarding house serves as a starting point for the 1920 rise-and-fall business play *Opportunity*, by Owen Davis. The hero's friend, working as an underling in a stock market concern, makes $20 per week (1–3). See Owen Davis, *Opportunity*. Typescript. NCOF+Davis, NYPL.
12. From "You Go to the Theatre," a feature in a theatre program from 1920: "Over 14,000,000 theatre programs were distributed in the past season. Of these, 25% went to visitors, leaving *more than 10,000,000* that were used by patrons living in and around New York. And remember, every one of these theatergoers paid a minimum of $1.00 for his seat." Program, George M. Cohan's Theatre, *The Tavern*, 15 Nov. 1920, NYPL.
13. The following programs were examined for this section: Madison Square Theatre, *Beau Brummell*, 13 Oct. 1890; Lyceum Theatre, *The Maister of Woodbarrow*, 26 Aug. 1890; Proctor's 23rd St. Theatre, *All the Comforts of Home*, 5 Sept. 1890; Madison Square Theatre, *Alabama*, 27 Apr. 1891; Bijou Theatre, *A Texas Steer*, 10 Nov. 1890; Daly's, *The Last Word*, 29 Oct. 1890; Star Theatre, *Mr. Potter of Texas*, 7 Mar. 1891; Niblo's, *Mr. Potter of Texas*, 8 Oct. 1892; Garden Theatre, *Cleopatra*, 16 Feb. 1891; Palmer's, *John Needham's Double*, 13 Feb. 1891; and Grand Opera House, *The Power of the Press*, 28 Dec. 1891. All programs are in NYPL. For the most part, I will be discussing the ads that appeared in these programs as a group, with a few exceptions—for example, only the Grand Opera House program (with a somewhat lower-priced 50 cents for reserved seats) ran ads for chewing tobacco.
14. Ibid.
15. Ibid.
16. As advertised in the Lyceum Theatre program for *The Maister of Woodbarrow*, 26 Aug. 1890.
17. In the Proctor's 23rd St. Theatre program, *All the Comforts of Home*, 5 Sept. 1890.
18. Garden Theatre, *Cleopatra*, 16 Feb. 1891. By way of comparison to Travelers' relatively small ad, Penn Mutual Life Insurance ads would take up half a page throughout the season at Philadelphia's Walnut Street Theatre circa 1889–1990. These ads tended toward the dramatic, as in the following: "What if I should die—die without a cent of provision for Mary!" Penn Mutual aimed their advertising directly at the professional salaried worker with limited disposable income, and—understandably, since the medium was a theatre program—a taste for sentimental melodrama. Such salaried workers, at least in part, could be considered part of the new PMC (Programs from the 1889–1890 season of the Walnut Street Theatre, vol. VII, nos. 1–37, courtesy of the Philadelphia Free Library Theatre Collection, Philadelphia, PA).

19. The following programs are referenced in this section: Madison Square Theatre, *The Prince Chap,* 4 Sept. 1905; Princess Theatre, *Zira,* 25 Nov. 1905; Lyceum Theatre, *Just Out of College,* 10 Oct. 1905; Belasco Theatre, *The Girl of the Golden West* (n.d.; 1905–1906); Princess Theatre, *Brown of Harvard,* 26 Feb. 1906; Wallack's, *Easy Dawson,* 4 Sept. 1905; Garden Theatre, *The Bad Samaritan,* 12 Sept. 1905; Wallack's, *The Squaw Man,* 1 Jan. 1906; and Garden Theatre, *The Galloper,* 26 Mar. 1906. All programs in NYPL. For the most part, I will be referring to these programs as a group, with occasional individual exceptions.
20. One of the first nationally sold products was, in fact, soap. An ad for "Hand Sapolio" in one of the nation's popular magazines urgently calls for a change of lifestyle: "you can't be healthy, or pretty, or even good, unless you are clean." The man in the tub scrubbing himself (seen naked from just above the navel) is flanked by one hand carrying a lit torch, and another carrying a bar of soap. An appeal to the exotic appears at the bottom of the ad: "Equals a Mild Turkish Bath." See Steven Heller, "1900–1919: Seducing the New Consumer." In *All-American Ads 1900–1919.* Ed. Jim Heimann (Los Angeles, CA: Taschen, 2005), 22; as well as Jim Heimann, ed., *All-American Ads 1900–1919,* 426.
21. Such ads appear in nearly all the programs noted above.
22. Program, Garden Theatre, *The Bad Samaritan,* 12 Sept. 1905.
23. The specific ad appeared in the Princess Theatre, *Brown of Harvard,* 26 Feb. 1906. Its copy, however, states specifically what is implied in various shirt and clothing ads of the period that emphasize "tighter fits" and less camouflaging of the male bodily form.
24. Velutina was still a prominent theatre program sponsor in 1905–1906, although the cost was now one-third (rather than one quarter) the cost of silk. The emphasis was now on the fact that Velutina was not only less expensive, but, in fact, "superior" to silk.
25. See John Berger, "The Suit and the Photograph," in *Rethinking Popular Culture: Contemporary Perspectives in Cultural Studies.* Ed. Chandra Mukerji and Michael Schudson (Berkeley, CA: University of California Press, 1991).
26. Emphasis in original. Program notes taken from the following programs: Lyric Theatre, *The Cheater,* 29 June 1910; Comedy Theatre, *A Man's World,* 7 Feb. 1910, and the West End Theatre, 7 Nov. 1910; Wallack's, *Alias Jimmy Valentine,* 4 Apr. 1910; Lyric Theatre, *The City,* 2 May 1910; Daly's Theatre, *The Inferior Sex,* 28 Feb. 1910, and Maxine Elliott's Theatre, 24 Oct. 1910; Cohan & Harris Theatre, *The Acquittal,* 12 Apr. and 19 Apr. 1920; Plymouth Theatre, *Little Old New York,* 8 Sept. and 11 Oct. 1920; Shubert Theatre, *The Blue Flame,* 19 Apr. 1920; Morosco Theatre, *Sacred and Profane*

Love, 22 Mar. 1920; The Playhouse, *The Wonderful Thing*, 19 Apr. 1920; Forty-Eighth Street Theatre, *Opportunity*, 4 Oct. 1920; George M. Cohan's Theatre, *The Tavern*, 15 Nov. 1920; Bijou Theatre, *The Skin Game*, 24 Jan. 1921; Princess Theatre, *Suppressed Desires* and *The Emperor Jones*, 2 May 1921. Programs found in NYPL. As before, I will generally be referring these programs as a collective group, as their formats and ads are similar, with two notable exceptions: the undated Criterion Theatre program of the first performances of O'Neill's *Beyond the Horizon* was a bare-bones printout listing only the play (on the inside page), cast, and crew; and The New Theatre's program for "The Nigger" (Dec. 1909) had all its ads printed in the form of business cards. The ads for the New Theatre, which catered to an exclusive and elite audience, were all for conspicuously high-end items such as champagne, jewelry, and expensive automobiles.

27. The New York Theatre Program Corporation (formerly Frank V. Strauss and Co.), "Why Is New York City the Theatrical Center of the World?" From theatre program "Little Old New York," Plymouth Theatre, 8 Sept. 1920, among others, in NYPL.

28. Nationally, the "player" piano was still riding its greatest crest of popularity in the early 1920s, reaching a sales peak of 200,000 in 1923. Record players, the radio, and "talking" motion pictures were chiefly responsible for the eventual falling off of the popularity of the player piano as home entertainment. See Lee Barnett, "Max Kortlander: King of the Player Piano." *Grand River Valley History* (vol. 18, 2001). <http://www.doctorjazz.co.uk/maxkort.html>.

29. These ads appeared regularly in the programs from the 1920–1921 seasons.

30. Ibid.

31. Ibid.

32. Guy Bolton's *Polly Preferred* (1923), for example, features an "effeminate" director—dressed in the now-familiar stereotypical move director's outfit (large cap, riding crop, etc.), and lisping in a pronounced way. See Guy Bolton, *Polly Preferred*. Typescript. NCOF+Bolton, 1923, NYPL.

33. Both the white Jolson and the black Williams greeted the reader smiling and in blackface.

34. Lewis J. Selznick's production company fizzled due to overexpansion by 1922; his son, David, became a major producer at MGM ("Selznick Presents," *Time* 26:1 [1 July 1935], <http://www.time.com/magazine/article/0,9171,770045,00.html>, par. 1 and 2). Olive Thomas's rather sordid death in 1920, possibly involving a fatal mix of alcohol and venereal disease remedy, provided early Hollywood with its first major scandal.

35. See Tice L. Miller, *Bohemians and Critics: American Theatre Criticism in the Nineteenth Century* (Metuchen, NJ: Scarecrow Press, 1981), as well as Miller,

"Criticism," in *Cambridge Guide to American Theatre*. Ed. Don B. Wilmeth with Tice L. Miller (New York, Cambridge University Press, 1996).
36. As noted earlier, the theatre itself would also conform to "big-business" models.
37. How the Syndicate damaged the theatre was not only the subject of many anti-Syndicate articles, but also augmented the criticism of the daily reviewers. Chief Syndicate "crimes" against theatre were monopolizing the theatre business, catering to "flighty females," and being a group of money-grubbing and uncultured Jews. Attitudes toward Jews among the critics (and the PMC) varied widely, from the *Dramatic Mirror* in early 1890 declaring onstage anti-Semitism "ungenerous, unjust, [and] un-American" to James Metcalfe of *Life* making blatantly anti-Semitic remarks throughout much of the Syndicate era. While, as Gerald Bordman points out, more Jews were patronizing the first-class theatres, their attendance was most likely a part of an assimilation process; moneyed Jews could conditionally "fit in" if they did not call undue attention to their Jewishness. See Mark Hodin, "The Disavowal of Ethnicity: Legitimate Theatre and the Social Construction of Literary Value in Turn-of-the-Century America." *Theatre Journal* 52.2 (2000) 211–226; Gerald Bordman, *American Theatre: A Chronicle of Comedy and Drama, 1869–1914* (New York: Oxford University Press, 1994) 446; and *Dramatic Mirror,* 11 Jan. 1890: 2.
38. Women also reaped the benefits of increased attention from the newspapers. As Jones points out: "The increasing newspaper emphasis on woman-interest was not due to the 'emancipation' of the sex, or to their new importance in industry and business, but mainly to the growth of department-store advertising." See Robert W. Jones, *Journalism in the United States* (New York: E.P. Dutton and Co., 1947) 599.
39. Nathan's greatest influence was most likely James G. Huneker, who spent two years as a daily critic for the *New York Sun* (1902–1904), but whose influence would prove far-reaching in the modern critical era. Huneker "brought serious public attention to continental dramatists," including Ibsen and Shaw. See Tice L. Miller, "James G. Huneker," in *Cambridge Guide to American Theatre* 242. Nathan admired Huneker greatly; as Connelly writes: "Nathan was delighted to be associated with Huneker. He closely identified himself with him personally and was proud to work with him professionally. When he coedited *The Smart Set* with Mencken, he solicited several short stories from his mentor." See Thomas F. Connelly, *George Jean Nathan and the Making of Modern American Drama Criticism* (Teaneck, NJ: Fairleigh Dickinson University Press, 2000) 50.
40. See also Connolly, *George Jean Nathan*, p. 94.

41. Connolly introduces his study of Nathan by referring to him as "the first modern American drama critic." See *George Jean Nathan*, p. 13.

3. THE PROBLEM OF NERVES

1. From the following programs: Madison Square Theatre, *Beau Brummell*, 13 Oct. 1890; Lyceum Theatre, *The Maister of Woodbarrow*, 26 Aug. 1890; Proctor's 23rd St. Theatre, *All the Comforts of Home*, 5 Sept. 1890; Madison Square Theatre, *Alabama*, 27 Apr. 1891; Bijou Theatre, *A Texas Steer*, 10 Nov. 1890; Daly's, *The Last Word*, 29 Oct. 1890; Star Theatre, *Mr. Potter of Texas*, 7 Mar. 1891; Niblo's, *Mr. Potter of Texas*, 8 Oct. 1892; Garden Theatre, *Cleopatra*, 16 Feb. 1891; Palmer's, *John Needham's Double*, 13 Feb. 1891; and Grand Opera House, *The Power of the Press*, 28 Dec. 1891. All programs are in NYPL.
2. See also John F. Kasson, *Rudeness & Civility: Manners in 19th Century America* (New York: Hill and Wang, 1990), especially the chapter "The Disciplining of Spectatorship."
3. While there was greater "depth" in the post-War era, there was still plenty of room for sex farces and other "frivolity."
4. Obviously, famous actresses of the period embodied the drawing room as well, but our primary concern is the male embodiments throughout this study.
5. Indeed, Towse and Winter were not the only ones who had difficulties making such distinctions, and the problem has remained with us, in one form or another, over one issue or another, to the present.
6. See Gerald Bordman, *American Theatre: A Chronicle of Comedy and Drama, 1869–1914* (New York: Oxford University Press, 1994) 297–298.
7. As one critic wrote: "There are no light effects. We are not permitted to look upon the sunset when it is red or the moonlight when it is an impossible but attractive shade of green. A servant does not once come upon a darkened stage with a simple lamp that causes an instantaneous and dazzling general illumination" See Bordman, *American Theatre*, pp. 297–298.
8. Quotations from *The Henrietta* are taken from Bronson Howard, *The Henrietta* (London: Samuel French, 1901).
9. "The Henrietta." *New York Times* 27 Sept. 1887: 4.
10. Gillette's views of acting were very much in keeping with the attitudes and *habitus* of the era in terms of "personality." He felt that an actor could not possibly perform in a way approaching realism unless his personality were incorporated: "As no human being exists without personality of one sort or another, an actor who omits it in his impersonation of a human being omits

one of the vital elements of existence." See William Gillette, "The Illusion of the First Time in Acting," in *Actors on Acting*. Ed. Toby Cole and Helen Krich Chinoy (New York: Three Rivers Press, 1970) 566.
11. Also quoted in Cullen and Wilmeth, "Introduction." In *Plays by William Hooker Gillette* (New York: Cambridge University Press, 1983).
12. "In the season of 1900–1901, Clyde Fitch made a sensational breach of the barrier against American playwrights. Four plays written by him were on the stage simultaneously. One commentator said that future generations would never believe that such a thing could happen and would have to turn back to 'musty records' to confirm it" (Atkinson 51–52). The plays Atkinson alludes to are *The Climbers, Barbara Frietchie, Captain Jinks of the Horse Marines,* and *Lovers' Lane*. See also Montrose Moses and Virginia Gerson, "Introduction," in *Clyde Fitch and His Letters*. Ed. Montrose J. Moses and Virginia Gerson (Boston: Little, Brown and Company, 1924) 177–178.
13. Fitch was nothing if not pragmatic regarding the Syndicate. As he wrote in one of his letters with regard to accepting a potentially lucrative deal from Frohman: "As Frohman has nearly *all* the theaters, & *nearly* all the actors, why not?" (author's emphasis). See Clyde Fitch, *Clyde Fitch and His Letters*. Ed. Montrose J. Moses and Virginia Gerson (Boston: Little, Brown and Company, 1924) 174.
14. The usually astute Brooks Atkinson, by misquoting one word from Fitch's essay, misses Fitch's point about the audience. Atkinson quotes the description of the gallery as having "*upholstered* hearts," implying a naturally inferior taste to that of the "plush" gentlemen and ladies occupying the orchestra seats. See Atkinson, *Broadway*, pp. 57–58. Indeed, Fitch's conflicted relationship with and attitude toward the "plush" elite drove the great majority of his work.
15. Adams and Fitch shared Charles Frohman as their principal producer. Frohman and Adams, in particular, would achieve great success inverting and complicating the male body, with Adams playing such roles as Peter Pan, Joan of Arc and the rambunctious rooster (or in the parlance of the play, "cock") Chantecler. See especially Kim Marra, *Strange Duets: Impresarios and Actresses in the American Theatre, 1865–1914* (Iowa City, IA: University of Iowa Press, 2006) 106–141. Marra's analysis is an informative "queer" approach to the issues of male bodies and masculinity.
16. Fitch's sexuality has been mostly a "hinty" subject until fairly recently. There were "whispers" of Fitch having "a hint of lavender" about him during his lifetime (See Peter Andrews, "More Sock and Less Buskin," *American Heritage Magazine* [Apr. 1972] 23: 48–57), and there existed what might be called a preponderance of circumstantial evidence, that is, his lifelong bachelorhood, his

flamboyant dress, his affinity for acting out the female characters of his plays, and the like. Kim Marra, in her article "Clyde Fitch's Too Wilde Love," cites letters exchanged between Oscar Wilde and Fitch as reasonable proof of Fitch's (secretly) gay orientation. See Kim Marra, "Clyde Fitch's Too Wilde Love," in *Staging Desire: Queer Readings of American Theater History*. Ed. Kim Marra and Robert A. Schanke (Ann Arbor, MI: University of Michigan Press, 2002).
17. One critical exception to pigeon-holing Fitch was William Dean Howells. In an exchange during January 1904, Howells received Fitch's letter with: "May I say that I do not know how it [your letter] could be *manlier?*" (author's emphasis). See Fitch, *Letters*, pp. 257–258.
18. From Program, Madison Square Theatre, *Beau Brummell*, 13 Oct. 1890, NYPL.
19. Fitch would collaborate with Wharton on a dramatization of Wharton's *The House of Mirth*, which opened on Broadway in 1906. While the play only enjoyed a brief run, Wharton and Fitch remained friends. See Glenn Loney, "Introduction," in *The House of Mirth: The Play of the Novel* (Rutherford, NJ: Farleigh Dickinson University Press, 1988).
20. See Bordman, *American Theatre*, p. 457; Atkinson, *Broadway*, p. 6; and John Houchin, *Censorship of the American Theatre in the Twentieth Century* (New York: Cambridge University Press, 2003), 40–52, on *Sapho* and its theatrical and social critics.
21. All references to *The City* are taken from *Plays by Clyde Fitch in Four Volumes*, vol. 4, with introduction by Montrose J. Moses and Virginia Gerson (Boston: Little, Brown, and company1915). The play was first performed 22 Dec. 1909.
22. Theatre historians tend to cite the line "You're a God damn liar!", which the villain Hannock says in Act II (580), as the ultimate shocker. Nevertheless, in Fitch's script, Hannock also uses the epithet earlier in Act I when he threatens to reveal Rand, Sr. as "a God damn whited sepulchre" (479). The second "God damn" comes at a much stronger moment in the play, as the hero has just revealed that Hannock has married his half-sister. It is not inconceivable that the first "God damn" was cut before the performance. See Gerald Bordman, *The Oxford Companion to American Theatre* (New York: Oxford University Press, 1984) 145–146.
23. Fitch had tried to introduce some "manly" cursing before, notably in the 1899 Nat Goodwin-Maxine Elliott vehicle, *The Cowboy and the Lady*. The dude-cowboy hero played by Goodwin introduces a "swear jar" at his ranch, and those who swore were obliged to sacrifice a quarter. The Goodwin character, after a couple of stray "damneds," contributes the first fifty cents. At the time, he was criticized by *The New York Dramatic Mirror* for exercising poor taste: "By actual count there are nineteen violent outbreaks of cursing in the first act

alone... This sort of thing is not amusing" ("Knickerbocker—The Cowboy and the Lady," *New York Dramatic Mirror* 6 Jan. 1900: 16).
24. It is one of the play's more unfortunate moments that Rand Jr. has to "forget" that his father has just died in the adjoining room in order for his younger sister to enter and provide some exposition: "Good God! I forgot!" See Fitch, *The City*, p. 502.
25. One can gain a measure of Fitch's excitement over the idea in his letters: "I know you'll say people won't stand for it, but wait till you hear how I shall treat it!" See Fitch, *Letters*, p. 365.
26. Moses is quoting Arthur Warren of the *New York Tribune*. Several reviewers emphasized the audience hysteria of the opening night performance, including J.C. Garrison of the *New York Press*, Joseph Meighan of the *New York Evening Globe* ("ushers will be needed to look after the fainting women at the matinees"), and the critic of the *New York Morning World* ("Hysterics Follow Climax of 'The City!'"). See Program Pamphlet, Lyric Theatre, *The City*; NYPL. The pamphlet includes reprints of the opening night reviews, opinions from William Lyon Phelps and George P. Baker ("The Opinions of Two Professors"), and cover descriptions of the play including the blurbs "His Posthumous Work," "Clyde Fitch's Greatest Play," and "An enduring monument to the genius of the American Playwright."
27. William Lyon Phelps, writing in 1921: "when he began to write, American drama scarcely existed; when he died it was reality.... He did more for American drama than any other man in our history;" also, "Walter Prichard Eaton said that modern American playwriting began with Clyde Fitch." See Andrews, "More Sock and Less Buskin," pp. 48–57.
28. See Montrose Moses, *The American Dramatist* (1925, rpt. New York: Benjamin Blom, 1964) 314, as well as a contemporaneous review of Fitch's *Letters* from the *Times:* "Yet will he [Fitch] live by his plays? When one thinks of the best of them, 'The Truth,' 'The Girl With the Green Eyes,' and 'The City,' the dust of time seems to be slowly settling upon them" ("'Letters' of Clyde Fitch and 'The Truth at Last' about Charles Hawtrey," New York *Times,* Book Review, 2 Nov. 1924: BR7). Once "modern American drama" had made its (PMC-endorsed) entrance onto the world stage, a recurring theme of criticism was to put as much distance between the present and the past as possible; thus were plays less than 20 years old often dismissed as "old" and "antiquated."
29. References to *The Moth and the Flame* are taken from *Representative Plays by American Dramatists*. Ed. Montrose Moses (1921, rpt. New York: Benjamin Blom, 1964).

30. By striking the mother of his child in church (and onstage), Fletcher went beyond nearly all of the era's stage villainy in terms of vile actions. Indeed, at the end of the 1950s, directors were still reluctant to stage the striking of a woman (e.g., Inge's *The Dark at the Top of the Stairs*, wherein the audience hears the husband violently slap his wife offstage).
31. That the "double standard" was accepted by Broadway audiences and "experts" (including the PMC) was also borne out by the later responses toward Rachel Crothers' *A Man's World* (1910) and Augustus Thomas's "answer" play, *As a Man Thinks* (1911). While critics respected Crothers' skill and thoughtfulness in presenting the injustice of the double standard from the "feminist" perspective, it was Thomas's play, with the pro-status quo message that "upon the golden basis of woman's virtue rests the welfare of the world," that found wider acceptance. See Arthur Hobson Quinn, *A History of the American Drama: From the Civil War to the Present Day*, Vol. 2 (New York: F.S. Crofts and Co., 1945); also Bordman, *American Theatre*, pp. 669, 687–688). There is no evidence, however, that Fitch himself believed in the double standard; to the contrary, as a writer who wrote and directed with great empathy toward and identification with his heroines, Fitch would most likely not have adopted such a standard as his own.
32. *The Climbers* found its way to Broadway without the help of Fitch's usual producer Charles Frohman. Frohman objected not only to the last-act suicide of the repentant but weak husband (which allowed the dutiful, heartbroken wife and the loyal best friend to get together), but also to the spectacle of the opening family catfight on the heels of a funeral. See Andrews, "More Sock and Less Buskin," pp. 48–57; and also Fitch, *Letters*, p. 174.
33. Fletcher, in *The Moth and the Flame*, is described on his entrance only as wearing "dark sailor clothes." See Fitch, *The Moth and the Flame*, p. 544. In all probability, this is because Fitch did not publish *Moth* himself—Montrose Moses published the play especially for his collection.
34. "Anti-hero" would not be an inapt description, except that these characters acted as catalysts, rather than leads.
35. See Tom Lutz, *American Nervousness, 1903: An Anecdotal History* (Ithaca, NY: Cornell University Press, 1991) 14–15, as well as Jackson Lears and Richard Wightman Fox, introduction to *Culture of Consumption: Critical Essays in American History, 1880–1980* (New York: Pantheon, 1983).
36. See Warren Susman, *Culture as History: The Transformation of American Society in the Twentieth Century* (New York: Pantheon Books, 1984) 273–274, and 277.

4. MUCKRAKING THE PLAYING FIELD: EMERGING PMC CLASS CONSCIOUSNESS

1. In general, the application of naturalist Charles Darwin's theories to human societies and economics. Thus, inequalities of wealth and power were justified as being the "natural" result of those being most fit to survive enjoying their success.
2. The expression "to shape up" first came into common parlance at the end of the nineteenth century. See Donald J. Mrozek, "Sport in American Life: From National Health to Personal Fulfillment, 1890–1940," in *Fitness in American Culture*. Ed. Kathryn Grover (Amherst, MA: University of Massachusetts Press, 1989).
3. See Wiebe, *The Search for Order: 1877–1920* (New York: Hill and Wang, 1967).
4. Seely also discusses this topic in Bruce Seely, "Research, Engineering, and Science in American Engineering Colleges: 1900–1960." *Technology and Cultur* 34.2 (Apr. 1993) 344–386.
5. Other institutions, of course, were turning out future PMC-types, including newly-created graduate institutions such as Clark University in Worcester, Massachusetts, and the University of Chicago, established in 1890 by John D. Rockefeller and the American Baptist Education Society, as well as the aforementioned separate professional schools of Yale and Harvard. The University of Chicago received something of a private "land grant" from department store magnate Marshall Field. See University of Chicago website, <http://www-news.uchicago.edu>. At the University of Chicago specifically, Joel Pfister notes that "between the early 1890s and 1930, almost two-thirds of the recipients of bachelor degrees from the University of Chicago took up professional occupations." See Joel Pfister, *Staging Depth: Eugene O'Neill and the Politics of Psychological Discourse* (Chapel Hill, NC: University of North Carolina Press, 1995) 276, ftn. 70. See also Martin Sklar, *The United States as a Developing Country*: *Studies in U.S. History in the Progressive Era and the 1920s* (New York: Cambridge University Press, 1992) 172. The point of import is that students who were seriously taking professional studies at college had little in common with the typical Broadway collegiate hero, and would appear onstage most likely as a "grind" to provide comic relief. To put the "grinds" in a more contemporary context, they occupied roughly the same position as "nerds" did in collegiate-based movies of the 1980s. And, just as real-life "nerds" frequently became enormously wealthy and powerful (Bill Gates, for example), the "grinds" would soon become the PMC experts so vital to American capitalist culture.

6. The expression "school of hard knocks" originates from this period. According to the OED, which defines the phrase as "the experience of a life of hardship, considered as a means of instruction," credit for first coining the phrase goes to George Ade, from his 1912 work *Knocking the Neighbors*.
7. U.S. Census Bureau, *Statistical Abstract of the United States*, 2003. Number of B.A. degrees conferred before 1960 include first professional degrees.
8. Arthur Hobson Quinn had this to say on *The College Widow*: "The whole college atmosphere seems to be written from the point of view of an outsider. This is not due to ignorance on Ade's part...but to the inherent weakness of the comedy of exaggeration.... Any real interpretation of college life is nonexistent." See Quinn, *A History of the American Drama: From the Civil War to the Present Day*, p. 114.
9. The Indiana Historical Society maintains a website that devotes a page to Ade: "George Ade: The Aesop of Indiana," a reference to the fables that first gained Ade national attention. See <http://www.indianahistory.org/pop_hist/people/ade.html>.
10. As Gerald Bordman points out, "*Charley's Aunt* [from October 1893] had employed an English university for its background, but its plot, relying on the need for a chaperone and the humor of a man masquerading as a woman, could have been set elsewhere. No way could *The College Widow* have been replanted to another setting" (p. 540).
11. Bordman offers this succinct definition of the title, whose meaning perhaps has been lost to modern audiences: "A college widow is a young lady, affiliated in some manner with a school, who loves or flirts with students, only to lose them on graduation day." See Bordman, *American Musical Theatre*, 3rd ed., p. 540. One of Ade's characters dispenses with the title with the terse description: "College widow. Buries one every commencement." See George Ade, *The College Widow: A Pastoral Comedy in Four Acts* (New York: Samuel French, 1924) 8. The type remained in the popular culture at least into the 1930s, with the Marx Brothers' film *Horsefeathers* centering around voluptuous college widow Thelma Todd.
12. This line would get as far as the typescript in the later musical version, *Leave It to Jane*, but would be, interestingly, penciled out. See Guy Bolton and P.G. Wodehouse, *Leave It to Jane* typescript, NCOF+Bolton, NYPL.
13. *Horsefeathers* would also adopt the exaggerated locutions for the academics, providing plenty of fodder for Groucho, as in this exchange: "The Dean is waiting in his office, and he's waxing wroth!" "Well, tell Roth to wax the Dean for a while," Groucho replies.
14. Ade thus touches on the point made by Harvey Green quoted earlier—football takes the place of religious rites, and both Witherspoon and Calvin are unable to interfere.

15. Prolific playwright Owen Davis also contributed a popular college sports drama to the same period, *At Yale* (1906). Strictly speaking, this was not a Broadway production; Davis's rah-rah comedy-drama played at the "popular theaters" around the country for a year, stopping in New York City in October 1907. The play, probably quite deliberately, echoes *Brown of Harvard*'s rowing competition, and was readily adaptable to localization by other college productions—for example, a 1912 University of Georgia production was called, appropriately enough, *At Georgia*. There are additional connections to the other college plays under consideration: Davis's hero, Dick Seely, is a poor "outsider" who has risen to gain the respect of his Yale teammates, and he is also falsely accused of sullying a girl's honor. *The New York Dramatic Mirror* liked Davis's effort enough to note that while "its story is a close copy of *Brown of Harvard*...in some portions it is superior to that play" ("Reviews of New Plays" 3). See Owen Davis, *At Yale* (New York: Samuel French, 1906), and "At Georgia," *New York Times* 3 Mar. 1912: X9.
16. References to *Strongheart* are from William de Mille, *Strongheart* (New York: Samuel French, 1909).
17. de Mille, in fact, initially planned to make his hero a Negro and not an American Indian. See Montrose Moses, *The American Dramatist* (1925, rpt. New York: Benjamin Blom, 1964) 331.
18. *Northern Lights,* by Edwin Barbour and James W. Harkins Jr., was a fairly recent attempt to deal with the Indian in White society (it opened in December 1895). This play focused on the character of John Swiftwind, a Yale-educated Indian who works as assistant surgeon at Fort Terra, MT. His treatment at the hands of both white doctors and members of his tribe are secondary themes, as the plot is driven by Swiftwind's efforts to save a spurned wife in distress and to prove the innocence of a supposedly cowardly soldier. See Bordman, *American Theatre*, pp. 390, 550–551.
19. The original production apparently lost a chance for some humor by having Strongheart delivering the line "seriously." This would be in keeping with the physicality of the almost 37-year-old Robert Edeson, an "exceptionally stern and mature" actor wearing dark make-up. See de Mille, *Strongheart*, p. 20, and Bordman, *American Theatre*, p. 551.
20. Robert Edeson, who played the title role, had this to say regarding the play and the character, in an interview a few weeks after the show opened: "I had this idea a long time ago. There seemed to me great possibilities in the red man. It was the only chance to touch on the race problem—to find the real American play. Why just think how cosmopolitan is the word American; it embraces every nationality. But the Indian is the real American, and I thought it best to go back to the starting point." To even "touch" on the race problem

would have been impossible if de Mille's character were a Black man. From "The Indian and the Drama," *New York Times* 19 Feb. 1905: X2.

21. Carlisle's most famous alumnus, the athlete Jim Thorpe, had just started at the school the year before (1904). He would not make an impression on a national level until later in the decade as a first-team All-American football player (in 1908 and 1909). Worldwide attention would accompany his triumphs at the 1912 Antwerp Olympics. See the official Jim Thorpe website at <http://www.cmgww.com/sports/thorpe/bio2.htm>.

22. Carlisle Indian Industrial School research specialist Barbara Landis maintains an active website on the school, including photos, primary records and testimony, and bibliography. See <http://home.epix.net/~landis/index.html>.

23. See Brewer, on O'Neill's *The Iceman Cometh:* "Whites perceive him [Joe] as a *good* Black because his desire for the privileges of Whiteness makes him useful in controlling other Blacks" (author's emphasis): Mary F. Brewer, *Staging Whiteness* (Middletown, CT: Wesleyan University Press, 2005) 71.

24. Rida Johnson Young is an interesting figure in the drama of the period—a woman equally at home in constructing comedies, musical librettos, and popular songs. Her skill and success in negotiating the male-dominated creative world of Broadway is worthy of note.

25. Henry Woodruff had knocked around Broadway for some years by the time he hit stardom in *Brown of Harvard*. As Bordman notes, "some critics felt he was always too self-conscious. Like so many others raised to stardom in this period, he was not a star for long." See Bordman, *American Theatre*, p. 573.

26. Of course, much of Carnegie's philanthropy was directed toward cultural improvement—libraries and concert halls being the prominent examples.

27. In Boucicault's famous melodrama *The Poor of New York*, the "true" poor is embodied by a once-prosperous hero who has lost his money, and must put on a front to hide his poverty.

28. See Ward and Trent et al. *The Cambridge History of English and American Literature*. New York: G.P. Putnam's Sons, 1907–21; (New York: Bartleby.com, 2000 <http://www.bartleby.com/cambridge/>), Sec. 20, Par. 32.

29. See also Fon W. Boardman Jr., *America and the Progressive Era 1900–1917* (New York: Henry Z. Walck, 1970) 15, and Howard Zinn, *A People's History of the United States, 1492–Present* (New York: Harper Collins, 2003) 323.

30. References to the play taken from Charles Klein, *The Lion and the Mouse* (New York: Samuel French, 1916).

31. Brooks Atkinson pokes fun at Klein's use of the plot device of "the papers" in *Broadway*, p. 71.

32. Klein most likely borrowed the "Octopus" analogy from Frank Norris's *The Octopus: A Story of California*. Norris's 1901 story of wheat farmers and their

struggles against the railroads (the titular "Octopus") was the first part of Norris's intended "epic of the wheat"—three novels that were to denounce capitalistic greed by tracing the path of wheat from farming to exportation. Norris only finished the second novel, *The Pit: A Story of Chicago*, before dying of a ruptured appendix.

Ida Tarbell's description of John D. Rockefeller in *The History of Standard Oil* (always "Mr. Rockefeller" when she does not include his full name) is rather less emotionally heated than that of Klein's dramatized counterpart. Tarbell tends to emphasize the cold, patient, and laconic qualities of Rockefeller—in one vignette, she recounts him idly rocking in a rocking chair while sizing up potential adversaries in the room (104–105). In the following passage, Tarbell describes a typical Rockefeller business maneuver:

> The Empire had gone systematically to work to develop markets for the output of its own and of the independent refineries. Mr. Rockefeller's business was to prevent any such development. He was well equipped for the task by his system of "predatory competition," for in spite of the fact that Mr. Rockefeller claimed that underselling to drive a rival from a market was one of the evils he was called to cure, he did not hesitate to employ it himself. Indeed, he had long used his freedom to sell at any price he wished for the sake of driving a competitor out of the market with calculation and infinite patience. Other refiners burst into the market and undersold for a day; but when Mr. Rockefeller began to undersell, he kept it up day in and day out, week in and week out, month in and month out, until there was literally nothing left of his competitor. (187)

See Ida M. Tarbell, *The History of the Standard Oil Company* (New York: McClure, Phillips and Co., 1904).

33. Generally speaking, 100 performances was the "magic figure" of the early twentieth century and carrying on into the 1930s—enough to repay backers, turn a profit, and show enough of a presence to prove that the show had built up an audience. One could, however, refer to the run of *The Boss* as "respectable."
34. References to *The Boss* taken from Edward Sheldon, *The Boss. Representative American Plays*, 6th edition. Ed. Arthur Hobson Quinn (New York: D. Appleton-Century-Crofts, 1938).
35. Blinn played the title role.

5. A SIZE THIRTEEN COLLAR: MUSICALS AND PMC CLASS CONSCIOUSNESS

1. Also qtd. in Bordman, *American Musical Theatre*, 3rd ed., p. 211.
2. See also Bordman, *American Musical Theatre*, 3rd ed., p. 269.

3. See Robert C. Allen, *Horrible Prettiness: Burlesque and American Culture* (Chapel Hill, NC: University of North Carolina Press, 1991); also Laura Mulvey, "Visual Pleasure and Narrative Cinema." *Screen* 16 (1975): 6–18. Mulvey quoted in Linda Mizejewski, *Ziegfeld Girl: Image and Icon in Culture and Cinema* (Durham, NC: Duke University Press, 1999) 31.
4. *The Summer Widowers* was also the title of a modestly successful musical that opened 4 June 1910. The plot involved a prima donna throwing a party for some men whose wives were on summer holiday. Although the party is innocent, complications ensue. See Bordman, *American Musical Theatre*, 3rd ed., p. 298.
5. The quote is from Atkinson's New York *Times* article of 28 Aug. 1927, "A New Theatrical Season Slowly Gathers Momentum."
6. There is a paradox between the "glorification" of the Ziegfeld Girls and the tawdriness of many of the individual girls' lives. As Ethan Mordden points out, "While he [Ziegfeld] did much to purge the chorus line of its smutty hangover from the Lydia Thompson days, he could not contain the steamy atmosphere in the end. Because he designed it." See Ethan Mordden, *Broadway Babies: The People Who Made the American Musical* (New York: Oxford University Press, 1983) 41.
7. Ade's story collections *Fables in Slang* (1899) and *More Fables in Slang* (1900) had already made him a favorite with the American public.
8. Quotations from *Very Good Eddie* from Philip Bartholomae and Guy Bolton (book), Schuyler Greene (lyrics), and Jerome Kern (music), *Very Good Eddie, Libretto* (New York: New York American Play Company, 1915); NCOF+Kern, NYPL.
9. In one of the funniest running gags, Madame Matroppo, who "always" remembers names through mnemonic devices, renders Eddie's last name as "Fish" (as in "kettle of") and "Pot." She does as much for Dick Rivers, referring to him as "Brooks," "Stream," and a few other bodies of water as well.
10. According to Bordman, the title echoes a phrase made popular in the Montgomery-Stone vehicle *Chin-Chin*, which had opened October of the previous year (1914), spoken by comic Fred Stone as a Chinese mannequin pretending to be a ventriloquist. Mordden attributes the title more generally to the typical ventriloquist act of the period, with the emphasis on Eddie in the play being, in effect, a "dummy" controlled by his wife. See Bordman, *American Musical Theatre*, 3rd ed., pp. 346, 357–358; and Mordden, *Broadway Babies*, p. 73, as well as Guy Bolton and P.G. Wodehouse, *Bring On the Girls! The Improbable Story of Our Life in Musical Comedy, with Pictures to Prove It* (New York: Simon and Schuster, 1953) 7, whose recollection most closely jibes with Bordman's account.

11. Also see Bordman, *American Musical Theatre* 3rd ed., p. 366.
12. Page 1–11, from the *Oh, Boy!* libretto; NCOF+ Bolton, NYPL. Bolton, Guy, and P.G. Wodehouse (book and lyrics), and Kern, Jerome (music), *Oh, Boy! Libretto* (New York: F. Roy Comstock, 1917). All quotations from *Oh, Boy!* are taken from this libretto.
13. Flatbush had become a "fashionable suburb" by roughly 1910. See "Flatbush, Long Island: Beauty in Diversity" <http://www.longislandexchange.com/brooklynqueens/flatbush.html>.
14. *Leave It to Jane* is usually classified as a "Princess" musical due to its style and the collaborators, even though, in fact, it played at the Longacre. *Oh, Boy!* was still playing at the Princess at the time of *Leave It to Jane*'s opening.
15. Guy Bolton, P.G. Wodehouse (book and lyrics), Jerome Kern (lyrics). *Leave It to Jane*. Typescript. NCOF+Bolton, 1917, 1–45. NYPL. All quotes from *Leave It to Jane* are taken from this typescript.
16. Despite the best efforts of the Castles and other experts, the "dance craze" still retained its sensational aspect, as witnessed by such headlines as "Parted by Dance Craze; Wife Says Husband Left Her to Fox Trot with Young Women" (*New York Times* 7 Jan. 1915: 22).
17. Along with the confusion between "musical comedies," "comic operas," and "operettas," there were disagreements as to whether *Watch Your Step* was a musical comedy or a revue. As Bordman notes: "With 'revues' still insisting on stories to hold them together and 'musical comedies' still accepting the most meager excuses for plots, *Watch Your Step* demonstrates the confusion between the genres at the time: the theatrical sheets of the day discussing the 'Rush of Revues' included the show…in their articles." See Bordman, *American Musical Theatre*, 2nd ed., p. 303.
18. According to the *Times* review of the show, Castle "knows how it feels to use automobiles, for he's a dancing teacher now." See "'Watch Your Step' Hilarious Fun." *New York Times* 9 Dec. 1914: 13.
19. Berlin's lyrics from <http://www.oldielyrics.com/lyrics/irving_berlin/watch_your_step.html>.
20. Astaire, with his frequent partner Ginger Rogers, would portray the Castles in the film *The Story of Vernon and Irene Castle*.
21. By contrast, after seductively dancing with Ginger Rogers to "Night and Day" in *The Gay Divorcee*, Astaire cheekily offers Rogers a "post-coital" cigarette.
22. Although Castle did see combat in Europe, his death was the result of a plane crash while training pilots stateside.
23. See also Susan C. Cook, "Passionless Dancing and Passionate Reform: Respectability, Modernism, and the Social Dancing of Irene and Vernon

188 Notes

Castle. In *The Passion of Music and Dance: Body, Gender and Sexuality.* Ed. by William Washabaugh (New York: Berg, 1998).

24. See especially Lewis A. Erenberg, *Steppin' Out: New York Nightlife and the Transformation of American Culture, 1890–1930* (Westport, CT: Greenwood Press, 1981)158–165. Irene Castle used the term "nigger dance" when describing the shimmy, around 1918 or 1919. See Erenberg, p. 174, ftn. 51.

6. SYSTEM AND FARCE: EMERGING PMC HABITUS

1. "George M. Cohan in America's Theater," <http://www.members.tripod.com/davecol8>.
2. As Ethan Mordden writes in *Broadway Babies*, "Critics couldn't understand why the public ignored their irritated reviews and acquired the taste for Cohan. Couldn't they see it? They saw it plain, and liked it." See Mordden, *Broadway Babies,* p. 26.
3. In the early twentieth century especially, Cohan's successes were not primarily a function of their initial Broadway runs—as noted in Chapter 2, most producers made their primary profits from tours, and Cohan was not an exception. Even his best-known early musical, *Little Johnny Jones,* ran only 52 performances in 1904. Prosperous road tours, successful Broadway revivals of *Little Johnny Jones* following "the road" in 1905, and brisk sales of sheet music (printed by Cohan's own publishing company) were more instrumental in fixing Cohan and such songs as "Give My Regards to Broadway" and "Yankee Doodle Boy" in the Broadway theatregoing consciousness. See John McCabe, *George M. Cohan: The Man Who Owned Broadway* (Garden City, NY: Doubleday and Co., 1973) 270–279. Following *Little Johnny Jones,* and the decline of "the road," nearly all Cohan productions were hits on Broadway during the period under study.
4. See McCabe, *The Man Who Owned Broadway,* and Ward Morehouse, *George M. Cohan: Prince of the American Theater* (Philadelphia, PA: J.B. Lippincott Company, 1943).
5. Eddie Cantor and Bert Lahr take us well beyond the 1920s, but I include this part of the quote to emphasize that Cohan's influence was not merely of his time, but exceptionally long-lasting. Indeed, as Mordden points out, such modern shows as *Annie* and *42nd Street* could also reasonably be considered "Cohanesque." See Mordden, *Broadway Babies,* p. 29.
6. As Ethan Mordden writes: "While Cohan laid down a few tracks himself, he was one of those performers you get live or not at all." See Mordden, *Broadway Babies,* p. 208. Cohan appeared in one movie musical, *The Phantom President,*

which biographers Morehouse and McCabe both describe as an unpleasant experience for the entertainer, not in small part because he disliked the songwriting team for the movie, Rodgers and Hart. In turn, Rodgers and Hart would also write the songs for Cohan's last Broadway hit, *I'd Rather Be Right*, although they never earned Cohan's friendship or respect. See Morehouse, *Prince of the American Theatre*, and McCabe, *The Man Who Owned Broadway*.
7. There were critics who disdained this trademark aspect of Cohan as well. For example, Frederick H. Young of the Providence *Journal* criticized Cohan's thank-you speech following *Little Johnny Jones*: "He delivered his speech... from the corner of his mouth, which did not impart a tone of sincerity to his remarks" (qtd. in Morehouse, *Prince of the American Theatre*, p. 69.
8. This photo and the one following appear in McCabe, *The Man Who Owned Broadway*, between pages 80–81.
9. Cohan's "identification" with the "little guy" remained with him as he worked on a script for the film *Yankee Doodle Dandy* toward the end of his life. According to McCabe, although Cohan's script was rejected by the studio, one key exchange, between the elder "Cohan" and "FDR," remained: Cohan remarks to Roosevelt that one of the great things about America is that "a plain guy like me can sit down and talk things over with the head man." "Well, now, you know, Mr. Cohan, that's as good a definition of America as I've ever heard," Roosevelt replies. See McCabe, *The Man Who Owned Broadway*, p. 266.
10. Two major figures of early twentieth century New York society. The implication is that Cohan in this production is extremely well-dressed, in contrast to the accusations of cheapness and "flashiness" regarding other Cohan costumes and characterizations of the period.
11. From the Robinson Locke collection of dramatic scrapbooks, NYPL.
12. This is not to imply that Butsch makes this assumption.
13. Imitations of Cohan (along with other popular Broadway stars) were prevalent in vaudeville. George Burns, for example, was part of a "Broadway Thieves" act early in his career, which consisted of imitations of Broadway personalities, including Cohan (Kate Davy, "An Interview with George Burns," *Educational Theatre Journal*, 27. 3, [Oct. 1975] 345–355.) Interestingly, some of the most successful imitations of Cohan on the vaudeville circuit were by women, including Elsie Janis and Venita Gould. See, for example, Susan Anita Glenn, "Give an Imitation of Me: Vaudeville Mimics and the Play of the Self," *American Quarterly* 50.1 (Mar. 1998) 47–76; as well as "Miss Venita Gould Pleases at Keith's," *The Tech,* Wednesday 17 May 1922: 2.

14. A Weber and Fields parody of one's work was considered something of an honor; producers would arrange special rehearsals in order for the vaudeville favorites to attend and take notes. In Fitch's *Letters,* compilers Moses and Gerson proudly list, along with Fitch's complete plays, the Weber and Fields parodies (there were four altogether, including *Sapolio,* for *Sapho*; and *The Curl and the Judge,* for *The Girl and the Judge*—see Fitch, *Letters,* p. 393.
15. See George M. Cohan, *Twenty Years on Broadway: And the Years It Took to Get There* (New York: Harper and Brothers, 1925).
16. See Bordman, *American Theatre,* p. 581.
17. Berlin, in fact, contributed his own PMC anthem to American popular culture for World War I: "Oh, How I Hate to Get Up in the Morning." While reveille took place much too early for most people not used to the military, a case could be made that a PMC worker in particular would be more accustomed to regular working hours that started considerably later. Also, the song's final joke constitutes a PMC way of looking at the army, as the singer, as soon as he murders the bugler, will then find a way to kill the soldier whose job it is to make sure the bugler wakes up.
18. By the time Cohan scored his late-in-the-day acting triumph in O'Neill's *Ah, Wilderness!,* Cohan felt he could communicate with O'Neill, the icon of Modern American Drama, as one "regular fellow" to another. See Louis Sheaffer, *O'Neill: Son and Artist* (Boston: Little, Brown and Company, 1973) 419, as well as Edward L. Shaughnessy, "A Connecticut Yankee in the Wilderness: The Sterner Stuff of O'Neill's Comedy," *The Recorder: A Journal of the American Irish Historical Society* (1989), <http://www.eoneill.com/library/on/shaughnessy/recorder.htm>.
19. Bringing Taylor into the discussion necessitates a clarification of what Taylor meant (and did not mean) by Scientific Management, as well as a stand regarding Taylor's character and legacy. For the former, Martha Banta, in *Taylored Lives: Narrative Productions in the Age of Taylor, Veblen and Ford* (Chicago: University of Chicago Press, 1993), offers this explanation:

> Two misunderstandings concerning the connections between Taylorism and time must be corrected from the outset: (1) Taylor did not originate time-motion studies. (2) Although Taylor paid great attention to methods for speeding up the work process, speeding is *not* what defines scientific management. The essential elements of scientific management include (a) the breaking down and analysis of each phase of the machine process; (b) the hastening of the demise of the skilled craftsman and jack-of-all-trades, and their replacement by unskilled workers assigned to isolated units of a work process rationalized to match machine standards; (c) the employment of

functional foremen restricted to single tasks; (d) the addition of a new layer of managerial elite. (Banta 330, ftn. 10, author's emphasis) This "new layer of managerial elite" represents one of the strongest statements and definitions of PMC identity of the period, as well as one of the most historically durable. For if we grant that Taylor exhibited a genuine and disturbing "mania" for control (see Banta 11 and 332, ftn. 26), we must also grant his lasting contribution to American corporate hierarchy—the continuing demand for an "educated" elite to determine how to get the most work from the workforce, complete with goals, bonuses, and strictly regulated time management.

20. Lawrence Lewis's March 1905 article, "Uplifting 17,000 Employees," highlighting the creation of a Sociological Department at the Colorado Fuel and Iron Company in 1901, is a prime example of a Scientific Management-driven tale of uplift, despite the fact that the employees were on strike at the time the article was written. See Martha Banta, *Taylored Lives*, pp. 103–106.
21. See Banta, *Taylored Lives*, pp. 113–135.
22. Banta makes a strong case for Chaplin's chief comic rival, Buster Keaton, as the exemplar of the comically Taylorized (and terrorized) individual in his short comedy *One Week*, which finds Buster negotiating human error and natural disasters in his attempts to build a do-it-yourself house. See Banta, *Taylored Lives,* pp. 8–9.
23. References to the play taken from Winchell Smith and Byron Ongley, *Brewster's Millions* (New York: Samuel French, 1907).
24. This is not to say that actors of the 1910s mumbled or muttered. There was, however, an attempt to more closely replicate the processes of speech and thought, prompted largely by an increasing interest in Freudian psychology.
25. The play apparently fell short of having universal appeal, however; although *Brewster's Millions* enjoyed long runs on Broadway and in London, it received a hostile reception for its German premiere in May 1909. With regard to the show's previous long runs, the *Vorsische Zeitung* opined with some contempt that "these figures speak less for the worth of the piece than for the easily appeased art requirements of our Anglo-Saxon cousins." See "American Play Rejected," *New York Times*, 30 May 1909: C2.
26. As it happens, Barnum *did* add the part about seeing the other fellow being humbugged.
27. Reference to *Get-Rich-Quick Wallingford* from George M. Cohan, *Get Rich Quick Wallingford,* typescript, NYPL. The typescript omits the familiar hyphens in the title.

28. Mitchell received considerable personal encouragement from Fitch, who saw great potential in the young actor. See Fitch, *Letters,* pp. 224, 234, and 308.
29. All references to *It Pays to Advertise* are from Roi Cooper Megrue and Walter Hackett, *It Pays to Advertise: A Farcical Fact in Three Acts.* In *Representative American Dramas: National and Local.* Ed. with introductions by Montrose J. Moses (Boston: Little, Brown, and Company, 1925).
30. Authors Cooper and Hackett employ the alternate spelling of "Pittsburgh" which was fairly common at the end of the nineteenth and the early twentieth century. Or else, they simply misspelled it; many people do.
31. There are contradictory accounts of the play's title and origin, partially tied to the status of Austria-Hungary that lasted until the end of the World War I. While Smith's sister identifies the play as Hungarian, the *Times* reviewer, mindful of the war effort, takes a couple of playful digs at the play's German origins: "On the basis of a Continental piece (let us not call it German) by Gabriel Dregley...its atmosphere is still Teut * * * that is, Continental" ("A Tailor-Made Man Is Amusing Comedy." *New York Times* 28 Aug. 1917: 5). Gerald Bordman provides more detail: "The comedy was based loosely on Gábor Drégely's *A szerencse fia* (The Son of Fortune)." See Gerald Bordman, *American Theatre: A Chronicle of Comedy and Drama, 1914–1930* (New York: Oxford University Press, 1995) 66.
32. References to *A Tailor-Made Man* from Harry James Smith, *A Tailor-Made Man* (New York: Samuel French, 1919).
33. Cohan, in fact, did take on the role of Wallingford toward the end of that play's run. See George M. Cohan in America's Theater, <http://www.members.tripod.com>.
34. Smith, *A Tailor-Made Man,* p. 50.

7. CONCLUSION: BUSINESS AS USUAL

1. References to *Clarence* from Booth Tarkington, *Clarence* (New York: Samuel French, 1921).
2. See Clark University website, <http://www.clarku.edu/aboutclark/timeline/1900s.cfm>, as well as David W. Sievers, *Freud on Broadway: A History of Psychoanalysis and the American Drama* (New York: Cooper Square, 1970) 35.
3. See also David Seabury, *Unmasking Our Minds* (New York: Boni and Liverwright, 1925) and Smith Ely Jeliffe and Louise Brink, *Psychoanalysis and the Drama* (Washington, DC: Nervous and Mental Disease Publishing Company, 1922) for contemporaneous commentary on the relationship

between the rise of psychoanalysis, the changing world of business, and the drama.
4. Other productions that inspired Freud-based theatrical criticism included William Legrand's *The Smouldering Flame*, on sexual repression, and Winchell Smith and Victor Mapes' *The Boomerang* (1913 and 1915, respectively). See Sievers, *Freud on Broadway*, p. 50.
5. O'Neill, *Beyond the Horizon*, pp. 201 and 206. All references to *Beyond the Horizon* from Eugene O'Neill, *Ah, Wilderness! and Two Other Plays* (New York: Modern Library, 1964). O'Neill's description of the younger brother, Robert, is similar to other "sensitive" and "poetic" (and autobiographical) O'Neill characters, including Richard in *Ah, Wilderness!* and Edmund in *Long Day's Journey Into Night*. O'Neill would also, of course, return to the description "a touch of the poet" in his play of the same title.
6. For O'Neill, the notion that Life is the enemy is closely related to God being the enemy. For example, in *All God's Chillun Got Wings*, the beleaguered Black hero Jim denounces God: "Maybe He can forgive what I've done to you; but I don't see how He's going to forgive—Himself." See O'Neill, *All God's Chillun Got Wings*, in *Ah, Wilderness! and Two Other Plays*, p. 194.
7. Probably a nod to Ibsen's Oswald, from *Ghosts*.
8. See the Internet Broadway Database, <http://www.ibdb.com/show.asp?ID=7163>.
9. Guy Bolton, *Polly Preferred,* typescript. NCOF+Bolton, NYPL, p. 1–13. All references to the play are taken from this typescript.
10. References to the play taken from Aaron Hoffman, *Give and Take* (New York: Samuel French), 1926.
11. Wainscott, in his analysis of *Give and Take,* in emphasizing the presence of the capitalist *deus ex machina*, ignores the large part that Jack's concept of industrial democracy plays in ensuring the happy ending. See Ronald Wainscott, "Commercialism Glorified and Vilified: 1920s Theatre and the Business World." In *The American Stage: Social and Economic Issues from the Colonial Period to the Present.* Ed. Ron Engle and Tice L. Miller (New York: Cambridge University Press, 1993) 178.
12. See the Internet Broadway Database, <http://www.ibdb.com/person.asp?ID=4388>, as well as Atkinson, *Broadway*, p. 80.
13. For example, the popular Laurel Drama Series, paperback collections of American plays by decade (with the titles *Famous American Plays of the...*), significantly begins with the 1920s.
14. In September 1929, Boston's Mayor Malcolm Nichols forbid the production of the play, saying that it was "a plea for the murder of unborn children, a breeding ground for atheism and domestic infidelity, and a disgusting spectacle

of immorality." Nichols had not gotten around to either seeing or reading *Strange Interlude*. See John H. Houchin, *Censorship of the American Theatre in the Twentieth Century* (New York: Cambridge University Press, 2003), esp. 111–116, "The Strange Journey of *Strange Interlude*," as well as Lane Lambert, "Banned in Boston, OK in Quincy: 1929 decision to invite O'Neill play 'Strange Interlude' to city thrust it into spotlight." *The Patriot Ledger*, 30 Sept. 2004. <http://ledger.southofboston.com/articles/2004/09/30/news/news04.txt>. See also " 'Strange Interlude' Barred at Boston," *New York Times* 17 Sept. 1929: 39; and " 'Strange Interlude' Wins Quincy's Favor," *New York Times* 1 Oct. 1929: 34. Quincy's Mayor, Thomas J. McGrath, felt that *Strange Interlude* was a "wonderful play."

15. References to the play from Eugene O'Neill, *Strange Interlude* (London: Jonathan Cape, 1928).

16. The complaint was that *Strange Interlude* violated the Wales Law, which outlawed "objectionable performances." The District Attorney's office also cleared a production of *Volpone* at the same time. Nevertheless, the Theatre Guild, which produced both shows, did agree to make some adjustments to more offensive lines. See Houchin 106–107; "One Year of 'Strange Interlude,' " *New York Times* 27 Jan. 1929: X1; and " 'Strange Interlude' Cleared By Benton," *New York Times* 2 May 1928: 16.

Bibliography

"The 1915 Follies Here Tomorrow." *New York Times* 20 June 1915: X4.

"An Absorbing Play of American Life." *New York Times* 21 Nov. 1905: 9.

Adams, Henry. *The Education of Henry Adams*. New York: Houghton and Mifflin Company, 1918.

Ade, George. *The College Widow: A Pastoral Comedy in Four Acts*. New York: Samuel French, 1924.

Allen, Robert C. *Horrible Prettiness: Burlesque and American Culture*. Chapel Hill, NC: University of North Carolina Press, 1991.

"American Play Rejected." *New York Times* 30 May 1909: C2.

Andrews, Peter. "More Sock and Less Buskin." *American Heritage Magazine* Apr. 1972: 48–57.

Aronowitz, Stanley. "The Professional-Managerial Class or Middle Strata." *Between Labor and Capital*. Ed. Pat Walker. South End Press Controversies Series, vol. 1. Boston, MA: South End Press, 1979.

"At Georgia." *New York Times* 3 Mar. 1912: X9.

"At the Theatres; Grand Opera House; 'A Gold Mine.'" *New York Dramatic Mirror* 1 Mar. 1890: 2.

"At the Theatres; Lyceum; 'The Master of Woodbarrow.'" *New York Dramatic Mirror* 6 Sept. 1890: 2.

"At the Theatres; Star Theatre; 'The Senator.'" *New York Dramatic Mirror* 18 Jan. 1890: 2.

Atkinson, Brooks. *Broadway*. New York: MacMillan Publishing Co., 1974.

———. "Laurels for 'Strange Interlude,'" *New York Times* 13 May 1928: 105.

———. "A New Theatrical Season Slowly Gathers Momentum." *New York Times* 28 Aug. 1927: X1.

"'A Bachelor's Night' Dull." *New York Times* 18 Oct. 1921: 20:1. *The New York Times Theater Reviews 1920–1970. Vol. 1.* New York: New York Times and Arno Press, 1971.

Baltzell, E. Digby. *The Protestant Establishment: Aristocracy and Caste in America*. New York: Random House, 1964.

Banta, Martha. *Taylored Lives: Narrative Productions in the Age of Taylor, Veblen and Ford*. Chicago, IL: University of Chicago Press, 1993.

Barck, Oscar Theodore, Jr., and Nelson Manfred Blake. *Since 1900: A History of the United States in Our Times*. 4th ed. New York: Macmillan, 1965.

Barnard, Charles. "Science on the Stage." *New York Dramatic Mirror* 4 Jan. 1890: 1.

Barnett, Lee. "Max Kortlander: King of the Player Piano." *Grand River Valley History* 18 (2001). 23 Aug. 2007. <http://www.doctorjazz.co.uk/maxkort.html>.

Barrymore, Ethel. *Memories, an Autobiography*. New York: Harper and Brothers, 1955.

Berger, John. "The Suit and the Photograph." *Rethinking Popular Culture: Contemporary Perspectives in Cultural Studies*. Ed. Chanddra Mukerji and Michael Schudson (Berkeley, CA: University of California Press, 1991).

Bernheim, Alfred L. *The Business of the Theatre: An Economic History of the American Theatre*, 1750–1932. 1932. New York: Benjamin Blom, 1964.

Blum, Daniel C. *A Pictorial History of the American Theatre*. New York: Greenberg, 1956.

Boardman, Fon W., Jr., *America and the Progressive Era 1900–1917*. New York: Henry Z. Walck, 1970.

Bolton, Guy. *Leave It to Jane*. Typescript. NCOF+Bolton, 1917. NYPL.

———. *Polly Preferred*. Typescript. NCOF+Bolton, 1923. NYPL.

Bolton, Guy, and P.G. Wodehouse. *Oh, Boy!* Typescript. New York: F. Roy Comstock, 1917. NCOF+Bolton, NYPL.

Bolton, Guy, and Schuyler Greene. *Very Good Eddie*. Libretto. New York: New York American Play Company, 1915. NCOF+Kern, NYPL.

Bordman, Gerald. *American Musical Comedy from Adonis to Dreamgirls*. New York: Oxford University Press, 1982.

———. *American Musical Theatre: A Chronicle*. 2nd ed. New York: Oxford University Press, 1992.

———. *American Musical Theatre: A Chronicle*. 3rd ed. New York: Oxford University Press, 2001.

———. *American Theatre: A Chronicle of Comedy and Drama, 1869–1914*. New York: Oxford University Press, 1994.

———. *American Theatre: A Chronicle of Comedy and Drama, 1914–1930*. New York: Oxford University Press, 1995.

———. *The Oxford Companion to American Theatre*. New York: Oxford University Press, 1984.

Botto, Louis. *At This Theatre: 100 Years of Broadway Shows, Stories and Stars*. New York: Playbill, 2002.

Bourdieu, Pierre. *Distinction: A Social Critique of the Judgement of Taste.* Trans. Richard Nice. Cambridge, MA: Harvard University Press, 1984.

———. "Habitus." *Habitus: A Sense of Place.* Ed. Jean Hillier and Emma Rooksby. Burlington, VT: Ashgate, 2002.

———. *In Other Words. Essays towards a Reflexive Sociology.* Stanford, CA: Stanford University Press, 1990.

———. "Sport and Social Class." *Rethinking Popular Culture: Contemporary Perspectives in Cultural Studies.* Ed. Chandra Mukerji and Michael Schudson. Berkeley, CA: University of California Press, 1991.

Braverman, Harry. *Labor and Monopoly Capital: The Degradation of Work in the Twentieth Century.* New York: Monthly Review Press, 1974.

Brewer, Mary F. *Staging Whiteness.* Middletown, CT: Wesleyan University Press, 2005.

Burns, Ric, and James Sanders. *New York: An Illustrated History.* Picture ed. Lisa Ades. New York: Alfred A. Knopf, 1999.

Butsch, Richard. *The Making of American Audiences: From Stage to Television, 1750–1900.* New York: Cambridge University Press, 2000.

Carleton, Henry Guy. "The Dramatic Millennium." *New York Dramatic Mirror* 1 Feb. 1890: 5.

Carroll, David. *The Matinee Idols.* New York: Arbor House, 1972.

Castle, Mr. and Mrs. Vernon. *Modern Dancing.* 1914. New York: DaCapo Press, 1980.

Chandler, Alfred D., Jr. *The Visible Hand: The Managerial Revolution in American Business.* Cambridge, MA: Belknap Press of Harvard University Press, 1977.

Chansky, Dorothy. *Composing Ourselves: The Little Theatre Movement and the American Audience.* Carbondale, IL: Southern Illinois University Press, 2004.

Clurman, Harold. "Introduction." *Famous American Plays of the 1930s.* New York: Dell, 1959.

Cohan, George M. *Get-Rich-Quick Wallingford.* Manuscript, 1910, NYPL.

———. *Twenty Years on Broadway: And the Years it Took to Get There.* New York: Harper and Brothers, 1925.

Cohen, Jean, and Howard, Dick. "Why Class?" *Between Labor and Capital.* Ed. Pat Walker. South End Press Controversies Series, vol. 1. Boston, MA: South End Press, 1979.

Coleman, Alta May. "Personality Portrait: Eugene O'Neill." *Theatre Magazine*, Vol. 31, No. 4, 1920. 23 Sept. 2007. <http://www.theatrehistory.com/american/oneill004.html>.

Conner, Lynne. *Spreading the Gospel of the Modern Dance: Newspaper Dance Criticism in the United States, 1850–1934.* Pittsburgh, PA: University of Pittsburgh Press, 1997.

Connolly, Thomas F. *George Jean Nathan and the Making of Modern American Drama Criticism.* Teaneck, NJ: Fairleigh Dickinson University Press, 2000.

Cook, Susan C. "Passionless Dancing and Passionate Reform: Respectability, Modernism, and the Social Dancing of Irene and Vernon Castle." *The Passion of Music and Dance: Body, Gender and Sexuality*. Ed. by William Washabaugh. New York: Berg, 1998.

Cooper, Roi Megrue, and Hackett, Walter. *It Pays to Advertise: A Farcical Fact in Three Acts*. *Representative American Dramas: National and Local*. Ed. with introduction by Montrose J. Moses. Boston, MA: Little, Brown, and Company, 1925.

Corbin, John. "The Play." *New York Times* 12 Jan. 1923: 3.

———. "Topics of the Drama." *New York Times* 11 Jan. 1903: 34.

Cromley, Elizabeth Collins. *Alone Together: A History of New York's Early Apartments*. Ithaca, NY: Cornell University Press, 1990.

Cullen, Rosemary, and Don B. Wilmeth. "Introduction." *Plays by William Hooker Gillette*. New York: Cambridge University Press, 1983.

Davis, Owen. *At Yale*. New York: Samuel French, 1906.

———. *Opportunity*. Typescript, 1923. NCOF+Davis, NYPL.

Davy, Kate. "An Interview with George Burns." *Educational Theatre Journal* Oct. 1975: 3.

de Mille, William C. *Strongheart*. New York: Samuel French, 1909.

Desmond, Jane C. "Embodying Difference: Issues in Dance and Cultural Studies." *Meaning in Motion: New Cultural Studies of Dance*. Ed. Jane C. Desmond. Durham, NC: Duke University Press, 1997.

Dithmar, Edward. "James A. Herne's Margaret Fleming." *American Theatre as Seen by Its Critics, 1752–1934*. Ed. Montrose J. Moses and John Mason Brown. New York: W.W. Norton and Co., 1934.

Dithmar, Edward A. "The Week at Theatres." *New York Times* 17 Apr. 1898: 9.

Dos Passos, John. *U.S.A.: The Big Money*. New York: Library of America, 1996.

Dreiser, Theodore. *Sister Carrie*. Cambridge, MA: Robert Bentley, 1971.

Ehrenreich, Barbara, and John Ehrenreich. "The Professional-Managerial Class." *Between Labor and Capital*. Ed. Pat Walker. South End Press Controversies Series, vol. 1. Boston, MA: South End Press, 1979.

Emery, Lynne Fauley. *Black Dance from 1619 to Today*. 2nd ed. Hightstown, NJ: Princeton Book Company, 1988.

Emery, Michael, and Edwin Emery. *The Press and America: An Interpretive History of the Mass Media*. 7th ed. Englewood Cliffs, NJ: Prentice Hall, 1992.

"The Emperor Jones." *Shadowland* Jan. 1921: 57. *Selected Theatre Criticism Volume II: 1920–1930*. Ed. Anthony Slide. Metuchen, NJ: Scarecrow Press, 1986.

Erenberg, Lewis A. *Steppin' Out: New York Nightlife and the Transformation of American Culture, 1890–1930*. Westport, CT: Greenwood Press, 1981.

Faulkner, Harold Underwood. *The Quest for Social Justice 1898–1914. A History of American Life*. Vol. XI. Ed. Arthur M. Schlesinger and Dixon Ryan Fox. New York: MacMillan, 1931.

Fiske, Minnie Maddern. "To the Actor in the Making." *Actors on Acting: The Theories, Techniques, and Practices of the World's Great Actors, Told in Their Own Words.* Ed. Toby Cole and Helen Krich Chinoy. New York: Three Rivers Press, 1970.

Fiske, Stephen. "The Acting of the Comedy." Souvenir 100th Representation of *Beau Brummell* Program. Philadelphia, PA: R.C. Hartranft, 1890.

Fitch, Clyde. *Beau Brummell. Plays by Clyde Fitch in Four Volumes.* Vol. 1. Ed. Montrose J. Moses and Virginia Gerson. Boston, MA: Little, Brown, and Company, 1915.

———. *The City: A Modern Play of American Life in Three Acts. Plays by Clyde Fitch in Four Volumes.* Vol. 4. Boston, MA: Little, Brown, and Company, 1915.

———. *The Climbers. Plays by Clyde Fitch in Four Volumes.* Vol. 2. Ed. Montrose J. Moses and Virginia Gerson. Boston, MA: Little, Brown, and Company, 1915.

———. *Clyde Fitch and His Letters.* Ed. Montrose J. Moses and Virginia Gerson. Boston, MA: Little, Brown, and Company, 1924.

———. *The Cowboy and the Lady.* New York: Samuel French, 1908.

———. *The Girl with the Green Eyes.* New York: Macmillan, 1905.

———. *Her Own Way.* Plays by Clyde Fitch in Four Volumes. Vol. 3. Ed. Montrose J. Moses and Virginia Gerson. Boston, MA: Little, Brown, and Company, 1915.

———. *The Moth and the Flame. Representative Plays by American Dramatists.* Ed. Montrose Moses. 1921. New York: Benjamin Blom, 1964.

———. "The Play and the Public." *Plays by Clyde Fitch in Four Volumes.* Vol. 4. Ed. Montrose J. Moses and Virginia Gerson. Boston, MA: Little, Brown, and Company, 1921.

"Follies of 1907." *New York Times* 9 July 1907: 7.

Gassner, John. "The Happy Years, the Advancing Theatre." *Twenty-Five Best Plays of the Modern American Theatre.* New York: Crown, 1949.

Rev. of *George Washington, Jr. New York Evening Post Mail*, 12 Feb. 1906. Robinson Locke collection of dramatic scrapbooks, New York Public Library, Lincoln Center, New York City.

Gillette, William Hooker. "The Illusion of the First Time in Acting." *Actors on Acting.* Ed. Toby Cole and Helen Krich Chinoy. New York: Three Rivers Press, 1970.

———. *Sherlock Holmes. A Drama in Four Acts. Plays by William Hooker Gillette.* Eds. Rosemary Cullen and Don B. Wilmeth. New York: Cambridge University Press, 1983.

———. "Will It Live?" *New York Dramatic Mirror* 25 Jan. 1890: 1.

"Girls and Glitter in 'Follies of 1911.'" *New York Times* 27 June 1911: 9.

Glenn, Susan Anita. "Give an Imitation of Me: Vaudeville Mimics and the Play of the Self." *American Quarterly* 50.1 (Mar. 1998): 47–76.

Golden, Eve. *Vernon and Irene Castle's Ragtime Revolution.* Lexington, KY: University Press of Kentucky, 2007.

Goodrum, Charles, and Helen Dalrymple. *Advertising in America: The First 200 Years.* New York: Harry N. Abrams, 1990.

Green, Harvey. "Introduction." *Fitness in American Culture: Images of Health, Sport, and the Body, 1830–1940.* Ed. Kathryn Grover. Amherst, MA: University of Massachusetts Press, 1989.

Greenfield, Thomas A. *Work and the Work Ethic in American Drama, 1920–1970.* Columbia, MO: University of Missouri Press, 1982.

Grimsted, David. *Melodrama Unveiled: American Theater and Culture, 1800–1850.* Chicago, IL: University of Chicago Press, 1968.

Hapgood, Norman. "Richard Mansfield's Henry V." *American Theatre As Seen By Its Critics, 1752–1934.* Ed. Montrose J. Moses and John Mason Brown. New York: W.W. Norton and Co., 1934.

Harris, Michael R. "Iron Therapy and Tonics." *Fitness in American Culture: Images of health, Sport, and the Body, 1830–1940.* Ed. Kathryn Grover. Amherst, MA: University of Massachusetts Press, 1989.

Hay, Peter. *Broadway Anecdotes.* New York: Oxford University Press, 1989.

Heimann, Jim, ed. *All-American Ads 1900–1919.* Los Angeles, : Taschen, 2005.

Heller, Steven. "1900–1919: Seducing the New Consumer." *All-American Ads 1900–1919.* Ed. Jim Heimann. Los Angeles, CA: Taschen, 2005.

"'Hello Broadway' Is Vastly Amusing." *New York Times* 26 Dec. 1914: 7.

"'The Henrietta.'" *New York Times* 27 Sept. 1887: 4.

Hillier, Jean, and Emma Rooksby. "Introduction." *Habitus: A Sense of Place.* Ed. *Jean Hillier and Emma Rooksby.* Burlington, VT: Ashgate, 2002.

Hischak, Thomas S. *The Theatregoer's Almanac.* Westport, CT: Greenwood Press, 1997.

Historical Statistics of the United States: Earliest Times to the Present. Vol. 2. Ed. Susan B. Carter, Scott Sigmund Gartner, Michael R. Haines, Alan L. Olmstead, Richard Sutch, and Gavin Wright. New York: Cambridge University Press, 2006.

Hodin, Mark. "The Disavowal of Ethnicity: Legitimate Theatre and the Social Construction of Literary Value in Turn-of-the-Century America." *Theatre Journal* 52.2 (2000): 211–226.

Hoffman, Aaron. *Give and Take.* New York: Samuel French, 1926.

"Holbrook Blinn Fine Figure in 'The Boss.'" *New York Times* 31 Jan. 1911: 10.

Holme, Bryan. *Advertising: Reflections of a Century.* New York: Viking Press, 1982.

Hornblow, Arthur. *A History of the Theatre in America from Its Beginnings to the Present Time.* Vol. II. 1919. New York: Benjamin Blom, 1965.

Houchin, John H. *Censorship of the American Theatre in the Twentieth Century.* New York: Cambridge University Press, 2003.

Howard, Bronson. *The Henrietta*. London: Samuel French, 1901.
Ignatiev, Noel. *How the Irish Became White*. New York: Routledge, 1995.
"The Indian in the Drama." *New York Times* 19 Feb. 1905: X2.
"It is...no more nor less than an outrage..." *New York Dramatic Mirror* 11 Jan. 1890: 2.
Jeliffe, Smith Ely, and Louise Brink. *Psychoanalysis and the Drama*. Washington, DC: Nervous and Mental Disease Publishing Company, 1922.
"John Drew at Palmer's." *New York Times* 4 Oct. 1892: 4.
"John Drew Thrown Off Horse and Hurt." *New York Times* 8 Dec. 1909: 2.
Jones, Robert W. *Journalism in the United States*. New York: E.P. Dutton and Co., 1947.
Kasson, John F. *Rudeness and Civility: Manners in Nineteenth-Century Urban America*. New York: Hill and Wang, 1990.
Kelly, Fred C. *George Ade: Warmhearted Satirist*. New York: Bobbs-Merrill, 1947.
Kerr, Walter. *Journey to the Center of the Theater*. New York: Alfred A. Knopf, 1979.
Kinsey, Sally Buchanan. "William Gillette: America's Sherlock Lived the Role." *Sherlock Holmes: Victorian Sleuth to Modern Hero*. Ed. Charles R. Putney, Joseph A. Cutshall King, and Sally Sugerman. Latham, MD: Scarecrow Press, 1996.
Klauber, Adolph. "The New George M. Cohan." *New York Times* 29 Sept. 1912: X2.
Klein, Alvin. "Theatre in Review; Oh, Boy! Is Delightfully Silly." *New York Times* 6 Nov. 1983. 23 Sept. 2007. <http://query.nytimes.com/gst/fullpage.html?res=950DE5D91739F935A 35752C1A965948260>.
Klein, Charles. *The Lion and the Mouse*. New York: Samuel French, 1916.
"Knickerbocker—The Cowboy and the Lady." *New York Dramatic Mirror* 6 Jan. 1900.
Lambert, Lane. "Banned in Boston, OK in Quincy: 1929 Decision to Invite O'Neill Play 'Strange Interlude' to City Thrust it into Spotlight." *Patriot Ledger* 30 Sept. 2004. 24 Sept. 2007. <http://ledger.southofboston.com/articles/2004/09/30/news/news04.txt>.
Lancaster, Albert Edmund. "The Secret of Popularity." *New York Dramatic Mirror* 17 May 1890: 2.
Leach, William. *Land of Desire: Merchants, Power and the Rise of a New American Culture*. New York: Pantheon Books, 1993.
Lears, T.J. Jackson. "American Advertising and the Reconstruction of the Body, 1880–1930." *Fitness in American Culture: Images of Health, Sport, and the Body, 1830–1940*. Ed. by Kathryn Grover. Amherst, MA: University of Massachusetts Press, 1989.
———. *No Place of Grace: Antimodernism and the Transformation of American Culture 1880–1920*. New York: Pantheon Books, 1981.
Lears, T.J. Jackson, and Richard Wightman Fox. "Introduction." *Culture of Consumption: Critical Essays in American History, 1880–1980*. New York: Pantheon Books, 1983.

"'Leave It to Jane,' The College Widow." *New York Times* 29 Aug. 1917: 6.

"'Letters' of Clyde Fitch and 'The Truth at Last' about Charles Hawtrey." *New York Times Book Review* 2 Nov. 1924: BR7.

Levine, Lawrence. *Highbrow/Lowbrow: The Emergence of Cultural Hierarchy in America*. Cambridge, MA: Harvard University Press, 1988.

Lewis, Emory. *Stages: The Fifty-Year Childhood of the American Theatre*. Englewood Cliffs, NJ: Prentice-Hall, 1969.

Loney, Glenn. "Introduction." *The House of Mirth: The Play of the Novel*. Rutherford, NJ: Farleigh Dickinson University Press, 1988.

Lutz, Tom. *American Nervousness, 1903: An Anecdotal History*. Ithaca, NY: Cornell University Press, 1991.

Mansfield, Richard. "Originality." *Actors on Acting*. Ed. Toby Cole and Helen Krich Chinoy. New York: Three Rivers Press, 1949.

Marbury, Elisabeth. "Foreword." *Modern Dancing*. 1914. New York: Da Capo Press, 1980.

Marra, Kim. "Clyde Fitch's Too Wilde Love." *Staging Desire: Queer Readings of American Theater History*. Ed. Kim Marra and Robert A. Schanke. Ann Arbor, MI: University of Michigan Press, 2002.

———. *Strange Duets: Impresarios and Actresses in the American Theatre, 1865–1914*. Iowa City, IA: University of Iowa Press, 2006.

Marx, Karl. *Capital*. Vol. 3. Trans. David Fernbach. New York: Penguin Books, 1991.

"The Matinee Girl." *New York Dramatic Mirror* 6 Jan. 1900: 2.

"Matinee Lady." *New York Dramatic Mirror* 6 Jan. 1900: 2.

Matthews, Brander. *On Acting*. New York: Charles Scribner's Sons, 1914.

McArthur, Benjamin. *Actors and American Culture, 1880–1920*. Philadelphia, PA: Temple University Press, 1986.

McCabe, John. *George M. Cohan: The Man Who Owned Broadway*. Garden City, NY: Doubleday and Co., 1973.

McConachie, Bruce A. "Case Study: Discoursing on Desire: Desire Under the Elms in the 1920s." *Theatre Histories: An Introduction*. Ed. Phillip B. Zarrilli, Bruce McConachie, Gary Jay Williams, and Carol Fisher Sorgenfrei. New York: Routledge, 2006.

———. *Melodramatic Formations: Studies in Theatre History and Culture*. Iowa City, IA: University of Iowa Press, 1992.

McNamara, Brooks. *The Shuberts of Broadway: A History Drawn from the Collection of the Shubert Archive*. New York: Oxford University Press, 1990.

McTeague, James. *Before Stanislavsky: American Professional Acting Schools and Acting Theory, 1875–1925*. Metuchen, NJ: Scarecrow Press, 1993.

Megrue, Roi Cooper, and Walter Hackett. *It Pays to Advertise: A Farcical Fact in Three Acts. Representative American Dramas: National and Local*. Ed. with introductions by Montrose J. Moses. Boston, MA: Little, Brown, and Company, 1925.

Metcalfe, James. "Brown of Harvard." *Life Magazine* 8 Mar. 1906. *Selected Theatre Criticism, Volume 1: 1900–1919*. Ed. Anthony Slide. Metuchen, NJ: Scarecrow Press, 1985.

———. "The College Widow." *Life* Magazine, 6 Oct. 1904. Slide, *Selected Theatre Criticism, Volume 1: 1900–1919*.

———. "Edward Shelton's The New York Idea." *American Theatre As Seen By Its Critics, 1752–1934*. Ed. Montrose J. Moses and John Mason Brown. New York: W.W. Norton and Co., 1934.

———. "George Washington, Jr." *Life Magazine*. 1 Mar. 1906. Slide, *Selected Theatre Criticism, Volume 1: 1900–1919*.

———. "George Washington, Jr." *New York Evening Post Mail* 12 Feb. 1906: n.p.

Miller, Tice L. *Bohemians and Critics: American Theatre Criticism in the Nineteenth Century*. Metuchen, NJ: Scarecrow Press, 1981.

———. "Criticism." *Cambridge Guide to American Theatre*. Ed. Don B. Wilmeth and Tice L. Miller. New York, Cambridge University Press, 1996.

———. "James G. Huneker." *Cambridge Guide to American Theatre*.

"Miss Venita Gould Pleases at Keith's." *Tech* 17 May 1922: 2.

Mizejewski, Linda. *Ziegfeld Girl: Image and Icon in Culture and Cinema*. Durham, NC: Duke University Press, 1999.

Mordden, Ethan. *Broadway Babies: The People Who Made the American Musical*. New York: Oxford University Press, 1983.

Morehouse, Ward. *George M. Cohan: Prince of the American Theater*. Philadelphia, PA: J.B. Lippincott, 1943.

Moses, Montrose. *The American Dramatist*. 1925. New York: Benjamin Blom, 1964.

———. "Introduction." *Representative Plays by American Dramatists, Vol. 3, 1856–1911*, 1921. New York: Benjamin Blom, 1964.

Moses, Montrose and Virginia Gerson. "Introduction." *Clyde Fitch and His Letters*. Ed. Montrose J. Moses and Virginia Gerson. Boston, MA: Little, Brown and Company, 1924.

———. "Introduction." In *Plays by Clyde Fitch in Four Volumes*. Vols. 1–4. Boston, MA: Little, Brown, and Company, 1915.

"Mr. Goodwin in 'Nathan Hale' at the Knickerbocker Theatre." *New York Times* 3 Jan. 1899: 9.

"Mr. Mansfield's endeavor…," *New York Dramatic Mirror* 25 Jan. 1890: 2.

Mrozek, Donald J. "Sport in American Life: From National Health to Personal Fulfillment, 1890–1940." *Fitness in American Culture: Images of Health, Sport, and the Body, 1830–1940*. Ed. Kathryn Grover. Amherst, MA: University of Massachusetts Press, 1989.

Mulvey, Laura. "Visual Pleasure and Narrative Cinema." *Screen* 16.3 (1975): 6–18.
Murphy, Brenda. *American Realism and American Drama, 1880–1940.* New York: Cambridge University Press, 1987.
"Musical Comedies' Vogue Said to Be on the Wane." *New York Times* 7 Sept. 1902: 10.
Nathan, George Jean. *The Theatre, the Drama, the Girls.* New York: Knopf, 1921.
———. *The World in Falseface.* New York: Knopf, 1923.
"New Dances that Have Smoothness as a Keynote." *New York Times* 1 Nov. 1914: SM2.
"New Plays Last Night—The Sultan of Sulu at Wallack's." *New York Times* 30 Dec. 1902: 9.
"New Princess Play Is the Best of All." *New York Times* 20 Feb. 1917: 7.
Noble, David. "The PMC: A Critique." *Between Labor and Capital.* Ed. Pat Walker. South End Press Controversies Series, vol. 1. Boston, MA: South End Press, 1979.
Norton, Elliot. "Puffers, Pundits and Other Play Reviewers: A Short History of American Dramatic Criticism." *The American Theatre: A Sum of Its Parts.* New York: Samuel French, 1971.
O'Neill, Eugene. *All God's Chillun Got Wings. Ah, Wilderness! and Two Other Plays.* New York: Modern Library, 1964.
———. *Beyond the Horizon. Ah, Wilderness! and Two Other Plays.*
———. *The Iceman Cometh.* New York: Vintage Books, 1967.
———. *Strange Interlude.* London: Jonathan Cape, 1928.
"One Year of 'Strange Interlude.'" *New York Times* 27 Jan. 1929, p. X1.
Park, Roberta J. "Healthy, Moral, and Strong: Educational Views of Exercise and Athletics in Nineteenth-Century America." *Fitness in American Culture: Images of Health, Sport, and the Body, 1830–1940.* Ed. Kathryn Grover. Amherst, MA: University of Massachusetts Press, 1989.
"Parted by Dance Craze." *New York Times* 7 Jan. 1915: 22.
"Pastors Approve Ban on the Tango." *New York Times* 5 Jan. 1914: 5.
Patterson, Jerry E. *The City of New York: A History Illustrated from the Collections of the Museum of the City of New York.* New York: Harry N. Abrams, 1978.
Peple, Edward. *A Pair of Sixes.* New York: Samuel French, 1917.
Pfister, Joel. *Staging Depth: Eugene O'Neill and the Politics of Psychological Discourse.* Chapel Hill, NC: University of North Carolina Press, 1995.
Poggi, Jack. *Theatre in America: The Impact of Economic Forces, 1870–1967.* Ithaca, NY: Cornell University Press, 1968.
Pollock, Channing. "Get-Rich-Quick-Wallingford." *The Green Book* (Dec. 1910). *Selected Theatre Criticism Volume 1: 1900–1919.* Ed. Anthony Slide. Metuchen, NJ: Scarecrow Press, 1985.
———. "It Pays to Advertise." *The Green Book* (Oct. 1914). Slide, *Selected Theatre Criticism Volume I.*

Postlewait, Thomas. "The Hieroglyphic Stage." *The Cambridge History of American Theatre, Vol. II: 1870–1945.* Ed. Don B. Wilmeth and Christopher Bigsby. New York: Cambridge University Press, 1999.

Postone, Moishe, LiPuma, Edward, and Craig Calhoun. "Introduction: Bourdieu and Social Theory." *Bourdieu: Critical Perspectives.* Chicago, IL: University of Chicago Press, 1993.

Quinn, Arthur Hobson. *A History of the American Drama: From the Civil War to the Present Day.* Vol. 2. New York: F.S. Crofts and Co., 1945.

Reed-Danahay, Deborah. *Locating Bourdieu.* Bloomington, IN: Indiana University Press, 2005.

Reid, Louis R. "Beyond the Horizon." *New York Dramatic Mirror* 14 Feb. 1920. Slide, *Selected Theatre Criticism, Volume II* 258.

"Reviews of New Plays: Yorkville—At Yale." *New York Dramatic Mirror* 10 Oct. 1907: 3.

"Revival Full of Laughs." *New York Times* 22 Oct. 1929: 33.

Robbins, Derek. *Bourdieu and Culture.* Thousand Oaks, CA: SAGE, 2000.

Roediger, David R. *Working Toward Whiteness: How America's Immigrants Became White.* New York: Basic Books, 2005.

Sachs, Curt. *World History of the Dance.* Trans. Bessie Schonberg. New York: W.W. Norton and Company, 1937.

Sayler, Oliver M. *Our American Theatre.* 1923. New York: Benjamin Blom, 1971.

Seabury, David. *Unmasking Our Minds.* New York: Boni and Liverwright, 1925.

Seely, Bruce E. "European Contributions to American Engineering Education: Blending Old and New." *Quaderns D'historia de L'enginyeria* III (1999):18–20.

———. "Research, Engineering, and Science in American Engineering Colleges: 1900–1960." *Technology and Culture* 34.2 (Apr. 1993): 344–386.

"Selznick Presents." Time 1 July 1935. *Time Archives*, Time 14 Sept. 2007 <http://www.time.com/magazine/article/0,9171,770045,00.html>.

Senelick, Laurence. *The Changing Room: Sex, Drag and Theatre.* New York: Routledge, 2000.

Shaughnessy, Edward L. "A Connecticut Yankee in the Wilderness: The Sterner Stuff of O'Neill's Comedy," *The Recorder: A Journal of the American Irish Historical Society* (1989). 19 Sept. 2007. <http://www.eoneill.com/library/on/shaughnessy/recorder.htm>.

Shawn, Ted. *Every Little Movement: A Book about François Delsarte.* Princeton, NJ: Princeton Book Co., 1976.

Sheaffer, Louis. *O'Neill: Son and Artist.* Boston, MA: Little, Brown, and Company, 1973.

Sheets-Johnstone, Maxine. *The Primacy of Movement.* Philadelphia, PA: John Benjamins, 1999.

Sheldon, Edward. *The Boss. Representative American Dramas.* Ed. Arthur Hobson Quinn. New York: Appleton-Century-Crofts, 1953.
Sievers, W. David. *Freud on Broadway: A History of Psychoanalysis and the American Drama.* New York: Cooper Square, 1970.
Sklar, Martin. *The United States as a Developing Country: Studies in U.S. History in the Progressive Era and the 1920s.* New York: Cambridge University Press, 1992.
Slosson, Preston William. *The Great Crusade and After: 1914–1928.* In *A History of American Life.* Vol. XII. Ed. Arthur M. Schlesinger and Dixon Ryan Fox. New York: MacMillan, 1930.
Smith, Edith, "Introduction." *A Tailor-Made Man,* by Harry James Smith. New York: Samuel French, 1919.
Smith, Harry James. *A Tailor-Made Man.* New York: Samuel French, 1919.
Smith, Winchell, and Bryan Ongley. *Brewster's Millions.* New York: Samuel French, 1907.
"The Stage To-day." *New York Dramatic Mirror.* 11 Jan. 1890: 2.
"'Strange Interlude' Barred at Boston," *New York Times* 17 Sept. 1929: 39.
"'Strange Interlude' Cleared By Benton," *New York Times* 2 May 1928: 16.
"'Strange Interlude' Wins Quincy's Favor," *New York Times* 1 Oct. 1929: 34.
"'Strongheart' Well Liked." *New York Times* 7 Feb. 1905: 9.
Susman, Warren. *Culture as History: The Transformation of American Society in the Twentieth Century.* New York: Pantheon Books, 1984.
"A Tailor-Made Man Is Amusing Comedy." *New York Times* 28 Aug. 1917: 5.
Rev. of *A Tailor-Made Man. New York Dramatic Mirror.* 8 Sept. 1917: 8. Slide, *Selected Theatre Criticism Volume 1: 1900–1919* 272.
Tarbell, Ida M. *The History of the Standard Oil Company.* New York: McClure, Philips and Co., 1904.
Tarkington, Booth. *Clarence.* New York: Samuel French, 1921.
Taylor, Frederick Winslow. *The Principles of Scientific Management.* New York: Harper and Brothers, 1911.
This Fabulous Century, vol. 1, 1900–1910. Series ed. Ezra Brown. New York: Time-Life Books, 1969.
Thomas, Augustus. *In Mizzoura. Representative Plays by American Dramatists, Vol. 3, 1856–1911.* 1921. New York: Benjamin Blom, 1964.
Tomkins, Vincent, ed. *American Decades 1910–1919.* Detroit, MI: Gale Research, 1996.
———, ed. *American Eras: Development of the Industrial United States, 1878–1899.* New York: Gale Research, 1997.
Towse, John Ranken. *Sixty Years of the Theater: An Old Critic's Memories.* New York: Funk & Wagnalls Company, 1916.

Trager, James. *The New York Chronology: The Ultimate Compendium of Events, People, and Anecdotes from the Dutch to the Present.* New York: Harper Collins, 2003.

U.S. Census Bureau. *Statistical Abstract of the United States, 2003.*

"Very Funny Satire of Common Failing." *New York Times* 20 Sept. 1910: 11.

Wainscott, Ronald. "Commercialism glorified and vilified: 1920s theatre and the business world." *The American Stage: Social and Economic Issues From the Colonial Period to the Present.* Ed. Ron Engle and Tice L. Miller. New York: Cambridge University Press, 1993.

———. *The Emergence of the Modern American Theater 1914–1929.* New Haven, CT: Yale University Press, 1997.

———. "Plays and Playwrights: 1896–1915." *The Cambridge History of American Theatre, Vol. II.*

Walker, Julia. *Expressionism and Modernism in the American Theatre: Bodies, Voices, Words.* New York: Cambridge University Press, 2005.

Walker, Pat. "Introduction." *Between Labor and Capital.* Ed. Pat Walker. South End Press Controversies Series. Vol. 1. Boston, MA: South End Press, 1979.

Ward, A.W., W.P. Trent, J. Erskine, S.P. Sherman, and C. Van Doren. *The Cambridge History of English and American Literature.* New York: G.P. Putnam's Sons, 1907–21. New York: Bartleby.com, 2000. 22 May 2007. 16 Sept. 2007. <www.bartleby.com/cambridge/>.

"'Watch Your Step' Hilarious Fun." *New York Times* 9 Dec. 1914: 13.

Webb, Jen, Tony Schirato, and Geogg Danaher. *Understanding Bourdieu.* London: SAGE, 2002.

Whaples, Robert. "Hours of Work in U.S. History". *EH.Net Encyclopedia.* Ed. Robert Whaples. 15 Aug. 2001. 20 Sept. 2007. <http://eh.net/encyclopedia/article/whaples.work.hours.us>.

Wharton, Edith. *A Backward Glance: An Autobiography.* 1933. New York: Touchstone, 1998.

Whorton, James C. "Eating to Win: Popular Concepts of Diet, Strength, and Energy in the Early Twentieth Century." *Fitness in American Culture: Images of health, Sport, and the Body, 1830–1940.* Ed. Kathryn Grover. Amherst, MA: University of Massachusetts Press, 1989.

Wiebe, Robert H. *The Search for Order: 1877–1920.* New York: Hill and Wang, 1967.

Williams, Raymond. *Modern Tragedy.* London: Chatto and Windus, 1969.

Wilmeth, Don B., and Christopher Bigsby, eds. *The Cambridge History of American Theatre, Vol. II: 1870–1945.* New York: Cambridge University Press, 1999.

Wilson, Garff B. *Three Hundred Years of American Drama and Theatre from Ye Bare and ye Cubb to Chorus Line.* Englewood Cliffs, NJ: Prentice-Hall, 1982.

Winter, William. *The Wallet of Time.* Vol. 2. 1913. New York: Benjamin Blom, 1969.

Wodehouse, P.G., and Guy Bolton. *Bring On the Girls! The Improbable Story of Our Life in Musical Comedy, with Pictures to Prove It*. New York: Simon and Schuster, 1953.

Woollcott, Alexander. "The Play" (Rev. of *Beyond the Horizon*). *New York Times*, 10 Mar. 1920: 9.

———. "The Play" (Rev. of *Ladies Night*). *New York Times* 10 Aug. 1920 10:1. *The New York Times Theater Reviews 1920–1970*, vol. 1.

———. "The Play." (Rev. of *No More Blondes*). *New York Times* 8 Jan. 1920 22:1. *The New York Times Theater Reviews 1920–1970*, vol. 1.

Wray, Matt. *Not Quite White: White Trash and the Boundaries of Whiteness*. Durham, NC: Duke University Press, 2006.

Wright, Erik Olin. "Intellectuals and the Class Structure of Capitalist Society." *Between Labor and Capital*. Ed. Pat Walker. South End Press Controversies Series, vol. 1. Boston, MA: South End Press, 1979.

———. "Social Class." *Encyclopedia of Social Theory*. Ed. George Ritzer. New York: SAGE, 2004.

Young, Rida Johnson. *Brown of Harvard*. New York: G.P. Putnam's Sons, 1907.

Zinn, Howard. *A People's History of the United States, 1492–Present*. New York: Harper Collins, 2003.

Index

Actors' Equity, 18, 165
  strike, 47–9
Adams, Henry, 24
Adams, Maude, 53, 65
Ade, George, 16, 52, 80–4, 107, 116
Adding Machine, The, 144, 166
advertising, 10, 17, 27, 33–5, 37, 44, 53, 66, 77, 103, 117, 143–6, 167
  theatre programs, 33–5, 37–9, 51
Aguinaldo, Emilio, 106
Ah, Wilderness!, 49, 126
  see also Cohan, George M.; O'Neill, Eugene
Allen, Robert C., 102
American Dance Club of Paris, 119
American Mercury, The, 45
American Society of Composers, Authors, and Publishers (ASCAP), 109
American Tobacco, 23
Anderson, Maxwell, 165
"Anglo-Saxon revitalization," 77
Anna Christie, 46, 166
Anti-Imperialist League, 106
Aristophanes, 82
Astaire, Fred, 120
Astor, The, 119
automobiles, 32
  in advertisements, 37
  see also advertising, theatre programs

Bachelor's Night, A, 165
Ballin' the Jack, 124
Baltzell, E. Digby, 29
Banta, Martha, 138
Barbara Fidgety, 131
  see also Fitch, Clyde
Barbara Frietchie, 131
  see also Fitch, Clyde
Barck, Oscar Theodore, Jr., 94
Barnum, P. T., 142
Barry, Philip, 166
Barrymore, Ethel, 48, 65
Barrymore, John, 18
Barrymore, Maurice, 15
Bartholomae, Philip, 109
Bass (Ale), 51
  see also advertising, theatre programs
Beau Brummell, 11, 34, 65
  see also Fitch, Clyde
Behrman, S. N., 166
Belasco (theatre), 28
Belasco, D., 53
Berlin, Irving, 109, 120, 135
Bernhardt, Sarah, 33
  see also advertising, theatre programs
Bernheim, Alfred L., 25, 26, 27, 53
Beyond the Horizon, 18, 156–9, 164, 167
  see also O'Neill, Eugene
Big Money, The, 24
Blake, Nelson Manfred, 94

Blinn, Holbrook, 99
Bloodgood, Clara, 65, 74
Bohemian, The, 45
"Bolshevikism," 161
Bolton, Guy, 109–11, 113–14, 116, 160–1
Booth, Edwin, 55, 133
Booth, The (theatre), 28
Bordman, Gerald, 72, 101, 108, 109, 113, 135
Boss, The, 94, 97–9
Boston Transcript, 131, 133
Boucicault, D., 90
Bourdieu, Pierre, 8–10, 16–17, 42, 86, 92, 118, 121
  on cultural capital, 8, 86
  on fields, 10, 16–17
  sociology of, 8
  theories of habitus, 9–10
Brando, Marlon, 133
"brave front," 36, 122, 146, 147, 149
Braverman, Harry, 5
Brewer, Mary, 30, 89
Brewster's Millions, 139–41
Bring on the Girls, 110
Brink, Louise, 159
Broadhurst, The (theatre), 28
Broadway, 1–2, 9, 10–13, 15–16, 19, 24, 40, 47, 58, 59, 60, 61, 62, 63, 65, 67, 72, 79, 87, 92, 105, 109, 117, 124, 125, 126, 128, 132, 133, 135, 136, 151, 153, 154, 155, 159, 160, 163, 164, 165, 166, 167, 168
  actors' strike and, 49
  audiences, 18, 58, 64, 68, 70, 79, 82, 97, 107–8, 114, 131, 139, 141, 143
  Broadway as field, 9–11, 16–17, 78, 133

building of theatres, 25, 28
business of, 18, 25, 33, 39
business plays on, 19, 94, 136, 138, 142, 146
collegiate plays on, 19, 78, 80–2, 84
cost of tickets, 32
evolution of critics on, 39–41, 45–7
geography of, 27
manners on, 51–2
musicals on, 101, 107–8, 113, 116, 120
portrayals of nervousness on, 19, 58, 74
Victorian sensibility on, 54–6
Brown of Harvard, 14, 15, 19, 26, 80, 84, 89–94, 114
Bunny Hug, 120, 121
Burke, Billie, 131
Burr MacIntosh Monthly, The, 45
Butsch, Richard, 41, 42, 81, 126, 131

Cake-Walk, 123–4
Calvin, John, 83
Cantor, Eddie, 128
Capital, 4
  see also Marx, Karl
capitalism (American corporate), 6, 7, 12, 95, 96, 98, 163
  failure of, 168
  Grant Mitchell's characters and, 146
  PMC stage characters preserving, 97
  psychoanalysis and, 155
  role of PMC in, 25, 30, 42, 117
  scientific management and, 135–6
  as subject for drama, 17, 19, 58, 94
  as subject for farce, 136, 138
  Ziegfeld Follies and, 105
Carleton, Henry Guy, 57
Carlisle Indian Industrial School, 88
Carnegie, Andrew, 90, 106, 117
Carpenter, Edward Childs, 46

"carriage trade," 36, 53, 61
Carroll, David, 63
Castle, Irene, 15, 20, 118, 120, 149
Castle, Vernon, 15, 20, 118, 120, 149
Castle House, 120–1
Castle Walk, 119
Catholics, 29
  assimilation of, 31
"Célibat et condition paysanne" (essay), 118
Century, The, 45
Chandler, Alfred Jr., 2
Chansky, Dorothy, 165
Chaplin, C., 138
Chester, George Randolph, 142
Chicago Tribune, 25
chief electrician, 26
chorus girls, 49, 53, 108, 109
  comparison with "Ziegfeld girls," 102–4
cigars, 51
  see also advertising, theatre programs
City, The, 63, 65, 67–70, 74, 96, 98
  see also Fitch, Clyde
Civil War, 18, 40
Claire, Ina, 103
Clarence, 153–4
Clark University, 154
cleanliness
  hygienic, 35
  in the theatre, 52
Climbers, The, 72
  see also Fitch, Clyde
Clurman, Harold, 160
Coca Cola, 145
Cohan, George M., 15, 17, 20, 26, 36, 49, 91, 101, 125–36, 139–43, 146–7, 151, 159, 165
"Cohanizing," 136, 139, 141, 148, 159

Cohen, Jean, 3
college degrees
  number conferred, 80–1
college football, 16, 77, 81–6, 88, 93
College Widow, The, 11, 16, 19, 80–4, 90, 114, 116
Collison, Wilson, 165
Columbia (University), 85, 86, 89
Columbia Records, 39
combination system, 25
comic operas, 101
Connolly, Thomas F., 41, 45
Conrad, Joseph, 46
Cook, Susan C., 118, 119, 121
Cooper Megrue, Roi, 143, 144
Corbin, John, 107, 108, 161
Cornell, 79
Cort, The (theatre), 28
Cosmopolitan, 53, 67
Craig's Wife, 99, 166
Crane, W. H., 59
Cromley, Elizabeth Collins, 31–2
Crothers, Rachel, 1
Cullen, Rosemary, 63
cultural capital, 8, 36, 42, 70, 74, 83, 86, 103, 155, 165
"cultured" elite, 40, 74, 77, 86, 90

Daly's, 58
Dana, Charles A., 43
"dance craze," 119
"dandies," 39
Darktown Follies, 124
Dartmouth, 79
Davis, Owen, 172n, 183n
de Mille, William C., 84–5, 87–8
Dean, James, 133
Delmonico's, 119
Delsarte, 170n

Depression, The, 33, 106
Desire Under the Elms, 160
   see also O'Neill, Eugene
Desmond, Jane C., 123
deWolfe, Elsie, 65
Dithmar, Edward A., 72
Dos Passos, John, 24, 138
Dostoyevski, Fyodor, 46
Doyle, Arthur Conan, 61
Drew, John, 15, 53, 63, 132, 133
Drieser, Theodore, 169n
Duke of Duluth, The, 108

Easiest Way, The, 66
Eaton, Rev. Dr. Charles A., 119
Edeson, Robert, 89
Ehrenreich, Barbara, 2, 3, 6, 7, 8, 30, 42, 114, 163
Ehrenreich, John, 2, 3, 6, 7, 8, 30, 42, 114, 163
Elliott, Maxine, 65
Ellis, Edward, 143
Emerson, R. W., 138
Emery, Lynne Fauley, 123–4
Emperor Jones, The, 18, 159
   see also O'Neill, Eugene
Encyclopedia of Social Theory, The, 3
Engels, F., 4
Erenberg, Lewis, 53, 122, 123
Essex Sedan, 37
   see also advertising, theatre programs
Everybody's Magazine, 132
executive staffs, 26

Fair and Warmer, 164
Famous American Plays of the 1930s, 160
farce, 14, 20, 21, 53, 69, 93, 110, 151, 153, 154, 160, 161, 163, 164, 166
   as response to American corporate capitalism, 136, 139, 141, 143, 144, 145
Father Knickerbocker, 23
Faulkner, Harold Underwood, 78
Fields, W. C., 104
Fiske, Mrs., 11, 53, 132
Fitch, Clyde, 11, 13, 17, 19, 34, 53, 59, 63, 96, 98, 99, 119, 121, 126, 131, 139, 147, 163
   plays, 63–75
   neurasthenic characters, 65–9, 71–5, 144, 158, 159
   problem of "manliness," 67–8, 70, 177–8n
"Floradora Girls," 53
"Flubby-dub the Caveman" (song), 115
Ford, Henry, 155, 156
"Freddy the Freshman," 84
"French vaudevilles," 101
Freud, Sigmund, 13, 20, 116, 160, 167
   and the PMC, 154–6
Frohman, Charles, 42, 52, 64, 66
   see also "The Syndicate"
Frohman, Daniel, 52
Follies Girls, 15, 102–5, 159, 165
   see also Ziegfeld, Florenz
"For the Automobilist," 37

"gab," 56, 141, 144, 146
"gallery gods," 64, 130, 131
Garfield Tea, 34
   see also advertising, theatre programs
Gassner, John, 1, 94
General Electric, 23
gentleman class, 93
   class consciousness of, 55, 151
   habitus of, 40, 151

reading newspapers, 44
  see also Habitus, of Victorian gentlemen
George Washington, Jr., 127–8, 130
  see also Cohan, George M
Gershwin, G., 109
Gerson, Virginia, 65, 66, 70
Get-Rich-Quick Wallingford, 20, 127, 142, 146, 160
  see also Cohan, George M.; Mitchell, Grant
Getting Gertie's Garter, 164
Gilbert and Sullivan, 113
Gillette, William, 57, 61
  as Sherlock Holmes, 61–3
  see also Sherlock Holmes (character)
Girl with the Green Eyes, The, 74
  see also Fitch, Clyde
Give and Take, 161–3
Globe, The (theatre), 28
Gold Diggers, The, 164
Golden, Eve, 121
golf, 38–9, 44
Good Housekeeping, 155
Good News, 84
Goodrich tires, 37
Goodwin, Nat, 65
Governor's Son, The, 129
  see also Cohan, George M
Grace Methodist Episcopal Church, 119
"Great White Way," 1, 27
  see also Broadway
Green, Harvey, 77
Green Book Album, The, 127
Green Book Magazine, 45, 146
Greenfield, Thomas, 97–8
"grinds," 12, 13, 14, 16, 79, 85, 89, 93, 139, 148, 163
  see also "Mr. Grind"
Grizzly Bear, 120, 121
Guam, 105
Guinness (ale), 51
  see also advertising, theatre programs

habitus, 8–12, 18, 28, 49, 60, 61, 86, 92, 125–6, 139, 148, 149
  PMC habitus; or Professional-Managerial Habitus (PMH), 8, 20, 40, 65, 136, 140, 151, 160
  of Victorian gentlemen, 19, 40–1, 51, 54–6, 124, 127, 134
  see also Bourdieu, Pierre
Hackett, Walter, 143–4
Hamilton, Hale, 142
Harbach, Otto, 164
Harlem, 124
Harper's Weekly, 45, 52
Harriman, Mrs. Oliver, 119
Harris, Sam, 17, 26, 141, 146, 147
Harvard University, 64, 79, 81, 91, 92, 106, 144
Haymarket Square, 47
Hearst, William Randolph, 41, 42, 43
Hello Broadway, 135
  see also Cohan, George M
Henrietta, The, 19, 58–61, 94
Her Own Way, 73
  see also Fitch, Clyde
Herbert, Victor, 101
Herne, James A., 28
History of the Standard Oil Company, 94
Hoffman, Aaron, 161, 163
Holland House, The, 119
Holme, Bryan, 103
Holmes, Sherlock (character), 61–3, 127, 149
Homestead, PA, 47
homosexuals, 39

214 *Index*

Hopwood, Avery, 163–4
Hornblow, Arthur, 132–3
Horrible Prettiness, 102
How the Irish Became White, 31
Howard, Bronson, 17, 19, 58–60, 94
Howard, Dick, 3
Howard, Sidney, 165
Hudson Super-Six, 37
   see also advertising, theatre programs

Ibsen, H., 56
Iceman Cometh, The, 78
   see also O'Neill, Eugene
Ignatiev, Noel, 31
"I'm a Dancing Teacher Now"
   (song), 120
immigrants, 6, 7, 24, 30, 31, 42, 77, 133
   "Americanization" of immigrants,
     24, 35, 88
   "inferior" immigrants, 67
   "upstart" immigrants, 128, 134–5,
     see also Cohan, George M
immigration, 23, 31
imperialism, 20, 102, 106
   as onstage trend, 108
In Other Words, 86
Indiana (state), 83
Indiana (University of), 81
"industrial democracy," 161, 163
"industrial psychology," 155
"intelligent playgoer," 102, 107, 108
Interborough Rapid Transit (I.R.T.), 23
Isle of Spice, The, 108
It Pays to Advertise, 17, 135, 143–7, 161
"It's Still Rock and Roll to Me," 34
Ivory Soap, 35, 145

James, William, 106
Jazz, 109

Jefferson, Joseph, 54
Jelliffe, Smith Ely, 159
Joel, Billy, 34
Jolson, Al, 39
Jung, Carl, 154

Kahn, Otto, 171n
Keith, B. F., 52
Kelly, Fred C., 81
Kelly, George, 99, 166
Kelly Springfield, 37
   see also advertising, theatre programs
Kern, Jerome, 109, 113–14, 116, 135
   see also "Princess" Musicals
Kerr, Walter, 62
Kinsey, Sally Buchanan, 61, 62
Klauber, Adolph, 134
Klaw, Marc, 53
   see also "The Syndicate"
Klein, Alvin, 114
Klein, Charles, 94–6
Knox Hats, 103
Kodak, 66, 71, 145

Labor and Monopoly Capital, 5
"ladder of Whiteness," 30–1
Ladies' Night (in a Turkish Bath), 164
Lafayette Theatre, 124
Lahr, Bert, 128
land-grant colleges, 20, 79–80
Lawson, John Howard, 160
League of Nations, 163
Lears, Jackson, 19, 33, 35, 52, 67, 77
Leave It to Jane, 16, 19, 84, 116, 155, 166
Lehr, Harry, 130
Levine, Lawrence, 52
Lewis, Emory, 28, 164
Life (Magazine), 15, 127
Lion and the Mouse, The, 94–7

Index   215

Lippman, Walter, 146
Little Johnny Jones, 26, 129
Little Theatre, The, 28
living space, 38, 117
Loney, Glenn, 66
Longacre, The, 28
Longacre Square, 27
Lowney's Chocolate Bonbons, 33
   see also advertising, theatre programs
Lunt, Alfred, 153
Lutz, Tom, 74
Lyceum, The, 28, 58

Macfarlane, Peter Clarke, 132, 133
Machinal, 160
Mackaye, Steele, 170n
Madison Avenue Baptist Church, 119
Madison Square (theatre), 58
Majestic, The, 119
Man Who Owned Broadway, The, 132
Mansfield, Richard, 65
Marbury, Elisabeth, 118, 120
Marshall, Tully, 68
Marx, Karl, 4–5, 8
Marxist approach, 4, 5
master machinist, 26
master of properties, 26
"Matinee Lady" (byline), 51, 61
"matinee girl(s)," 42, 64, 70, 97, 133
Matthews, Brander, 10, 11
McArthur, Benjamin, 48, 49
McCabe, John, 49, 127, 128, 129
McConachie, Bruce, 160
McCutcheon, George Barr, 139
McKinley, William, 105
McLure's, 45
McNamara, Brooks, 17
Mencken, H. L., 45, 47
Mendum, George Drew, 48

Metcalfe, James, 15–16, 127, 128, 129
Miller, Marilyn, 18
Miller, Tice, 40, 41, 43, 47
Mitchell, Grant, 141–51, 153, 155, 167, 168
Mizejewski, Linda, 103, 104
Modern Dancing, 118
Modern Times, 138
Modern Tragedy, 157
"moneyed" elite, 74–5, 77
Montgomery, Walter, 55
Mordden, Ethan, 104, 105, 128
Morehouse, Ward, 131, 132
Morrill Act, 79
Moses, Montrose, 65, 66, 70, 71, 94, 143–4, 146
Moth and the Flame, The, 64, 71–2
motion pictures, 25, 33
Mr. Can-Do, 12, 14, 61, 140, 143, 151, 166
Mr. Grind, 12–14
Mr. Nervous, 12–14, 19, 56, 58, 59, 61, 73, 166
Mrozek, Donald, 78
"muckrakes," 1, 69, 94–5
Mulvey, Laura, 102
Munsey's Magazine, 45
Murphy, Brenda, 1, 15
Murray, Mae, 104
musical comedy, 75, 100–2, 105, 107, 108, 109, 113, 115, 120, 128, 135, 160, 165
musical plays, 101, 115

Nathan, George Jean, 18, 41, 45–7
Nathan Hale, 65
Nelson, Thomas L., 26, 27
"Nesting Time in Flatbush" (song), 114–15

neurasthenia; neurasthenic, 13, 19, 20, 62–3, 65, 71–5, 83, 119, 139, 144, 155, 158, 162
New Amsterdam (theatre), 28, 103
New Theater, The, 28
"new women," 102
New York Building Loan Banking Company, The, 34
  see also advertising, theatre programs
New York City, 2, 18, 23–4, 37, 40, 68
New York Dramatic Mirror, 51, 54, 57, 135, 150, 158
New York Evening Post, 40, 130
New York Herald (Tribune), 23, 45
New York Sun, 43, 67, 113, 121
New York Theatre Program Corporation, 37
New York Times, 28, 44, 34, 87–9, 96, 99, 101, 104, 107, 113, 114, 116, 119, 135, 142, 143, 146, 151, 155, 158, 161, 165, 167, 168
  identity of, 43
New York World, 41, 43, 58
Niagara Falls, 34
  see also advertising, theatre programs
"nigger dances," 123
No More Blondes, 164
No Place of Grace, 52
Noble, David, 3
Norton, Elliot, 43, 44

Ochs, Adolph, 43–4
Odets, C., 100
Oh, Boy!, 113–15
Ohio State, 81
Oklahoma!, 115
On Acting, 10
"One Step," 120

O'Neill, Eugene, 2, 18, 19, 21, 45–7, 49, 72, 75, 78, 126, 140, 154–60, 164–8
Ongley, Byron, 139
"opera tango," 119
"opera waltz," 119
Outing, 45
"Ovalesque" Dress Shirt, 35–6

Pair of Sixes, A, 11, 20, 125
Pennington, Ann, 104
Peple, Edward, 125
"Pfaffians," 40, 41
Pfister, Joel, 155
Philippines, 105, 106
Phoebe Snow, 145
"photographic," 62, 66, 69
Pinkerton detectives, 47
Pittsburg(h), 145
"Play and the Public, The," 64
  see also Fitch, Clyde
"pluck," 146
Plymouth, The, 28
Poggi, Jack, 25, 52, 126
Pollock, Channing, 127, 142, 146
Polly Preferred, 160, 161
"pop" psychology, 20, 155
Popularity, 132
  see also Cohan, George M
Porter, Cole, 109
Postone, Moishe, 126
Presbyterians, 29
press agents, 27, 144
"Princess" musicals, 16, 20, 100, 101, 109, 113, 117, 160
Princess Theatre, 26, 27, 109, 115
Princeton, 16, 163
Principles of Scientific Management, The, 137

Processional, 144
Professional Managerial Class (PMC), 2, 16, 18, 60
  anti-imperialism and, 106
  audience maturing, 165
  on Broadway "field," 10–11
  business plays and, 94–8, 100
  buying habits of, 33–8
  buying tickets for shows, 32–3
  class formation, 6–9, 17, 25, 46
  class identity
  Cohan and, 126, 134, 136
  college plays and, 78–9, 81–2, 84–6, 88–9, 93–4
  Craig's Wife as cautionary tale for, 166
  creation of modern American drama and, 12, 21, 154
  daily life of, 18
  dancing and, 118–20, 122–3
  definition of, 2–6
  distinction between habitus and class consciousness of, 12
  as dramatic expert, 47
  emerging habitus of, 20, 40, 56, 65, 93, 124, 136, 151, 160
  ethnicity and race of, 29–31, 88–9
  executive positions on Broadway, 26
  farce and, 138–41, 143–4, 146–9, 151
  in Fitch plays, 19, 64, 65, 71
  Give and Take and, 161, 163
  influence of psychology on, 20
  living conditions of, 32
  musicals and, 101–2, 105, 107–8, 110–12, 114–17
  nerves, neurasthenia and, 58, 65, 71, 74, 75
  newspapers read by, 42–4
  O'Neill as dramatic hero of, 49, 156, 159, 164
  PMC expert hero, 61, 124, 139, 153
  "PMC-ing" of Broadway, 49, 56, 62, 65, 141, 151, 166, 168
  psychology and, 154–5
  "regular fellows" and, 140
  religion of, 29
  rhetoric of "thinking," 10–11
  role in American corporate capitalism, 6
  salary of, 29
  shift from Victorian gentlemen, 18
  stock market crash and, 168
  F.W. Taylor and, 136–8
  as theatergoing public, 28
  "types" of, 12–15
  university and college training of, 7–8, 79
  working life of, 29, 63
Professional Managerial Class consciousness, 10, 12, 18–20, 42, 75, 79, 85, 93, 94, 96, 100, 101, 105, 108, 110–12, 115, 117, 146, 160
Progressive Era, 6, 24
"Providences of God," 106
Puck, 45
Puerto Rico, 105
Pulitzer, Joseph, 41, 42, 43
Pulitzer Prize, 156, 166, 167
Purdue, 80, 81

Quaker Oats, 145

"rag," 109, 121
Reed-Danahay, Deborah, 9
Republic Theatre, 28
revues, 101, 120, 135–6
Rice, Elmer, 166
Riesner, Dr. Christian F., 119

"the road," 25, 33, 39, 126
Robbins, Derek, 118
Robson, Stuart, 59, 60
Rodgers and Hammerstein, 115
Rodgers and Hart, 109
Roediger, David, 30, 31
Roosevelt, Theodore, 67, 69, 78, 91, 136, 145, 156
Ross, Edward A., 6
Runaway, The, 108
Russell, Lillian, 53
Ryder, John (actor), 55

Sachs, Curt, 122
Sag Harbor, 28
Sappho, 67
   see also Fitch, Clyde
Sayler, Oliver M., 155–6
Scientific management, 11, 20, 33, 136–9
Scientific Management (book), 98
Seely, Bruce E., 79
Selwyn, The, 28
Selznick Pictures, 39
Senelick, Laurence, 12
Shakespeare, 18, 82, 93
Shannon, Effie, 65
Shaw, Oscar, 110
Sheldon, Edward, 94, 97–9
"Show Us How to Do the Fox Trot" (song), 120
Showboat, 165
Shubert, Lee, 17, 26
Shubert, the (theatre), 28
The Shuberts, 17, 27, 44, 53
Sievers, David, 156
"Simple Life, The" (song), 110
"Size Thirteen Collar" (song), 112
"skyscraper," 23

Smart Set, The, 45
"Smiling Isle, The" (song)
Smith, Charles Emory, 106
Smith, Edith, 147
Smith, Harry James, 147–9
Smith, Winchell, 46, 139
social Darwinism, 77
Sohmer Pianos, 33
   see also advertising, theatre programs
Sothern, E.H., 15
Southern Baptists, 29
Spain, 105
sports (athletics), 16, 19, 78, 82
stage manager, 26
Stages: The Fifty-Year Childhood of the American Theatre, 164
Stallings, Laurence, 165
"Standard Eight," 37, 38
   see also advertising, theatre programs
Standard Oil, 23, 95
"Star-Spangled Banner, The," 91
Steffens, Lincoln, 23
Steinway, 145
Stickiness of Gelatine, The, 131
   see also Fitch, Clyde; Weber and Fields
stock market crash, 168
Strange Interlude, 21, 141, 166–7
   see also O'Neill, Eugene
Street Scene, 166
Strenuous Life, The, 78
Strongheart, 19, 80, 84–9, 93, 114
Stubbornness of Geraldine, The, 131
Sudermann, H., 52
Sultan of Sulu, The, 20, 105–8
"summer widowers," 102–3, 105
Susman, Warren, 56
   "culture of character," 56

"The (Theatrical) Syndicate," 16, 17,
  42, 53, 127
  Syndicate agreement; mode of
    operation, 26

Tailor-Made Man, A, 146–51, 155,
  161, 168
"talking cure," 160
tango, 119, 120, 122
Tarbell, Ida, 94
Tarkington, Booth, 153–4
Taylor, Frederick Winslow, 10, 11, 20,
  33, 98, 136–8, 148, 150, 155, 162
"Taylorism," 138
"theater district," 27
Theatre, The, 44
theatre criticism, 10
  critics as thinkers and experts, 10,
    51, 64, 104, 126, 134
  and the "death" of the musical,
    101, 113
  and end-of-the-century optimism,
    51, 57
  evolution of, 39–41
  and fight with Shuberts, 44
  geared toward playgoer/
    businessman, 43
  "genteel" criticism, 11, 19, 40–1,
    54–6
  and George Jean Nathan, 45–7
  and the "intelligent playgoer," 102
  and "jazz," 109
  and magazines, 45
  and modern American drama, 154
  and newspaper circulation boom, 42
  and "photographic" realism, 66
  and PMC consciousness, 42
  and psychology, 155
  and race issues, 87–9
  and sentiment, 97
  shift from Victorian to PMC, 18,
    46–7, 54
  and the Syndicate, 55
Theatre Magazine, 52, 127, 159
theatre seating, 28
They Knew What They Wanted, 165
Thomas, Augustus, 46, 56
Thomas, Olive, 39
ticket prices, 33
"Till the Clouds Roll By" (song), 113
Times Square, 27
"tired businessman," 13, 63, 102, 112,
  133, 159, 164
Towse, John Ranken, 19, 40–1, 45,
  54–6
Travelers Insurance Company, 35
Treadwell, Sophie, 160
Truex, Ernest, 110
Truth, The, 65
  see also Fitch, Clyde
turkey trot, 119, 120, 121
Twain, Mark, 106
Twelfth Night, 93

Uneeda, 145
union suits, 38
  see also advertising, theatre
    programs
United States Tires, 37
  see also advertising, theatre
    programs
University of Michigan, 81
Urban, Joseph, 104
U.S. Census, 29
U.S. Steel, 23

Vanderbilt, Mrs. Reginald, 119
Vanity Fair (magazine), 45

vaudeville, 46, 52, 53, 81, 110, 126, 129, 131, 133, 135, 137
Veblen, Thorstein, 24
Velutina, 34, 36
   see also advertising, theatre programs
Very Good Eddie, 146, 109–13
Victorian era, 13, 40, 51, 54
Viennese operetta, 101, 113
Visible Hand, The, 2

Wainscott, Ronald, 1, 47, 108, 153, 154, 160, 161, 164
Waiting for Lefty, 100
Walker, Pat, 3
Wall, Mrs. Berry, 119
Walter, Eugene, 66
wardrobe mistress, 26
Warfield, David, 54
WASPs, 29, 133, 140
Watch Your Step, 120, 135
Webb, Creighton, 130
Weber and Fields, 110, 131, 135
"Well-Fitting Dress Coat, The," 147
West, Mae, 81
Wharton, Edith, 66
What Price Glory?, 164
"What the Man Will Wear," 35, 38
"What the Woman Will Wear," 35
whiteness as a social category, 30–1
"Why is New York City the Theatrical Center of the World?", 37
Why Men Leave Home, 164
Wiebe, Robert, 3, 7–8, 78
Williams, Bert, 39, 104
Williams, Raymond, 157

Wilmeth, Don B., 63
Wilson, Garff B., 28
Wilson, Woodrow, 163
Winter, William, 19, 40, 41, 45, 54–6
Winter Garden, 28
Wodehouse, P. G., 110, 113–14, 116
Woodruff, Henry, 15
Woollcott, Alexander, 11, 43, 44, 153, 158, 164
Work and the Work Ethic in American Drama, 1920–1970, 97
working class, 43, 81, 106, 108
   as social process, 5
World in Falseface, The, 45, 46
World War I (the Great War), 2, 41, 43, 51, 53, 109, 121, 123, 153, 155, 165
Worthing, Frank, 54
Wright, Erik Olin, 3–4
Wynn, Ed, 104

Yale, 16, 64, 79, 81
Yankee Consul, The, 108
"Yankee Doodle Dandy," 91, 124, 135
   see also Cohan, George M
yellow journalism, 42
Y.M.C.A., 71
Young, Rida Johnson, 15, 88, 90–3

Ziegfeld, Florenz, 15, 102, 159, 165
   effect on fashion, 103–4
   Follies, 18, 20, 102–5, 159
   Ziegfeld Girls, Follies Girls, 15, 21, 102–5, 159, 165
Zinn, Howard, 47, 67, 105, 106

GPSR Compliance
The European Union's (EU) General Product Safety Regulation (GPSR) is a set of rules that requires consumer products to be safe and our obligations to ensure this.

If you have any concerns about our products, you can contact us on

ProductSafety@springernature.com

In case Publisher is established outside the EU, the EU authorized representative is:

Springer Nature Customer Service Center GmbH
Europaplatz 3
69115 Heidelberg, Germany

www.ingramcontent.com/pod-product-compliance
Lightning Source LLC
LaVergne TN
LVHW011816060526
838200LV00053B/3807

9781349380046